PUBLIC OPINION AND POLITICAL CHANGE IN POLAND, 1980–1982

T0381798

SOVIET AND EAST EUROPEAN STUDIES

PUBLIC OPINION AND POLITICAL CHANGE IN POLAND, 1980–1982

DAVID S. MASON

Butler University

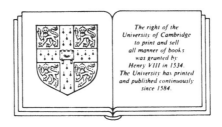

The right of the
University of Cambridge
to print and sell
all manner of books
was granted by
Henry VIII in 1534.
The University has printed
and published continuously
since 1584.

CAMBRIDGE UNIVERSITY PRESS

CAMBRIDGE

LONDON   NEW YORK   NEW ROCHELLE
MELBOURNE   SYDNEY

To Sharon, Dana and Melanie

CAMBRIDGE UNIVERSITY PRESS
Cambridge, New York, Melbourne, Madrid, Cape Town, Singapore,
São Paulo, Delhi, Dubai, Tokyo

Cambridge University Press
The Edinburgh Building, Cambridge CB2 8RU, UK

Published in the United States of America by Cambridge University Press, New York

www.cambridge.org
Information on this title: www.cambridge.org/9780521124423

First published 1985
This digitally printed version 2009

A catalogue record for this publication is available from the British Library

Library of Congress Cataloguing in Publication data

Mason, David S. (David Stewart), 1947–
Public opinion and political change in Poland, 1980–
1982.
(Soviet and East European studies)
Bibliography: p.
1. Poland—Politics and government—1980–
2. Public opinion—Poland. I. Title. II. Series.
DK4442.M37   1985   943.8′056   85-5280

ISBN 978-0-521-30798-7 Hardback
ISBN 978-0-521-12442-3 Paperback

Contents

List of tables

Preface

In 1980 and 1981, Poland became a remarkably open society, with a proliferation of new and independent ideas, organizations and publications. This openness also affected sociological research, and in particular public-opinion research. The government, academic research institutes, and even Solidarity conducted and published public-opinion surveys on all manner of subjects, including the most highly charged political issues. These surveys offer us a unique and candid snapshot of Polish society during one of the most turbulent and exciting periods of modern history.

In relying on public opinion data, this study focuses on the public rather than the elite, and on the public's perceptions of the elite (both Solidarity and the regime) rather than the elite's perceptions or policies. This work differs, then, from political histories of the Solidarity era, which largely focus on the top of the political system: on the composition, makeup and policy debates within the Party and within Solidarity, and the political competition between Solidarity and the Party. This, of course, was an important aspect of the events of 1980–2, but in some respects misses the unique features of the situation. To the extent that society, or the workers, had taken over the 'leading role' in Polish society, it is important to understand the values, attitudes, and beliefs of the workers and other social groups.

In showing the interaction between the political elites and the general population, the approach of this book is different from most other Western studies of communist political systems. The latter usually concentrate on elites, institutions, dissidents, and ideology. These emphases are largely a result of the available resources: we have information on the composition and (to a lesser extent) the

ix

politics of the political elites; on the structure and functioning of the political institutions of communist regimes; on the activities and writings of dissident individuals and groups; and on ideological debates within these societies. Unfortunately, these topics overlook the main subject of politics: the citizens. Because of the closed nature of these countries, the lack of institutionalized forms of opposition, and censorship, Westerners have had little opportunity to investigate the role and orientations of the public in communist societies.

While the East European regimes have increasingly conducted and published public opinion surveys in recent years, they rarely reveal (or conduct) surveys touching on the sensitive issues of support for the regime and its ideals or policies. There have been few exceptions to this rule. Politically oriented surveys did appear in Czechoslovakia in 1968 and help us to understand much about the sources of support for and opposition to that regime and for the Dubček reforms. The other exception is Poland during the Solidarity era. Polls conducted and published in Poland in 1980 and 1981 asked remarkably open questions about popular support for the Party, socialism, Solidarity, and religion, among many other subjects. These surveys offer an unprecedented opportunity to study the public's attitude towards, and effects on, political change in that country. They also offer the chance to study a society in the process of profound social, political and economic transformations. Seldom have such studies been conducted in a 'revolutionary' environment, even if this revolution was a limited and truncated one. This material, then, should not only help us better understand the events of 1980–2, but should provide insight into the nature of a socialist society, and the extent and sources of support and opposition to the principles and practice of communist politics.

The approach of this book is partly chronological and partly topical. There is some movement through history, in that the early chapters focus on the period before and after 1980, the middle chapters on the Solidarity era, and the last ones on the imposition of and reaction to martial law; but the chapters focus on issues rather than on particular periods of time. The chapters on the Party and on Solidarity, for example, each take different 'cuts' through the same time period. There is no attempt here to provide a comprehensive history of the Solidarity era; that is provided, and will be provided, in other books (e.g. Ascherson 1981; Ruane 1982; Ash 1983b).

The book is organized in the following manner. Chapter 1

provides an overview of the nature of public opinion research in communist countries, and the role of public opinion research in Poland in the tumultuous years from 1980 through 1982. Chapter 2 sets the stage by tracing the major developments in Poland during the 1970s that led to the explosion in the summer of 1980. This political setting is followed by an investigation of the social setting in Chapter 3, which focuses on the basic values of Poles on the eve of 1980. Chapter 4 traces the causes and consequences of the 1980 events, and how these were perceived by the population. Chapters 5 and 6 focus, respectively, on Solidarity and the Party and the changes that each went through during 1981. These changes were substantial: both Solidarity and the Party matured during 1981, but in the process, both lost some of the unity and elan they had had earlier. By the end of 1981, the public had changed as well. While popular support for Solidarity was still strong, there was increasing recognition of the long-term problems Poland was facing and recognition of the need for compromise. These issues are addressed in Chapter 7. Chapter 8 treats the imposition of martial law, and the reaction of Solidarity and the public to this traumatic event. This subject, of course, remains an open chapter in Poland's history. I have arbitrarily limited the discussion to the end of 1982, the end of one year of martial law, without implying that this is in any way a time of closure. Chapter 9, the conclusions, reviews the role of the public, and of public opinion, and the extent to which Solidarity and the regime adequately responded to the population. It also attempts to assess the state of the public mood, of Poland's values and expectations, in the aftermath of Solidarity and martial law.

I am deeply indebted to a large number of institutions and individuals for support in preparing this book. The International Research and Exchanges Board supported my research in Poland during the first half of 1982. The National Endowment for the Humanities allowed me a summer of uninterrupted writing through its Summer Stipend program, and a grant from the American Council of Learned Societies provided partial release time from teaching during the fall of 1983. Butler University supported my research and writing with a sabbatical leave in 1981–2 and a Faculty Fellowship during 1983–4.

This institutional support provided the opportunity for research and writing. This could not have succeeded, however, without the encouragement and assistance of family, friends and colleagues in

Poland and the United States. In Warsaw, I was assisted by dozens of scholars, many of them associated with the Institute of Sociology of the University of Warsaw or the Academy of Sciences. While I cannot hope to name all of them, I am especially grateful to Witold Morawski, Kazimierz Słomczyński, Renata Siemieńska, Aleksandra Jasińska-Kania, Władysław Adamski, Krzysztof Jasiewicz, and Zbigniew Sufin. Upon my return to Indiana, Karen Ledwin provided valuable research assistance. For reading all or parts of this manuscript, I would like to thank Edward Buehrig, Jack Bielasiak, Tim Wiles, Mary McGann, Witold Morawski, Krzysztof Jasiewicz, Georges Mink, and Richard Fredland. Burt Woodruff introduced me to the world of word processing and helped me out when things got tough. Our departmental secretaries, Charlene Clements and Ellen Thorn, assisted me with typing, correcting and proofreading.

Finally, I would like to thank the three wonderful ladies to whom this book is dedicated. My daughters Dana and Melanie cheerfully accompanied me to Poland, distracted and entertained me, and only occasionally erased part of my manuscript from the computer. And most importantly, for sharing the Polish experience, for reading and re-reading drafts, for lending encouragement, and for bearing with me, I extend love and thanks to my wife Sharon.

Introduction: public opinion and politics

Some fifteen years ago, Herbert McClosky (1969, p. 10) called for more rigorous research techniques in the study of politics. He suggested that public opinion data could help balance traditional political and historical studies, which would often 'infer a nation's climate of opinion from a relatively small number of books, articles, speeches, editorials, or legislative acts'. 'When one observes political phenomena anecdotally', he wrote, 'one's eye is drawn to whatever is dramatic and exciting, which means, often, to whatever is idiosyncratic and atypical.' Systematic use of public opinion data could help provide a more accurate view of a nation's climate of opinion.

Since that time, such techniques have become commonplace in the study of politics in Western societies and have added a great deal to our understanding of political processes in general. Studies of politics in communist societies, however, are still mostly in the traditional mode, in spite of numerous efforts to apply more rigorous social-science methods in this area (e.g. Fleron 1969). To a large extent, the problem is due to the lack of available and reliable data from these countries; this has been the case especially with public opinion data. In recent years, such data from Eastern Europe and the Soviet Union have become somewhat more available. Poland has been the most advanced country in the region in conducting and publishing such research, and the Solidarity era stimulated a flood of open and provocative public-opinion surveys. This book examines political change in Poland during 1980–2 through the medium of public opinion research.

The use of public opinion data to analyze political developments in a communist party state raises a number of issues about the role of public opinion data in social science research and about the concept of political culture. Public opinion can be defined as 'the distribution of personal opinions on public objects in the population outside the government' (Davison and Leiserson 1968, p. 198). Through scientific sampling techniques, it is possible 'to reproduce in miniature and with remarkable accuracy the characteristics of a given universe' (McClosky 1969, p. 4). The 'universe' may be either the whole population of a country, or certain groups within it. The sample survey, then, allows one to study the values, beliefs, attitudes, and activities of a given population, as well as the underlying attitudinal structures or personality characteristics and the relationships among these numerous variables. This book will focus on the values, beliefs, and attitudes of Poles rather than on personality characteristics and their relationships with attitudes, largely because of the derivative nature of this research. While I was able to do some of my own multivariate analysis, I was largely dependent on the results of analysis done by Polish researchers. In Poland as elsewhere in the Soviet bloc, raw data are seldom made available to Western scholars.

Despite the useful and revealing nature of public opinion research, one does have to be careful of such data, which are subject to error, bias, distortion and manipulation. This, however, is true of all data, and indeed of all research. These problems are likely to affect survey results in communist countries just as they do in the United States (see Wheeler 1976). However, this occasions the need to be careful in drawing inferences from the data, not to reject them. The special problems of dealing with such data from communist countries are addressed below.

Most of our knowledge about public opinion is derived from research conducted in the United States and Western Europe. In some respects, then, what we know is culture bound, in that it reflects characteristics, values and attitudes of people in one particular type of culture and political system. Nevertheless, many of the conclusions from such research are interesting to us, if only for purposes of comparison with a communist society. Survey research has shown, for example, that there is no *single* public opinion on any particular issue; political issues are often salient for one group and irrelevant for another. Most people are not well informed on public issues and pay little attention to political personalities and issues, even when they are prominent in the mass media. Partially because of this low information level, public opinion on political questions is highly unstable, changing frequently in reaction to events and trends. The less informed people are, the more changeable are their opinions. In fact, 'people tend to adjust their opinions to conform to the situation in which they find themselves' (Davison and Leiserson, p. 190). Consequently, those who are opposed to a particular course of action beforehand may come to approve it after it has been adopted.

The story is quite different with political activists. The number of people in this 'political class' in Western democracies is quite small, probably less than 10% of the population. These people, obviously, are more informed on political matters, and are more ideological, more partisan, and more likely to have coherent and consistent political beliefs. Their attitudes are much more resistent to change. In the United States, at least, political competition takes place largely within this political class, seldom involving their rank and file supporters. Democratic and Republican activists, for example tend to be much farther apart in their stands on issues than the rest of the population (McClosky 1969, pp. 21–6). This low level of popular involvement in politics is not necessarily detrimental for democratic societies. In fact, as Robert Dahl (1956) has argued, a situation in which there are strong and intense feelings on both sides of an issue, with few people undecided, can be destabilizing; if the issue is critical, it may even presage the breakdown of democratic government.

Despite the contextual differences, many of the above generalizations may apply to public opinion in Poland as well. As Zvi Gitelman (1977, p. 5) has pointed out, 'the modernization of East European society has resulted in the partial emergence of publics – collectives that confront issues, discuss them, and divide over them, in place of masses'. Just as in the United States, one cannot speak of a single undifferentiated public opinion in the East European states. As will be seen in this book, many of the other generalizations about the US hold in Poland as well. Opinions are highly unstable, and are affected by changes in the political and economic environment. Most people, most of the time, are uninformed on and uninterested in politics. When circumstances change and many people become intensely involved, as they did during the Solidarity era, political stability becomes endangered. But even during the period of mass involvement, the major political competition occurred between the 'activists' in Solidarity and in the government. And, as will be seen in later chapters, the leaders of Solidarity and the governing regime were more deeply divided on the critical issues than was the public.

Survey research in the United States has shown that there are seldom direct links between public opinion and public policy. As V. O. Key (1961, pp. 409–24) contends, the relationship is a complex one with 'government (and other centers of influence as well) affecting the form and content of opinion; and in turn, public opinion may condition the manner, content, and timing of public action'. According to Key, 'all governments ... must concern themselves with public opinion. They do not maintain their authority by brute force alone; they must seek willing acceptance and conformity from most of their citizens.' Public opinion in democracies, then, often acts as a negative factor; it sets the boundaries for action but does not assure that action will be taken.

In the East European societies, public opinion has often not had even this boundary-setting function; however the role and influence of public opinion on policy has grown in recent years. In the Stalinist era, public opinion was viewed as something to be guided rather than followed (Inkeles 1958, p. 24) and there were few challenges to this way of thinking until the late 1960s. Since knowledge of public opinion was viewed as being an instrument of social control, the means to ascertain public opinion were also controlled. Thus survey research, which can often elicit disquieting results, was played down in this role. Rather, public opinion was discovered by feedback through official channels of the bureaucracy (the party apparatus, the secret police) and through 'voluntary channels' such as articles and letters to newspapers by citizens, meetings of mass organizations such as trade unions and youth organizations, and meetings of citizens with local officials and deputies to soviets or local councils (Mickiewicz 1983, p. 98).

Eventually, even in the Soviet Union, there was some recognition that these traditional channels did not always provide full or accurate information. The increasingly complex nature of the society fostered social and attitudinal differentiation, challenged the assumptions about the unity of public opinion, and necessitated more accurate measurement of public opinion for policy making. In the Soviet Union, consciousness of these problems was spurred by a number of survey research studies whose results contrasted with official views. One, for example, revealed a startling lack of success in the effects of socialization of the population through the media. Over half of the respondents did not understand some important ideological terms which appear frequently in the media, such as 'dictatorship', 'imperialism', and 'leftist forces' (Mickiewicz 1983, p. 106). The results of such surveys often provided information quite different from that derived from official channels. In part, no doubt, this was due to the overrepresentation of party members in official channels; they were likely to convey views and information that fit the official line. Survey research results did not always bend so well to ideological demands.

Such developments strengthened the hand of the 'pluralist' school of public opinion research in the communist states, who argued that socialist public opinion is pluralistic on all but the most fundamental issues, and that the sample survey can reveal important information about society and social cleavages. The pluralists argued that public opinion has a broader role than previously perceived. Public opinion is not simply a passive force to be manipulated, but an active one that can yield important benefits to the regime. Survey research can make governments more effective by helping them better understand the needs and concerns of their citizens. It can also fulfill a 'democratic' function in allowing for a sense of popular participation and expression of interests. More detailed information about social differentiation and group values and behavior can also enhance the monitoring and control of such behavior (Gitelman 1977, pp. 13–18; and Welsh 1981, p. 1).

The expanded role for public opinion was a function of the evolution of the political systems of these countries. In the totalitarian stage, public opinion was tolerated only when passive and supportive, and then only on issues selected by the regime. With the relaxation of totalitarian rule and the greater visibility of the publics, public opinion was taken more into account, and assumed a 'permissive' as well as a supportive role. This is essentially the status of public opinion in the Soviet Union and Eastern Europe now. Public opinion polls are conducted, and often published, but the samples are often limited in scope, typically to one region or city, and the topics are usually restrictive and non-political. Areas of frequent research include the attitudes and worldview of young people, workers' attitudes towards their work and workplaces, and the role and position of women in socialist society.

But occasionally, in periods of reform, public opinion can even come to play a decisive role on certain issues, as has been true in both Yugoslavia and in Czechoslovakia during the Prague Spring (Gitelman 1977, p. 7). As will be shown below, public opinion also assumed such a role in Poland during the year and a half of Solidarity. As William Welsh (1981, p. 11) has sugggested, there is a strong relationship between a regime's confidence and the openness of public opinion research. As these reformist regimes have sought to strengthen their legitimacy by responding to public needs, it becomes imperative to have the information about these needs that survey polls provide. To the extent that this succeeds, the governments have less to fear from the results of openly conducted and published opinion polls.

The impact of public opinion on policy in communist regimes is limited, though, by the absence of independent interest groups and competitive parties to aggregate and process alternative demands and to pressure the authorities to recognize and act on them (Gitelman 1977, p. 32). When the population organizes such groups to push their demands, as the Poles did in 1980 (and the Czechoslovaks in 1968), the authorities have reacted with force. With the crushing of Solidarity, the regime in Poland demonstrated that the authorities insist on defining the political agenda and controlling the channels of public opinion. If, however, these regimes refuse to allow the emergence of independent parties and interest groups, they may have to rely even more heavily on ascertaining public opinion through survey research, to elicit that information about society otherwise provided by interest groups.

There is another side of the relationship between public opinion and policy that is particularly but not solely true in authoritarian regimes: the possibility that governments might deliberately manipulate public opinion. Key and others acknowledge that democratic governments seek to mold and shape public opinion. However, just as it is difficult to prove any direct impact on policy by public opinion, studies of government efforts to manipulate public opinion have also not been able to show any clear causal links (Davison and Leiserson, p. 193). The situation is somewhat different in Eastern Europe than in the United States where the government does not have the advantage of a virtual monopoly on propaganda. Indeed, in Eastern Europe, 'the deliberate use of public opinion for the purpose of social control occupies a prominent place in the writings of contemporary socialist scholars' (Gitelman 1977, p. 21). Even in these countries, though, the success rate in this regard is probably quite low. While the populations of these societies have internalized some of the official values and points of view, the dominant values of the society often diverge sharply from the official ones. This has especially been the case in Poland. This raises a set of related issues relating to the idea of political culture.

POLITICAL CULTURE

Political culture, in the words of Lucian Pye (1968, p. 218), 'is the set of attitudes, beliefs, and sentiments which give order and meaning to a political process and which provides the underlying assumptions and rules that govern behavior in the political system'. A nation's political culture is rooted in both national history and individual experience. It embraces the political orientations of both the leaders and the citizens. As an element of the broader culture, it consists of values that are passed down from one generation to the next.

The concept of political culture represents an attempt to relate research results from depth psychology and public opinion surveys to dynamic political analysis (Pye 1968, pp. 218–19). Or, as Almond and Verba suggested in their pathbreaking volume on *The Civic Culture* (1963, pp. 32–3), political culture constitutes the link between 'micropolitics' (political attitudes and motivations) and 'macropolitics' (the structure and function of the political system and its institutions). The impact of *The Civic Culture* was felt even in communist states, where the terms 'civic culture' and 'political culture' entered the lexicon of Marxist political scientists (Wiatr 1980, p. 106).

There may be competing or conflicting political subcultures within a society. Archie Brown (1977, p. 8), in a book on political culture in communist states, observes that 'to speak of *the* political culture of a society is almost always an oversimplification'. He calls attention in particular to the possible discrepancy between the 'dominant' political culture of the society and the 'official' one of the regime. The relationship between elite and mass subcultures is an important element in the performance of the political system. The greater the conflict between them, the greater the likelihood of political conflict or political stagnation. This was certainly the case in Poland, where certain aspects of the official political culture are at sharp variance with the dominant culture of the society (e.g. Catholicism).

Polish society was particularly divided over the issue of the scope of politics. As Lucian Pye notes, every political culture must define for its society the generally accepted scope of politics, which includes a definition of the accepted participants in the political process, the range of permissible issues, and the functions of the political process and various agencies of the political system. By 1980, many Poles, especially skilled workers, were challenging the regime's norms on all of these issues. The workers demanded a widening of the scope of politics. During 1981, Poland was beginning to move from a 'subject' political culture to a 'participant' one. As Almond and Verba (1963, p. 35) point out, such changes may produce psychological confusion and instability in society. As will be seen in later chapters, this was indeed the case in Poland.

As with public opinion, a political culture has little direct impact on policies or political change. Rather, political culture shapes the political environment, which in turn affects public opinion. In addition, political culture acts as a filter for popular demands and helps to limit them. Only those popular wants and desires that survive the filter can be considered public opinion, and only public opinion can influence political activity (Devine 1972, p. 24).

Political culture may also be the object of policy, as it is especially in communist states. The creation of a 'new socialist man' is, as Jack Gray puts it, 'the end product of the official political culture'. But this effort has been 'on the whole a depressing failure':

the authoritarian, bureaucratic practice of most of these regimes (as opposed to the long-term ideal) has quite clearly scotched the development of the sort of participatory democracy through which the new socialist citizen must be created if he is to be created at all. Indeed, the effort to create him has visibly slackened as the acceptance of 'legal consciousness', expressed obliquely in Kadar's 'He who is not against us is for us', has spread. Almost everywhere apathy, privatism, and 'economism' are prevalent and tolerated and sometimes even encouraged (Brown and Gray 1977, p. 270).

This is all the more striking given the advantages possessed by communist regimes in their domination of the processes of education and political socialization. These failures are particularly evident in Poland, where the pattern of responses to survey questions often reflects that of any industrial society (Kolankiewicz and Taras,

1977). The failure of the Polish regime to shape the dominant political culture into the form of the official one perpetuates the division between the authorities and the society. It is also a major source of the increasingly frequent upheavals in Polish society.

This book will focus on public opinion and the changes in public opinion on specific and current issues during the Solidarity era, rather than on developing a political culture of Poland. The concept of political culture is a difficult one to define, and has little explanatory power apart from the survey research material that helps constitute it. Since a political culture consists of basic and widespread beliefs, knowledge and attitudes, it should be a relatively stable feature of the political system. Research more recent than *The Civic Culture*, though, has shown that even basic political attitudes may change in reaction to specific political events (Almond and Verba 1980, p. 401). As we will see, this also has been the case in Poland. Except for Chapter 3, on the values of Polish society, we will focus on the more dynamic characteristics of public opinion, and its relationship to political events.

DATA SOURCES AND RELIABILITY

As noted above, one needs to treat the results of survey research with some caution. Students of public opinion research in the West have pointed out the numerous problems with validity and reliability with the resulting data. Public attitudes are highly volatile and dependent on situation and circumstances. One must be wary of the possibility that respondents provide dishonest answers, that their recall may be faulty, that they may be providing answers they think the interviewer wants to hear, or that they simply do not care enough to provide thoughtful and accurate responses (Gitelman 1977, pp. 25–8). One cannot assume, therefore, that any particular survey necessarily reflects deep-seated or permanent beliefs or attitudes, or that public opinion has any particular effect on the political process. All this is true even in Western democratic societies.

The difficulties are multiplied with such research in communist countries. Respondents are even more likely to be intimidated by interviewers, particularly those from governmental or other official research centers. Direct political questions may not be asked in the first place, or if they are, they may be skewed in such a way as to elicit favorable responses. Sensitive results may not be reported at all, or only partial results may be released. This is part of a larger problem, which is the more politicized nature of public opinion research in communist states. While a number of sociologists have, over the years, appealed for treatment of such research as objective information, the official line has been closer to the idea of public opinion research as a propaganda tool. In a book on public opinion published in Poland in 1980, only three functions of public opinion were identified: the integrative role, the consultative role, and control. There is no mention of the role of public opinion research in providing information, as a policy tool, or as a form of scholarly inquiry. The author of that book sees such research in a narrowly instrumental and manipulative role (Kuśmierski 1980, pp. 309–19). Finally, perhaps because of these many problems, policy makers may not rely on public opinion research. This was especially the case in Poland between 1975 and 1980, when the limited public opinion surveys often produced results the regime did not want to know about (see following chapter).

Despite all of these caveats, public opinion surveys can provide useful and reliable information. They add an important extra dimension to our understanding of Polish society beyond that which is provided by the speeches, writings, or interviews of the elite, on the one hand, or by reporters' interviews or conversations with individual Poles, on the other. Both of these sources of data are as subject to unreliability and pitfalls as is public opinion research. Focusing on the elite tells us little about the attitudes, beliefs or behavior of the mass public. Interviews with 'typical' Poles are even more dangerous in the absence of any accurate determination of what is typical. Western reporters tend to seek out, find, and associate with those who are hostile to the regime or its ideology. The official Polish media, on the other hand, report interviews with those who are favorably disposed to the system. Public opinion surveys, based on large samples usually representative of the population, give us a better indication of the 'typical' attitudes, as well as providing information about attitudinal differences and the sources of such differences.

The problems of reliability and validity of such research were greatly reduced after August 1980, for a number of reasons. The new Kania regime, first of all, recognized the need for accurate representations of the public mood, and encouraged the development of public opinion research. The more open atmosphere during the period of renewal no doubt reduced the fear element when citizens were asked to respond to survey questionnaires.

More surveys were being conducted by non-official organizations or institutes (e.g. universities and the Academy of Sciences), whose interviewers were less intimidating to most Poles than those from Polish Radio and Television or the Party's research institutes. By the spring of 1981, even Solidarity was conducting survey research, providing additional information about Solidarity members, and providing useful points of comparison with official poll results. Furthermore, the proliferation of survey research centers and of surveys provided the opportunity to compare results to similar or identical questions in different locales, occupational settings, or time periods, or by different research organizations, lending additional confidence to the results. This book, for example, includes repetitive surveys conducted by the University of Warsaw in 1964, 1976 and 1980 and by the Academy of Sciences at the end of 1980 and again at the end of 1981. It also refers to essentially identical surveys on confidence in institutions conducted by the official Center for Public Opinion Research of Polish Radio and Television (OBOP) and by Solidarity's Center for Social Research (OBS). Some surveys focused on just one city, such as the University of Warsaw's repetitive surveys in Łódź; while others (most others, in fact) consisted of nationwide representative samples of the adult population. Solidarity's OBS generally asked questions only of Solidarity members. Other surveys, such as the Academy of Sciences' two surveys (*Polacy '80* and *Polacy '81*) included questions on union membership, allowing comparisons of the views of Solidarity members and non-members. Each of these research institutions, their surveys and methodologies, are discussed more fully in Chapter 1.

All of these factors taken together, the more open and participatory atmosphere in Poland during 1980–1, the multiplication of public opinion research centers, the more sophisticated and penetrating nature of survey research, contribute to the reliability and usefulness of the results of such research. The public opinion data provide a rich resource for the study of this epochal period of Poland's history.

I

Public opinion research in Poland

Public opinion research became part of the 'renewal' that swept across Poland in 1980 and 1981. The topics available for study during this period were practically unlimited, and studies that would have been kept under lock and key before 1980 were now made available to the public. Universities, periodicals, and even Solidarity conducted public-opinion surveys with little central supervision or censorship. All of this was a function of the changed environment, but also became an important factor in shaping the political environment. Political actors on both sides attempted to use the survey data issuing from this period to bolster their positions. Public opinion research, like so much else in Poland, became highly politicized.

POLISH PUBLIC OPINION RESEARCH BEFORE 1980

The development of public opinion research in Poland is thoroughly addressed in Sicinski (1963, 1967), Huszczo (1977) and Ward (1981) and will be only summarized here. The evolution of official attitudes towards public opinion research and its use was similar to the regional pattern described in the Introduction. Poland, however, has been slightly ahead of the pack on most of these issues. Poland has the richest tradition in sociological research in Eastern Europe, and was the first to begin systematic public opinion polling. Polish sociologists were among the first to take advantage of the 'thaw' in the region after the death of Stalin, with the establishment by the Polish Academy of Sciences (Polska Akademia Nauk, hereafter PAN) of a Center for Sociological Research in 1954. In the aftermath of the 'Polish October' a large number of sociological research institutes were set up by PAN, the universities in Warsaw and other cities, the (communist) Polish United Workers' Party, and various government agencies. A number of media research centers were also constituted, some of which conducted their own public opinion surveys of the media habits of the public and the influence of the media on public opinion. The most important of these were the Center for Press Research in Kraków and the Center for Public Opinion Research (Ośrodek Badania Opinii Publicznej, hereafter OBOP) set up in Warsaw in 1958 and later reconstituted and subordinated to the government Committee on Polish Radio and Television. Later on, OBOP polls focused on the popularity and attention to various radio and television programs, but at first they surveyed a much broader range of issues. In the early post-October period the results of OBOP and other polls were widely publicized and generated a great deal of interest. Huszczo (1977, p. 43) characterizes the period from 1958 to 1963 as 'the heyday of Polish public opinion studies'. Sociologists who conducted these surveys were relatively autonomous, and did not have to justify public opinion research in terms of Marxist ideology, as was being done in the Soviet Union (Mink 1981, p. 127). The new emphasis on public opinion research was praised for its function of reflecting the moods, goals, and needs of the population and for its usefulness in 'the democratic guidance of society' (cited in Huszczo 1977, p. 68).

Surveys conducted and published during this period included some controversial polls of student attitudes on Marxism, socialism, and religion; popular assessments of the standard of living and especially of food supplies; support for private vs. socialized agriculture; perceptions of the existence and sources of social and class distinctions; and popular impressions of other countries, including the U.S. and the Soviet Union. The result of these surveys likely caused the regime both satisfaction and concern. On the one hand, most Poles approved the basic tenets of socialism and applauded the accomplishments of the regime in raising the standard of living, reducing social class differences, and expanding social and occupational mobility. On the other hand, the effects of fifteen years of socialization seem to have been slight. Few students described themselves as Marxists and most were still practicing Catholics. There was widespread dissatisfaction with the availability of food and other consumer goods. And in the 1961 poll on other countries, the United States came out about as well as the Soviet Union (see Huszczo 1977, p. 64).

The slowdown in public opinion research

The renaissance of public opinion research began to fade in the early 1960s, just as Gomułka's reform program did. The Polish October had opened up a two-way flow of information between the population and the leadership, and public opinion research was one means to convey information from below. As the political system increasingly returned to its authoritarian pattern, the upward flow of information was cut off, and public opinion research became less useful.

After the early 1960s, there were few published national surveys, and the more sensitive political issues were avoided. The 1961 Warsaw University study, for example, which was meant to be the first of a series of periodic investigations into student attitudes, turned out to be the last. Most of the polls of the 1960s were restricted in scope, testing opinions in a particular locality, or on narrowly defined issues. OBOP, which had previously conducted such interesting surveys, was in 1965 reorganized and attached to the Committee on Radio and Television, and confined most of its research to the media habits of the population.

There was some widened scope for sociological research, however, in terms of cross-national surveys. In the 1960s, the Academy of Sciences participated in a survey of local leaders that was part of comparative study of the United States, Yugoslavia, India and Poland (see Jacob 1971). In the 1970s, Słomczyński, Miller and Kohn (1981) executed a replication in Poland of some American surveys on social stratification, values, and authoritarianism. And Renata Siemieńska (1982) has compared 'materialist' and 'post-materialist' values in Poland with those in West European countries. Most of the results of these works were published outside Poland, however, and had little impact on the debate over public opinion research within the country.

The retreat from surveys of public opinion did occasion some criticism from the academic community. In 1967, Andrzej Siciński complained that public opinion research was being slighted because of the emphasis on the 'one-way flow of information from the center of power to the society at large' (cited in Gitelman 1977, p. 5). He also pointed out that the research that was being conducted was not being used by the authorities. In words that were to reflect almost exactly similar complaints fifteen years later, Siciński pointed out the 'lack of properly organized and institutionalized channels for conveying the data and conclusions from the research centers to the executive authorities. As yet, no satisfactory mechanism has been developed for introducing research data into the policy-making process' (cited in Gitelman 1977, pp. 29–30). The neglect of public opinion research was only one symptom of the increasing alienation of the Gomułka regime from the population. Gomułka's lack of understanding of the popular mood, and the failure to foresee the public's reaction to the December 1970 food price increases, contributed to the collapse of his government that month.

The new Gierek leadership pledged to be more open and responsive to public needs. Stefan Nowak, the dean of public opinion researchers in Poland, took the opportunity to appeal for a revitalization of public opinion research, in an article that appeared in the Party's monthly theoretical journal (Nowak 1971). Nowak criticized the past attitudes towards sociological research, which was assessed primarily for its propaganda value rather than a source of information. Social research should be accepted and encouraged even if the results were complex and controversial. This would help in the determination of individual and social needs, and provide practical information for policy-makers for the allocation of resources, and the assessment of the impact of policy decisions on the population.

Gierek largely ignored Nowak's advice. Opinion was to be gauged in the more traditional fashion through the mass membership organizations, the Party, and meetings of Party and government leaders with ordinary workers. Polls were still taken, but they were usually restricted to 'internal use only'. The Gierek regime was hoping to avoid significant political reform by pacifying the population with improvements in the standard of living. The years 1970–5 saw dramatic increases in real wages, availability of food and consumer goods, and foreign imports. Public opinion polls during this period concentrated on popular satisfaction with material things and the standard of living. In 1974 the Central Committee set up its own public opinion research center to monitor worker attitudes in 164 key industrial enterprises. This Center for Research on Social Opinion was attached to the Party's 'think tank', the Institute of Basic Problems of Marxism–Leninism (Instytut Podstawowych

Problemów Marksizmu–Leninizmu – hereafter IPPML), and therefore gave the regime more control over the content of the surveys and the distribution of the results. While the results were provided to Party and government leaders, they were generally not published, except *post facto* after August 1980.

That the strategy of consumerism paid off is evident from the annual OBOP polls on whether the previous year was good or bad. In 1974, 60% assessed the previous year positively, and in 1975, 81% did (Siemieńska 1982). At the same time, in the early 1970s, the public expressed satisfaction with the accomplishments the regime had made since 1970, and expressed confidence in the political leadership. Young people were more interested in a 'peaceful' life than an 'active' one, and few expressed any particular interest in political activity or political reform (Gołębiowski 1976 and Ward 1981, p. 423).

The slowdown in economic growth in 1975 and 1976 and the protests in Radom and Ursus in the summer of 1976 ended the honeymoon period for the Gierek leadership. As the regime became less confident, it put even further restrictions on public opinion research. Information became scarce on both survey results and on the polling institutes themselves, as they were instructed not to disseminate results (Mink 1981, p. 130). Although OBOP had initiated its own quarterly journal (*Przekazy i Opinie*) in 1975, it seldom carried survey results, emphasizing survey methodology. Even the quantity of OBOP polls decreased after 1975, from about ten a year in the early 1970s to five a year after 1975 (Ward 1981). And while surveys continued to be conducted by other organizations, most were of a non-political nature, questioning attitudes on labor, wasted time, press readership, expectations of the future, etc.

Albin Kania, the Director of OBOP, later discussed the institute's problems in the latter 1970s. After 1976, OBOP continued to investigate attitudes on the standard of living, confidence in the mass media, societal optimism, and even attention to foreign radio stations. But the results were so 'glaringly' at odds with the demands and expectations of the authorities that OBOP was required to classify the results and restrict circulation. They ended up 'on the shelf, forgotten' (Kania 1981).

A similar assessment was provided by Zbigniew Sufin, the sociologist in charge of the surveys at the Party's IPPML. Research was rarely initiated by the Party leadership, and the results were usually ignored. Sufin later wrote that the results of the research sent to the Party leadership 'was a sufficiently strong signal of the growing difficulties, but unfortunately these signals were ignored'. A series of results prepared for use at the 8th Party Congress in early 1980 contained 'a strong critical current', but these results also were 'wasted' (Sufin 1981a, pp. 2–4).

Public opinion research on the eve of 1980

The official attitude toward public opinion research at the end of the 1970s is revealed in an article by Lesław Wojtasik appearing in *Polityka* in April 1980. While this article takes a somewhat 'progressive' attitude toward the need for more accurate information in Polish society, it is distinctly conservative on public opinion and other sociological research. It is clear from this article how far away the regime was from the suggestions made by Stefan Nowak in early 1971. Wojtasik addresses the 'public mood' and admits that it is not just influenced by material conditions. The public also has certain informational needs which, if not satisfied, will lead people to turn to 'other sources which are not always friendly towards us'. To avoid this, it is necessary to improve the quantity, quality and accuracy of information disseminated through the media. Various representative organs need also to be 'put to better use than has been done until now'. These are mild criticisms, but reflect some recognition of the lack of success of the socialization process in Poland (on which more below).

The author argues the importance of gauging *and modifying* the public mood, but diminishes the role of survey research for this purpose. The public mood, he says, can simply be defined as 'good' or 'bad', and the best way to determine this is not through polls and sociological interviews, but through direct contact with people. This would include the organized activities of agitators, the copying down of comments in discussions at gatherings, conversations between workers and managers, and the observation of collective behavior. Such means can provide an accurate measure of the public mood, and facilitate efforts to counteract negative moods through the 'mass system of agitation'.

A similarly restrictive view of survey research is provided in a 1980 book on the *Theoretical Problems of Propaganda and Public Opinion*.

The author treats public opinion as an element of propaganda. He does not arrive at 'the idea and essence of public opinion' until the second half of the book, and then hardly mentions survey research as a method of ascertaining public opinion. Public opinion, as he defines it, serves only three functions: integration, consultation and control. 'Consultation', though, needs to be carried out 'through existing party and social organizations' and through the mass media (Kuśmierski 1980, pp. 309–19). He does not mention systematic polling in this context. Survey research apparently serves no function in providing information or facilitating decision-making, or as a form of scholarly inquiry.

These are extremely retrograde views of public opinion research, and are not much different from that put forward in the Stalinist era. The article confirms Nowak's 1971 contention that the authorities distrusted not only the results of public opinion research, but also the scientific method of doing so. As Gitelman points out, surveys of public opinion are midway between 'traditional communist channels of opinion expression', such as letter writing and group meetings, and 'the still inadmissable system of interest groups' (1977, p. 32). Wojtasik's article suggests a retreat even from this midway, with a return to the more traditional methods. It also reflects the increasing weakness and lack of legitimacy of the Gierek regime. Increasingly isolated from the public and unaware of the rising 'bad mood' in society, Gierek continued to push unpopular policies. Without adequate information about public opinion, he was unable to avoid the catastrophe that befell the regime in the summer of 1980.

In a way, the regime had dug its own grave during the early 1970s. During that time, the population was persuaded to accept the political regime, even if grudgingly, in exchange for improvements in the economy. Indeed, the survey polls of the 1970s indicate increasing attention to material needs and concerns. At the same time, most people had become largely apolitical. Youth surveys from the late 1970s showed declining interest in public life and increasing attention to friends and families at the expense of the larger community and country. Of thirteen goals and life aspirations, 'the ability to influence affairs of the state' was in 12th place in one survey (Siemieńska 1982, p. 17). Young people were even more apolitical. When they were asked what qualities they valued, 'ideology' appeared in *last* place on a list of fifteen (Wolski 1980). In shifting the attention of workers and young people from politics to the economy, the success of the economy became of crucial importance to the legitimacy of the regime. This worked fine during the early 1970s, but when the economy began to falter, so did the legitimacy of the regime. People were not generally interested in politics, but they did expect steady increases in the standard of living.

The inattention to political things was in large part due to the nature and influence of the media. Most people read either the local or national party papers (Ward 1981, p. 395). Both Polish radio and television are widely followed by the population. Despite the attention to the official media, they have less impact on the formation of opinions than do families, friends and other sources. In a survey reported in 1977, it was found that the family (by far the most important) and books were more significant in forming public opinion than was the press. Furthermore, only half of the sample in this survey acknowledged the moral right of the Party to form public opinion (cited in Mink 1981, pp. 131–2).

This survey did not mention some other important media: foreign radio stations and the Catholic Church. Mid-1970s polls by Radio Free Europe of listeners in Poland found 55% of the respondents saying that RFE helped them to form opinions (Hart 1980, p. 19). Polish surveys of young people from the same period show about a third listening to foreign radio stations, including 12% to RFE (Olędzki 1983, p. 257). The Church also played and continues to play, an important role in the formation of public opinion. Most Poles attend Sunday masses, where the celebrant often reads pronouncements and communiques from the Pope, the Primate, or the Polish bishops.

The lack of effectiveness of media socialization of the public, in combination with the worsening economic situation and an increasingly surly population, made even more imperative the need for effective public opinion research. Scholars later complained that in the late 1970s, their research on public opinion, 'manifestations of social pathology', and other research was virtually ignored by the authorities. In the absence of accurate information about what the public thought and what it wanted, the regime increasingly relied on coercion to stifle dissent. But when, in the summer of 1980, dissent engulfed virtually the entire population, coercion was no longer a viable tool.

PUBLIC OPINION RESEARCH DURING THE SOLIDARITY ERA

With the signature of the Gdańsk agreements in August 1980, and the subsequent formation and growth of the Independent Self-governing Trade Union Solidarity, the whole of Polish society became more open, pluralistic, and critical. This was also true of academic researchers, especially sociologists. During the end of 1980 and 1981, public opinion research was more openly pursued, discussed, and published, and conducted by a wider variety of institutions, than ever before in Poland. Indeed, the openness of survey research in Solidarity's Poland was unprecedented for any communist country, surpassing even the rush of public opinion surveys from Czechoslovakia in the spring of 1968 (see Piekalkiewicz 1972).

In the more open 'post-August' atmosphere, there was frequent discussion in the press over the failure of the Gierek regime to adequately account for public opinion. Jacek Maziarski, writing in *Kultura* on January 25, 1981 addressed the causes of the 1980 events:

> The authorities, free of public opinion's control, had the feeling of complete freedom of action, but it was a misleading and dangerous freedom ... Restrictions of free speech and manipulative propaganda gimmicks created a pacifying image of unanimity and approval. In effect, the authorities were misled by the fiction created by themselves. They did not know what the public really thought.

In ignoring public opinion, the leadership had become overly dependent on 'interest groups, industry lobbies, particular factions and cliques'.

The new Kania leadership apparently agreed with this assessment, and allowed a wide range of public opinion polls to be conducted and published by the official polling organizations, academic institutions, newspapers, and even Solidarity. Some of the results were of doubtful validity, but the academic institutions, in particular, made a major effort to meet some of the criticism and suggestions raised by Stefan Nowak ten years earlier. While OBOP and other official organizations accelerated the pace and publication of their research efforts, there was an even more rapid expansion of survey research by the universities and the Academy of Sciences. Nowak had noted earlier that the affiliation of the pollsters could have important effects on the responses elicited from the population.

Pollsters from research institutes tend to obtain more 'objective' responses than do those from governmental or party polling organizations. So with surveys increasingly conducted both inside and outside the government, there was an opportunity to compare results, and to balance the data obtained by different sources. There were other novelties in this period. There were a number of systematic national representative samples of public opinion, in contrast to the usual practice of focusing on one particular group or region. This provided a better picture of the public mood, but also allowed more sophisticated analysis of the differentiation of public opinion by region, occupational groups, union and party membership, religious belief, etc. Finally, surveys in 1980 and 1981 often posed questions about specific policies already adopted or being contemplated by the regime. This was highly unusual for a communist country, and came to function as a kind of continuing referendum on the policies and the programs of both Solidarity and the regime. The following sections will review the survey research efforts during 1980–1 of the official polling organizations, the 'semi-official' ones in the academic and journalists' communities, and of Solidarity.

Official polling organizations

The two main official polling organizations after 1980 were Polish Radio and Television's OBOP and the Central Committee's IPPML. There were significant changes in the activities of both after 1980, though in different forms. OBOP, on the one hand, expanded the frequency and distribution of its polls, while IPPML proceeded to publish the results of some earlier surveys that had received limited press coverage.

OBOP had been fairly active in the later 1970s but, as mentioned above, there was little publicity about the nature of its research, or the results of the surveys. All of this changed dramatically at the end of 1980. OBOP increased the frequency of its polls (national representative samples of several thousand adults) to twice monthly or more. During the first seven months of 1981, OBOP conducted 26 surveys. It expanded the list of recipients of its communiques to 200 people, including government and party officials, academics and journalists. By the middle of 1981, OBOP was even circulating its reports to Solidarity headquarters and to the editors of *Tygodnik Solidarność*. As Albin Kania, the Director of OBOP, declared 'there is no secret research any more' (*Wall Street Journal*, July 6, 1981, p. 17).

Kania asserted that the government was taking account of public opinion before making decisions, 'which is something of a novelty in our political and social life'. For the first time now, *government* offices addressed requests to the center to conduct polls on policy issues such as taxes, prices, rationing, social benefits, etc. Kania asserted a new role for public opinion research – to educate the society about itself:

> Showing that other people have different opinions about the same thing teaches tolerance and respect – that differences of opinion must be settled by presenting arguments in a discussion, not by imposing one's view. It's good for both the authorities and Solidarity ... The polls tend to discourage the radicals and extremists in both the party and Solidarity. That's why it's very important for the society to know what it thinks as a whole (*Wall Street Journal*, July 6, 1981).

Even though there was much greater press coverage of OBOP polls than before August, Kania thought there should be more. He complained that while all OBOP results were sent to editors, the results rarely appeared in the press. It is a pity, he said, that 'old ways still persist' (Kania 1981).

During 1980 and 1981, OBOP conducted surveys on a wide range of issues, and many of these were summarized in *Życie Warszawy*, *Kultura*, *Polityka*, or other newspapers. One standard question, asked at least several times a year before 1980 and almost every month after August was on people's assessment of the past year and expectations of the future. This 'optimism index' provides a useful indicator of the changing public mood over this period. The radical fluctuations in this index also confirm Western findings that attitudes and opinions, as opposed to 'orientations', are highly unstable and respond sharply and quickly to political and economic developments.

OBOP conducted many other surveys on some of the most controversial and important issues of the day. In November 1980, OBOP surveyed public opinion on the causes of the 1980 crisis and the issues of primary concern to the population (reported in Maziarski 1981). In early March, it surveyed popular attitudes towards the new Jaruzelski government and its '10 point program' (Radio Warsaw, March 30, 1981). In May OBOP approached the highly sensitive subject of public confidence in various institutions.

The results, which showed the Party in last place of fifteen, were presented in summary form in *Kultura*. In the spring, OBOP also surveyed attitudes on how best to deal with the budget crisis, whether through price increases, income taxes, or wage freezes. These surveys on specific policy issues are virtually unprecedented in the communist countries. In the fall, OBOP polls concentrated on the increasingly tense situation in the country, the culpability of the government vs. Solidarity for the crisis, and the possible avenues of resolution of the crisis.

The OBOP polls tackled some sensitive and important issues, attracted unprecedented publicity, and apparently were actually used in policy formations. The published results were often unfavorable to the regime. But they were not free of some of the errors of validity and reliability that were characteristic of the pre-Solidarity era, and they were more likely to serve the purposes of the regime than were the semi-official polls to be discussed below. Not all of the OBOP results were reported in the press. Some of them received no media mention at all; others were selectively quoted. Furthermore, often the results were portrayed in a way that supported the regime's point of view. The November 1980 poll discussed in *Kultura*, for example, reported a high level of public interest in 'calm and stability', much higher than the expressed interest in 'democratization of life', limitations on censorship, etc. This issue of 'calm and stability' was used by the regime all during 1981 in its criticism of Solidarity and the societal disruptions caused by the union. Similarly, certain results of a series of fall polls on the levels of trust in the government and the leadership of Solidarity were not released at first, when many more people indicated trust in Solidarity than in the government. But by the end of November, the polls showed a trend, with increasing numbers trusting the government, and declining trust in Solidarity. At that point, shortly before the declaration of martial law, the communique was released, showing the whole series of results. By referring to this poll, the government could claim, as it later did, that people were becoming disillusioned with Solidarity, but felt that a confrontation between the two sides was inevitable. Martial law, then, was billed as having saved Polish society from chaos, instability, and perhaps even civil war.

The public opinion research center of the Central Committee's Institute of Basic Problems of Marxism–Leninism (IPPML), which was created in 1975, had also been very active in surveying public attitudes during the late 1970s. The results of these surveys were even more closely guarded than those of OBOP. Between 1975 and 1980, the Institute carried out ten major survey research projects, each based on national samples of 2000 to 5000 people; it also carried out a number of surveys of a large sample of some 20,000 workers in 164 large enterprises. In addition, the Institute did analysis of other survey data, including a 1975 survey by the Main Statistical Office (Główny Urząd Statystyczny) of 22,000 people on living conditions and societal needs (Beskid and Sufin, 1981). Most of these surveys concentrated on living conditions, assessments of developments in the early 1970s, and opinions about local government and party organizations. There were few sensitive political issues addressed in these surveys (at least as far as subsequent publications indicate). Even so, virtually none of these results were reported in the press, or even published by IPPML itself, until *after* August 1980.

Some of the results of these surveys began to appear in the press in 1981, and the Institute itself published four volumes of data and analysis of these 1970s surveys in the spring of 1981 (Beskid and Sufin, 1981; Sufin 1981a and 1981b). Despite the fairly non-controversial nature of the results, the size of the editions were quite small, numbering only 500 each. Presumably this was sufficient for distribution to most top government and party offices, but not even all members of the Central Committee saw these volumes, and few sociologists in the universities did. This limited distribution is even more surprising in that the Director of IPPML, Jerzy Wiatr, was himself a sociologist at the University of Warsaw. The secretiveness with which IPPML protected its data perhaps reflects the Party leadership's continuing concern with its image and its legitimacy. The volumes that were finally released contained little that was directly critical of the regime or the leadership, at a time when polls released by OBOP, the Academy of Sciences, and Solidarity did. The coordinator of the IPPML research project, Zbigniew Sufin, complained in one of the volumes that *before* 1980 the authorities had paid little attention to the results of their research, and implied that the crisis of 1976 and 1980 could have been avoided or mitigated by paying more attention to public opinion data. The handling of IPPML research results (in 1981 and after) suggests that the party leadership remained highly suspicious of the use of public opinion research and the dissemination of its results.

'Semi-official' polling organizations

Many surveys were conducted during 1980 and 1981 by organizations that were not so closely tied to, or controlled by the authorities; these included newspapers, the universities, and the Academy of Sciences. Newspaper surveys generally were not systematic or representative, and focused on public reaction to immediate political events and the economic situation. An example of this is a poll conducted by the weekly *Polityka* on September 4, 1980, just a few days after the signature of the Gdańsk Agreements (results presented in T. A. Jones, *et al.*, 1984). The *Polityka* survey asked 500 employees of large industrial plants their assessments of the causes, results, and likely consequences of 'the latest developments'. Most people believed that the strikes were 'an unavoidable consequence of existing policies' or 'a justified protest of working people'. The most important results were perceived to be the creation of the new trade unions and the commitment to an improvement of the standard of living. People were quite optimistic about the potential impact of these events on the society, the economy, and the political system. The publication of these data signals a change already in the openness of the press and in the willingness to address and publish public opinion on politically sensitive subjects. These kinds of questions had rarely been asked in the previous decade, and had certainly not appeared in the popular press. These results were not entirely out of line with the official position on these events. The authorities were already (half-heartedly) admitting that the strikes were justified, that past policies had been mistaken, and that the future would be better. But in some respects public opinion was ahead of the leadership, and these results, in conjunction with the strikes themselves, probably contributed to the removal of Gierek on September 5. His resignation made it easier for the new Kania regime to pursue the line that the events of the summer had been an inevitable consequence of bad policies implemented by Kania's predecessors.

This *Polityka* survey with quantitative results was an unusual one for a newspaper. The more typical newspaper survey was a series of interviews with a number of workers, students, managers, etc. with the results presented 'qualitatively' by quoting the respondents and summarizing the results. An example of this was a fall 1980 poll of 205 enterprise directors on economic reform. The results showed that, as a group, the directors favored decentralization, self-management, a greater role for workers' councils, and flexibility in the setting of wages and prices (Chmielewski 1981). Like the *Polityka* poll mentioned above, these results were unlike anything that had appeared before in the Polish press, but they were also in line with the official plans for economic reform at the time of their publication. Of course, much public opinion research conducted by other organizations was published in the official press. *Życie Warszawy* was particularly active in this regard, frequently presenting results of OBOP and other surveys. The weekly *Kultura* had several long pieces on the results of surveys by OBOP and by the Academy of Sciences. And a number of unlikely publications (for example, *Przeglad Techniczny*) often carried results of some of the more interesting and potentially sensitive surveys conducted by academic sociologists. All of this reflected the renewal and pluralization of Polish society that was strongly supported in the journalists' community. Publishing surveys showing popular support for change was itself a political act. Their appearance contributed to the sense of solidarity in the population.

With the arrival of the Solidarity era, academic sociologists were able to conduct surveys with an unprecedented degree of freedom. They were able to ask questions that had not been permitted before, or to ask them in a much more direct manner. Given the general relaxation of controls in society, respondents were more willing to provide honest answers, providing greater validity to the results. And many results, which previously would have been restricted in circulation, were now published in the press or circulated in the academic community.

A few diverse examples will illustrate these points. At the end of 1980, the Institute of Sociology of the University of Warsaw, in cooperation with the Institute of Philosophy and Sociology of the Polish Academy of Sciences (hereafter by the Polish acronym IFIS PAN) conducted the fourth of a series of surveys of working males in the city of Łódź. Similar surveys, asking many of the same questions, had been done in 1960, 1964 and 1976. The previous surveys had focused primarily on the questions of equality, social stratification, and social mobility. The same questions were asked in 1980, but there were additional questions including those about the late 1970s and about union membership. This then enabled the testing of views on some fundamental issues by union membership. Unfortunately, little analysis of these data was done in Poland before the declaration of martial law.

There was also a very interesting survey on political socialization in the schools conducted by a doctoral candidate in the Institute of Sociology at the University of Warsaw. The main thrust of the project was to examine the influence of parents' and teachers' attitudes on elementary school students in Warsaw. But the questions included some remarkably sensitive ones on Poland's best friends and worst enemies, the sense of political efficacy (questions drawn from the *Civic Culture* surveys), and the most admired living persons (the Pope was the first choice of every group). This survey was interrupted by martial law, and the researchers had to content themselves with truncated data, but preparation of the results continued after martial law.

A third project at the University of Warsaw was an international collaborative effort that involved in-depth interviews with Solidarity activists. The project was led by French sociologist Alain Touraine, but most of the work in Poland was conducted by Polish sociologists. Some of these results have been published in Touraine's *Solidarity* (1983). This whole project was unique both because of the subject matter and the international team. It was remarkable enough that the 'leaders of the opposition', Solidarity activists, were the subject of such a major project. To allow the participation of Western sociologists in the study was even more remarkable, and attests to the extraordinary degree of autonomy and academic freedom achieved by the universities during 1981.

The most interesting public opinion surveys of the Solidarity era were two national representative samples taken at the end of 1980 and the end of 1981 by IFIS PAN, entitled *Polacy '80* (Poles '80) and *Polacy '81*. These were highly unusual surveys in that they were large national representative samples, with extensive questions on the backgrounds of the respondents, and a large number of questions about the political and economic environment as well as on more fundamental ideological issues. The first survey was more cautious than the second, but asked a number of questions about the Gdańsk Agreements, the strikes of 1980, the causes of the crisis, and support for Solidarity. It also asked opinions about the role of the Party and the Church in Polish society, and support for policies associated with political and economic decentralization and with egalitarianism. The larger number of questions allowed fertile field for analysis, in which seven sociologists participated. Each of them contributed a chapter in the final report, which was published in two small editions and sold in bookstores. One of the chapters attempted to construct from the data various 'models' of opinion along two dimensions: 'monocentric–pluralistic', and 'egalitarian–non-egalitarian effectiveness'. The authors concluded that there was strong support both for a more pluralistic society and a more egalitarian one, though support for these principles did not always come from the same people.

The *Polacy '81* survey was conducted at the end of 1981, just before the declaration of martial law. This survey asked many of the same questions as the earlier survey, allowing a comparison of attitudes between the beginning and the end of the Solidarity era. But it also added a number of new questions that addressed even more openly the hot political issues of the winter of 1981. These included questions on the locus of responsibility for the crisis, the perceptions of the source of the threat to Poland's sovereignty (asked but not reported in the *Polacy '80* survey), and the perceived need for various emergency measures to cope with the crisis. Most interesting of all, this survey asked about the Party's role in Polish society, whether it should retain its monopoly of power, and whether *new* political parties should be constituted, including by Solidarity. Never before had such questions been asked and reported so openly in Poland.

The large number of opinion questions and background characteristics on the respondents allowed the researchers to do a considerable number of cross-tabulations and statistical tests of significance of relationships between certain variables and also to examine in some detail the sources of support for various policies and ideas. The *Polacy '81* report included, for example, the most detailed treatment available of the membership of Solidarity, by occupational category, religious belief, and even Party membership.

The project director, Władysław Adamski, asserted that the major task of the survey was to better understand the sources of conflict in a socialist society. But unlike in past studies, the researchers looked for such sources not only in the economic sphere, but *primarily* in the political realm. In the introduction to the final report of this survey, Adamski noted the lack of congruence between social needs and aspirations and the effectiveness of economic and political institutions in satisfying them. He also noted the increased feelings of weakness and disenfranchisement in the population (pp. 5–11). Like some of the other public opinion surveys of 1981, the *Polacy '81* survey was cut short by the declaration of martial law. As the last national survey before December 13, though, it provides a fascinating portrait of the attitudes of Poles a year after the formation of Solidarity and on the eve of martial law. At first there was some doubt about whether the *Polacy '81* report would see the light of day, given its controversial and sensitive findings. These included more detail and substantiation for the abysmally low reputation of the Party; the open expression of the belief that the Soviet Union was the main threat to Poland's sovereignty; and the continued widespread support for the activities of Solidarity. By the spring of 1982, though, the chapter drafts of the report were circulating in the Academy of Sciences (though not outside that institution), which held a number of seminars on the major findings. Eventually the report was published in house in a small edition of 500 copies 'for internal use only'. It was not, however, distributed for public consumption as had been the *Polacy '80* book. The *Polacy '81* report seems to have 'slipped through the cracks' of martial law, as a number of other controversial books had by virtue of being in process at the time martial law was declared. It is unlikely that such public opinion surveys will be published again under the present regime.

Solidarity's public opinion polls

Public opinion research was pluralized even further with the establishment of a Solidarity public opinion research organization. The Center for Social Research (Ośrodek Badań Społecznych, hereafter OBS) attached to Solidarity's Mazowsze (Warsaw) region organization, was set up in October 1980 as the union's official research institute (Dorn 1981). Later, a similar research organization was set up in the East-Central (Lublin) region.

The OBS was charged with polling the union's members and proposing ideas for the programs, activities, and strategy of the movement. The OBS polls were random samples of Solidarity members, usually several hundred in a particular region. They provided the union leadership with feedback from its members, and provide us, retrospectively, with a useful set of data to balance the official and semi-official polls. The most direct comparison is provided by a survey conducted by Solidarity in October 1981, replicating the spring OBOP poll on confidence in fifteen institutions. The poll of Solidarity members showed roughly the same rankings of the institutions, though Solidarity, as might be expected, scored even higher and the Party, in last place, even lower than in the OBOP poll.

Probably the most thoroughgoing Solidarity poll was one conducted in April 1981 among some 695 union members in the Lublin region. This survey attempted to ascertain the basic orientations of the union's members towards the union, it accomplishments, its leadership, and its future (Krasko 1981). It asked general questions about Solidarity (e.g. whether one's expectations about the union had been fulfilled) as well as questions about the past and future policies and tactics of the union. The results revealed continued strong support for the union, though the support was more conditional than it had been at the end of 1980. By the fall of 1981, Solidarity's public opinion research effort was becoming more extensive and more sophisticated. By this time, OBS was conducting nationwide polls of about 1000 Solidarity members. Some surveys were designed to measure the level of support for the union's leadership while others tested the waters on specific issues, such as the use of the strike weapon and the government's proposal for a temporary suspension of strikes. In October, OBS polled the delegates at Solidarity's national congress on some fundamental issues, then compared the results to those obtained from the national sample. Here too, one sees continued strong support for the union's national leadership and its policies, but also some sharp cleavages in the attitudes and orientations of the activists at the Congress and the general union membership.

The Solidarity polls provide much information that is not available from the official and semi-official polls. They specifically tap the opinions of Solidarity members on both national issues and Solidarity policies. The later polls, especially, provide insight into the differentiation of views within the movement, and the sources of tension between the activists and members, and the national and regional leadership. And the fact that Solidarity itself conducted these surveys suggests that the results on some issues may be somewhat more reliable than official surveys; people had less to fear from Solidarity pollsters than from official ones, and may have provided more open responses.

On the other hand, the Solidarity results should be treated with some caution too. Respondents may have exaggerated support for the policies and leadership of Solidarity as a sign of support for the union. And many of Solidarity's polls were conducted in the big factories where opinions were likely to be more radical than in the membership at large.

PUBLIC OPINION RESEARCH UNDER MARTIAL LAW

The imposition of martial law on December 13, 1981 terminated the activities of public opinion research as much as those of Solidarity. A number of interview projects, including the major *Polacy '81* survey, were ended before they were completed. There were no new polls at all in the first months of martial law, except by the official OBOP. The changed situation was very much as Gitelman described such trends:

As regards public opinion, when the possibilities of influencing politics and social life appear to be expanding, there is a growing interest in public opinion surveys in the population as a whole. When the activist period is ended, polls cease to be taken at all or are concentrated on more specialized and less controversial issues, and interest in public opinion wanes, as does belief in its importance and efficacy (Gitelman 1977, p. 23).

This phenomenon prevailed in Czechoslovakia in the year after August 1968, and was also true in Poland during 1982.

This did not mean that academic research on public opinion stopped. In fact, there was a remarkable degree of normality in the academic community under martial law, as sociologists continued to discuss and analyze the data that they had collected during the previous year. Some of these results were quite controversial and were unlikely to be published, but work continued anyway. Indeed some of these results *were* published. The *Polacy '81* report was printed and distributed, albeit in limited numbers, and was eventually discussed in *Polityka* and on Polish radio. A summary of the report, however, prepared for the journal *Studia Socjologiczne*, was rejected by the censors. Some of the results of *Polacy '80* were analyzed in a remarkable issue of *Sisyphus* (in English) which addressed the causes of the conflicts of 1980 and 1981.

But few new polls were conducted in 1982, and even fewer were publicized. The martial law regime, uncertain of its support and legitimacy, refused to allow either independent organizations or independent public opinion polling. The only sanctioned polls during 1982 were by the official polling organizations, and few of these were published. After martial law, the Party's IPPML did not publish any of its survey results until July of 1983. Both the methods of polling, and the popular reaction to such research, had reverted to the pre-August period. Most survey questions were, as before, framed in such a way to suggest the right answer, or dealt with non-controversial subjects. The exceptions to these results simply were not made public. In March 1982, for example, OBOP and IFIS PAN conducted a survey of attitudes towards trade unions, including Solidarity. Apparently, the poll showed that over 70% of the population favored immediate reinstatement of Solidarity. The results were never made public. And in the face of this evidence, the regime continued to claim that the public no longer supported the independent trade union.

By the end of 1982, as the regime became somewhat more confident, some polling results were discussed more openly. In November, *Życie Warszawy* carried an analysis of a May 1982 survey of youth attitudes by the Institute of Research on Youth. The author of that article tried mightily to find positive elements in the results, but the best he could do was claim that 'it is not true that there is a total disbelief in socialism' among young people (Gołębioski 1982). This must have been small comfort to the authorities; but the fact that the issue was even addressed publicly suggests some continued interest in public opinion on the part of the regime. Similarly, at the end of 1982, OBOP released figures from its annual survey on how people assessed the previous year; only 17% found the year of martial law to have been 'good' (*Życie Warszawy*, December 30, 1982).

By the middle of 1982, though, there was a reassessment of the role of public opinion research. Jaruzelski may have stimulated this by asserting in a speech to the Sejm that the authorities must become accustomed to the systematic use of public opinion research. A major article in the government newspaper by the former chief of OBOP asserted that one of the major reasons for the 'current crisis' was the failure of the authorities to take into account 'the state of social consciousness and real social attitudes'. He admitted that public opinion was especially important under martial law precisely because 'public life is not conducted in normal conditions' (Łukasz Szymański 1982).

The ambivalent position of the government toward public opinion research became even more curious when it was announced in the spring of 1982 that the government would establish a new public opinion research organization. Warsaw sociologists (in conversations with this writer) were puzzled by the need for such an organization, given the continued activity of OBOP and the existence of IPPML (though the latter conducted no opinion research at all during 1982). Despite the uncertain mission of the new Public Opinion Survey Center (Centrum Badania Opinii Publicznej, hereafter CBOP), it began operations in early 1983, under the direction of Colonel Dr Stanisław Kwiatkowski. Kwiatkowski asserted that the survey results would be used both to support decision making and to provide the public with 'knowledge about itself'. He indicated a recognition of some of the recent lessons of survey research in stating: 'the awareness of public opinion, gathered mostly from individual talks and peoples' pronouncements at public meetings and employees' meetings with management, is very helpful, but is incomplete. The concurrence of several opinions cannot be taken to represent ... the opinions of the majority of the population (Kwiatkowski 1983). The tone of this suggests that public opinion research would not return to the old-fashioned methods of the 1950s. But given the mood of the population, and the continuing restrictive political environment, it was also unlikely to return to the free-wheeling days of Solidarity.

CONCLUSIONS

The role and use of public opinion research expanded dramatically during the Solidarity era in Poland. This was partly an inevitable consequence of the sudden shift in the political environment occasioned by the rise of Solidarity. As Karl Deutsch, David Apter and others have pointed out, highly coercive political systems tend to be 'low information systems', and vice versa. As the more coercive 'command' system of the Gierek regime gave way to the more pluralistic atmosphere of the Solidarity era, both the regime and Solidarity came to rely more on public opinion in the fashioning and justification of their policies. Such polls were also popular in the population, in that they acted as a channel for the expression of attitudes, needs, demands, and criticism. Through public opinion polls, as through Solidarity, some of these feelings were being openly addressed and expressed for the first time since the establishment of communist rule. The polls provided a means for the academics to help represent the interests of the workers. They provided another channel of communication from below, just as Solidarity did. In 1981, Poland had become a pluralist society without pluralist and representative institutions, so public opinion acted as a surrogate for those institutions. In this respect, public opinion played a stronger role in the political process than it does in most democratic societies.

The increased openness to public opinion research contributed to an improvement in the techniques of such surveys. Many of the pitfalls of public opinion research raised by Stefan Nowak in his 1971 article were addressed in the surveys of 1981. Nowak called for truly representative samples, which were not often used before or after his article. But during 1981, the *Polacy* surveys of IFIS PAN were true national representative samples, and both the official OBOP and Solidarity's OBS moved in this direction as well. Another problem had been with the way in which survey questions were formulated, such that the question often suggested the 'correct' response. In the mid-1970s, for example, IPPML asked people if things had improved since 1970; the positive responses were largely a foregone conclusion. Later, however, OBOP simply asked if the previous year was 'good' or 'bad', allowing for the expression of more gut-level feelings and more differentiated responses. And during 1981, virtually all of the polling organizations posed quite direct and open questions about confidence in institutions, support for various policies, and support for basic changes in the economy and the political system. Perhaps the most significant change in public opinion research was simply the diversification of organizations conducting polls. As Nowak pointed out, the responses people give often depend on who is asking the questions. When the Party's IPPML and the government's OBOP were asking the questions, people were bound to be cautious in their responses. Experience had shown, according to Nowak, that the best atmosphere for honest responses appears when research is conducted by purely scholarly institutions (as opposed to government ones). Thus the results obtained by the universities, the Academy of Sciences, and Solidarity (as an independent institution) provide more reliable results than those of the official institutions. Furthermore, the more open environment of 1981 undoubtedly contributed to popular willingness to be more open in their responses. Consequently, the survey results of 1981, whether or not they were effectively used by the authorities at the time, provide a uniquely accurate and revealing portrait of the basic orientations and short-term opinions of the population. Solidarity itself helped to focus, channel and institutionalize the rather diffuse sense of dissatisfaction in the population. Before Solidarity, there was little opportunity for Poles to collectively discuss their grievances and develop a hierarchy of needs and demands. Solidarity was beginning to fulfill this function. The public opinion polls of this period played a similar role in focusing public needs and demands and in creating what Edward Keenan has called 'a sense of statistical community'. The same process was at work in Czechoslovakia in 1968, when polls were one of the ways people felt they could influence events, and the widespread publicity of the results contributed to the individual's sense that he was not alone in his feelings (Gitelman, 1977, p. 22). In Poland, the first polls after the Gdańsk Agreements demonstrated the overwhelming popular support for the strikes and for the idea of an independent trade union. This contributed to the new and exciting sense of community and contributed both to the regime's acquiescence to the formation of Solidarity, and to the flood of members to the new union. This sense of community even extended to members of the Polish United Workers' Party (PZPR), many of whom sided with Solidarity or even joined the organization.

There were contrary tendencies in the public opinion data that did not bode so well for Solidarity. Over the course of Solidarity's sixteen months, there were some marked changes in public opinion that indicated two parallel processes: increasing divisions within the organization; and a 'demythification' of the movement. In the heady days of August and the fall of 1980, Solidarity enjoyed support that was both universal and unquestioning. By the end of 1981, while support was still solid, it was not nearly as uncritical. As the charismatic and revolutionary features of the movement gave way to a more institutionalized one, absorbed with policy debates and organizational detail, the bright image of Solidarity was bound to tarnish a bit. The public opinion polls both reflected and contributed to this process.

The poll results also became sources of public debates, and were used by both supporters and opponents of Solidarity. The more radical supporters of Solidarity could point to spring 1981 data showing that a majority of members supported the union's tactics, including warning strikes and general strikes. Solidarity members favoring a more moderate course could point to the *declining* support for the leadership and its tactics (including the strike) and to the members' support of a more restricted field of activities for the union. Opponents of Solidarity cited polls showing increasing confidence in the government, declining confidence in Solidarity, and widespread support for a return to 'law and order', anyway. Just as the public and professional interest in opinion polls came to replicate that in democratic societies, so did the political exploitation of the results of the surveys. The poll results themselves became a political tool, used by both Solidarity and the regime to justify their policies and to discredit the other side. Oftentimes, just as in the West, the same polls or the same data were used to support precisely opposite positions.

In a broader context, the public opinion polls of 1980–1 also revealed much about the political culture of Polish society. On the one hand, they largely confirmed the official line that most Poles supported the basic principles of socialism, and appreciated some of the long-term accomplishments of the post-war regime. On the other hand, the polls also revealed how deep were the feelings of dissatisfaction, betrayal, and cynicism. Popular trust in the political leadership was virtually nil, and most Poles felt that the self-interest and corruption of the leadership had led Poland off the path of socialism. The widespread dislike of the Soviet Union was also revealed in these polls. One can infer from all of this that the process of political socialization in this communist country, at least, has not been very effective. After thirty-five years of communist rule, during which an entire generation has been schooled and socialized to support and respect the system, Poles are deeply skeptical of Poland's political system, its economic organization, its ideology, and its foreign alliances.

Certainly, both Solidarity and the regime learned much about the role, influence, and potential of public opinion research. From the regime's point of view, much of this influence was negative; so it would like to exert more control over the process and results in the future. This may explain the establishment of the new Center for Public Opinion Research, which is strictly under government (and military) control. But the genie of public opinion cannot be put back in the bottle. People now *know* what Poles think, and it is unlikely that martial law has greatly affected the more deep-seated attitudes.

As Walter Connor (1977) has said, both communist and democratic regimes are increasingly willing to tolerate 'mass apoliticism' rather than commitment. Given the hopelessness for the post-Solidarity regime of trying to foster commitment, probably the best it can hope for is apathy.

2

The public and policy change in the 1970s

The disturbances of 1980 were a result of a number of long-term factors in Poland's postwar history. The Polish workers had come to use protest and revolt as an almost institutionalized mechanism for achieving political and economic change. The years of these protests had become virtually a litany by 1980: 1956, 1968, 1970, 1976. In fact, given the apparent petrification of the political system in Poland, protest was often seen as the *only* means of effecting change in the society. On the issue of food price increases, societal protest had achieved particular success: in both 1970 and 1976, the regime was compelled to rescind already announced increases in retail food prices.

The authorities had responded to these protests in a patterned way. Popular protests were followed by attempts to mollify the population with increased wages and consumer goods and, in 1956 and 1970, with a change in the top Party leadership position. Changes in the position of First Secretary resulted in a short-term emphasis on 'mass oriented policies' as the leadership tried to consolidate its position (Bunce 1980). As Bogdan Mieczkowski (1978) describes the situation, consumption has been inversely proportionate to the power of the Party. When the Party is weak, it uses consumption to win popular support. Once the new leadership has consolidated power, consumer interests once again recede, and the standard of living again declines. This has resulted in a kind of cyclical pattern in which dissatisfied Poles protest, leading to a change in policies or leaders, which causes a temporary improvement in the situation. Then, however, old leadership patterns reemerge, popular dissatisfaction resurfaces and tensions build up toward another series of protests.

This model focuses on the economic elements of the policy process; it is economic issues that spark protests, and it is through economic measures that the regime hopes to defuse tensions. While political issues have been raised in most protests (e.g. the slogan 'without freedom there is no bread' in 1956), these were always secondary and tended to be added on to primarily economic demands. Before 1980, the demands for political reform issued largely from intellectuals rather than from workers. As Zvi Gitelman (1981, p. 133) puts it:

For certain elements in Eastern Europe – intelligentsia, religious believers, some young people – consumer satisfaction is not an acceptable yardstick by which to judge the leadership, but for the large majority consumer satisfaction is the most important influence of their attitudes toward the leadership and the political system generally.

A second important long-term factor was the 'revolution of rising expectations'. All during the 1950s and 1960s, there had been a high rate of social and occupational mobility for workers. The rapid industrialization and economic development of the country, in fact, necessitated this kind of mobility; but this mobility also helped to counteract somewhat the deprivations of industrialization. As the regime concentrated on building up industry at the expense of consumer goods, the overall standard of living declined, but each *individual* worker had considerable opportunity to move ahead. Polish workers *perceived* high levels of inter-generational upward mobility as well. In surveys done among urban workers in 1964 and 1976, 70–85% thought that their occupational positions were higher or much higher than those of their fathers (Janicka 1981). This high degree of mobility generated even higher expectations. Polish sociologist Jan Szczepański called attention to this problem already in the late 1960s: the standard of living was increasing more slowly than expectations (1970, p. 128). All of this contributed to 'the revolution of rising expectations'.

There had also been steady and significant change in the composition of society that was to affect the outlook and behavior of workers in the 1970s. The industrialization and urbanization of Poland, particularly during the 1950s, had led to substantial shifts in the social composition of the population. In 1950, 28.3% of the population were workers and 47% were farmers. By 1970, 38% were workers and only 30% were farmers. This high rate of movement into the cities and factories had contributed to the high rate of occupational mobility: the children of farmers were now workers and enjoying the higher status and standard of living of the working class. These shifts also led to other changes in the social fabric, especially in education and technical skills. In 1970 there were three times as many students graduating from both secondary vocational schools (*szkoły zawodowe*) and from higher educational institutions as there had been in 1950. As the economy became more complex and diversified, so did the workforce. And, as has been true in other developing societies, it became less and less possible for the regime to rely on compulsion to achieve economic growth, as it had done in the 1950s. Increasingly, the regime came to rely on economic incentives, and the legitimacy of the communist state came to rest on consumer satisfaction.

By the late 1960s, it had become increasingly difficult to sustain the levels of economic growth that Poland had enjoyed in the previous twenty years. During the 1960s, real wage increases were much less than they had been in the second half of the 1950s. All during that decade, there was a decline in the share of national income devoted to consumption. Poland, more than most of the European communist states, was unsuccessful in adopting the economic reforms necessary to shift from the old pattern of forced industrialization. This was at least partly due to the lack of unity within the PZPR leadership. In most East European countries, economic reforms have only been possible when the party is united. Elite factionalism in Poland was thus an additional obstacle to economic reform (Gitelman 1981, p. 130).

THE 1970 EVENTS AND THEIR AFTERMATH

The factionalism in the leadership was temporarily overcome in 1968, allowing some efforts at economic reform. Student unrest in the spring of 1968 gave Mieczysław Moczar and the conservative 'Partisan' faction an opportunity to bid for power. Party First Secretary Władysław Gomułka was able to resist the pressure by accepting an alliance with the regional party bosses (including Edward Gierek) and the economic 'pragmatists' whose strength was considerably increased in the top Party posts after the Fifth Party Congress in November 1968.[1]

---

[1] For more detail on the 1968–70 period, see Johnson (1971) and Pelczynski (1973).

The economic reforms instituted after the Fifth Congress contributed to dislocations in the economy, resulting in inflation and unemployment. By 1970, widespread food shortages led to protests and considerable public apprehension over a new wage structure adopted in May 1970. This structure was ineptly explained and threatened hardships in the less productive sectors of the labor force. As a result of the poor harvest in 1970, the Party decided to raise the prices of some foods, and announced the new price system by radio and television on December 12, and in the press several days later. At the same time the new wage incentive plan was announced. The announcement sparked five days of rioting, looting, work stoppages, and protests, starting in the port cities of Gdańsk and Szczecin and spreading to most of the nation's cities. The police reacted with force, and at the end of the disturbances official figures listed 45 dead and 1,165 injured.

The two mid-December announcements touched on two sensitive nerves in Polish society: egalitarianism and the standard of living. As will be discussed in the next chapter, egalitarianism is a deep-rooted value among Poles. Most people supported the egalitarian policies of the socialist regime, including the gradual reduction in the wage spread between rich and poor. After 1967, there had been an increase in this gap (in aggregate statistics) for the first time since the mid-1950s (Beskid 1976, pp. 196–7). And the *perception* of increased social differences and privilege also increased in the late 1960s. The new incentive system threatened to worsen these inequalities. That these issues were important to the workers was evident in their meetings with Gierek in Gdańsk after Gomułka's removal. They complained about unequal bonuses favoring management, asked about the high salaries of directors and ministers, and called for limitations on the perquisites afforded to those in management and leadership positions.

The food price increase was the spark that ignited the protests, which reflected concern over the deteriorating standard of living. Real wage increases in 1968–70 had been among the smallest since the early 1950s. Food price increases hit especially hard in a society where food expenditures were already almost half (47%) of total individual consumption (compared, for example, to only 32% in East Germany). And the price increases were bound to affect the poorest in the most direct way. It was estimated that in 1970, a third of all four-person households were below the 'social minimum' for consumption (Pitus 1975, p. 58). For them, food constituted an even larger proportion of their budgets.

As in 1956, the demands of the workers were largely economic ones, not political. Some political demands did emerge in continuing strikes at the beginning of 1971, but they were not part of the original spontaneous strikes, and appeared after the situation had largely stabilized. Even so, these non-economic demands did not have nearly the political hue of those from the dockyards ten years later. They were much more limited: release of arrested demonstrators, the ending of sanctions against strikers, the punishment of those responsible for violence in December, and the improvement of public information on state policies (*Poznań 1956–Grudzień 1970*).

The lack of a strong political dimension to the 1970 disturbances was partly due to the lack of input from intellectuals. Up until the late 1970s, there was no significant convergence in the demands of intellectuals and workers. Demands for political reform emanated mostly from the former. In the spring of 1968, intellectuals and students had protested over political and cultural restrictions. The workers did not join or help the intellectuals in 1968; in 1970 the intellectuals did not join with the workers. As portrayed in Andrzej Wajda's film 'Man of Iron', this was often deliberate retribution for the lack of support from the workers in 1968.

Results of 1970

The workers' protests of 1970 scared the Party leadership more so than the student protests of 1968, and elicited a more positive response. Gomułka was replaced as Party First Secretary by Edward Gierek, the Party leader in the coal-mining region of Silesia and a man who was considered closer to the workers and more sympathetic to their needs. In a radio and television speech the day after he was appointed, Gierek reversed the Party's initial condemnation of the riots and admitted that they were a manifestation of legitimate working class grievances. In a speech to the Sejm shortly thereafter, Gierek and Prime Minister Jaroszewicz promised more housing, better market supplies, a revision of the new wage system (including a 7 billion złoty increase for the lowest paid workers), a two year freeze on prices, and full normalization of relations between Church and state (*Trybuna Ludu*, December 24, 1970). The food price increases were rescinded on March 1.

At the beginning of 1971, the Gierek regime embarked on a new economic policy with two major goals: to increase consumption and the availability of consumer goods; and to improve social welfare benefits for the most vulnerable groups in society. The first moves were designed to alleviate the plight of the neediest. In a speech to the Central Committee in February 1971, Gierek promised to improve the living conditions for large families and those with the lowest incomes, to raise the lowest old-age pensions, to freeze food prices for two years, and to fight hidden price increases. Indeed, the regime followed through on most of these promises in the succeeding years. Between 1970 and 1979 paid maternity leave was increased from 12 to 18 weeks; leave without pay for child care was extended from one to three years; nursery school capacity was increased by 50% and preschool facilities doubled; and the minimum monthly wage increased from 850 złoty to 1800 (*Polityka*, November 2, 1979). Some social welfare benefits that had been available only to workers in socialized industries, such as social security and free health care, were extended to private farmers and their families in 1971 and 1972.

Despite the gains in these areas, the main focus of the new economic policy was on consumption. To achieve this goal, Gierek pledged in his February 1971 speech that there would be increased production of meat, expanded imports of grain from the USSR and other countries, an effort to secure foreign loans for increased imports of both investment and consumer goods, and increased investments in consumer industries (Mieczkowski 1975, pp. 172–5).

There was remarkable success in achieving these goals as well. Between 1971 and 1975, Poland's economy and standard of living grew at an unprecedented rate. National income grew at an average annual rate of almost 12% and real wages by over 7% a year. Gross agricultural output grew at 3.7% a year, and livestock production at 5.3% annually. Per capita meat consumption grew from 53 kilograms in 1970 to 70 kilograms by 1975, higher than in some West European states. All of this occurred despite a declining share of the national income for consumption, as capital investments also increased at a record pace. By the end of the decade, more than half of Poland's industrial capacity had been built since 1971.

Effects on society of 1970–5 economic growth

These rapid economic changes had a dramatic impact on the perceptions and expectations of society. In a survey conducted in

1975, over 90% of those questioned believed that there had been an improvement in the standard of living in the country since 1970, though a somewhat smaller percentage perceived improvements for their own families (see Table 2.1).

Table 2.1. *Popular assessment of improvement in living conditions between 1970 and 1975*

Has situation improved?	In country	For family
A great deal	27.4	16.0
Somewhat	64.4	57.1
No change	4.1	7.9
Has worsened	1.0	8.1

Source: Sufin 1981b, p. 24.

Even discounting the possible bias toward a positive response in this survey, these results indicate a highly favorable assessment of the regime's economic accomplishments since 1970. These positive feelings were also reflected in the responses to more general questions about one's place in society and style of life. Eighty-five percent or more of each social group expressed satisfaction with their 'place in society' and with their lives overall. When asked, 'in the future, would you like to occupy the same place in society as presently, or would you like to change?', over 80% of each social class responded, 'the same' (Beskid and Sufin 1981, pp. 229–32, 245–8).

Despite these positive assessments of the gains of the early 1970s and of the general living conditions, there was still considerable dissatisfaction with purchasing power and market conditions. In another 1975 survey (of 22,000 adults), 16.8% said they had enough money only for the cheapest food and clothing, and another 44.1% identified with the statement that 'we live very frugally in order to set aside money for the most important purchases' (Sufin 1981a, p. 6). The most frequent source of dissatisfaction for people in 1975 was the market situation and supplies, especially of meat and meat products. While two-thirds or more thought that the availability of butter, poultry, bakery and dairy products was good or very good, only 11% identified the meat situation that way (Sufin 1981b, p. 9). This was in spite of dramatic increases in both meat production and consumption in the previous five years, and speaks again of the rising expectations occurring in Polish society. Meat supplies had increased, and without price increases, but the demand for meat, and the expectations of Poles, had increased even faster. The improvements of the past five years had also engendered high hopes for the next five years. Almost 60% of a 1975 sample expected an improvement in their families' living standards in the second half of the decade (Sufin 1981a, p. 8). On average, Poles desired per capita incomes 84% higher than their actual incomes. And this was after they had already achieved a 60% growth in real incomes in the years since 1970. For some groups, there was an even wider spread between actual and desired incomes. Farmers, in particular, desired incomes 2.3 times their actual incomes. As economist Lidia Beskid pointed out, these expectations were impossibly unrealistic:

The high level of growth of the national economy and consumption in the years 1971–1975 created very high consumption expectations in the population. In the first half of the 1970s, one may speak of an interdependence of the development of expectations and real growth in consumption. In the second half of the 1970s, and especially in 1978 and 1979, the situtation changed. The subjectively expected tempo of growth of consumption significantly exceeded the possibilities of the economy (in Sufin 1981a, p. 36).

These hopes for further improvements were to be dashed in the next years as the economic miracle of Poland came to a grinding halt. This was bound to increase social tensions.

Popular assessment of politics

The positive assessments of economic developments. in the mid-1970s found reflection in a positive evaluation of Poland's national political leadership as well, as indicated in Table 2.2.

Table 2.2. *Confidence in local and national leaders, 1975 (%)*

Response	Do people have confidence in:	
	Local authorities?	Leadership of country?
Yes	27.5	48.4
Rather so	40.3	36.4
Rather not	14.0	4.8
No	6.3	1.1
Hard to say	11.9	8.9

Source: Sufin 1981b, p. 181.

According to this poll, almost 85% of the population believed that 'society has confidence in the leadership of our country'. No doubt this figure is exaggerated somewhat due to the intimidation factor in such polls. However Table 2.2 provides the figures for trust in local authorities as well as a point of comparison. Confidence in the national leadership, which was primarily responsible for the economic developments of the previous five years, was much higher than that for the local authorities. The survey on confidence in the national authorities is, to my knowledge, the first such poll published in Poland (though in a very limited edition of 500 copies, intended for use by the Central Committee). The fact of its publication probably reflects the favorable nature of the responses. One can assume that such questions were posed in unpublished surveys prior to this time. That *this* one was published suggests that the favorable rating was higher than at other times, an assumption that accords with the positive ratings of the economy by the population. When this same question was asked two years *later*, in December 1977, the positive assessment of the national leadership had dropped from 85% to 78%. This change also coincided with a deteriorating economic situation. As we will see below, by 1980 there had been a sharp decline in the percentage of those expressing confidence in the government. The link between economic satisfaction and confidence in government is indicated by another question in the 1975 poll: 'in the last several years, has the leadership of the country adequately attended to the satisfaction of the needs of the population?' Almost 90% of the sample responded positively to this question with 51.3% answering 'yes' and 38.4% 'rather so' (Sufin 1981b, p. 20).

The attitudes of Polish farmers to the Gierek regime were also quite favorable in 1975. During the first half of the decade, the regime had taken numerous measures to improve the lot of private farmers and to stimulate agricultural production. There was an increase in the prices paid to farmers for their food, and farm families had been brought into both the social security and free health care plans. In 1975, the government's agricultural policies were rated favorably by 81% of farmers; only 8% viewed those policies as not beneficial. And farmers gave positive ratings of from 80 to 93% on each of the specific agricultural policies adopted after 1970 (Sufin 1981b, p. 12).

It is apparent that these surprisingly positive assessments of the political leadership were based on the regime's performance and promises in the economy rather than the *processes* leading to those changes. The economic changes were initiated and carried out from the top, with little consultation or involvement by the workers or local institutions. In fact, the decision-making process became even further centralized during the 1970s 'to mobilize society around the goals set by the central decision-makers' (Siemieńska 1982). The regime was banking on continued economic success to shore up its political legitimacy. In the process, though, the channels of communication from the citizens to the leaders were becoming increasingly ineffectual. When the workers did later develop grievances, there were no official institutions through which they could be heard.

The Gierek regime had failed to deliver on its 1970 promises of 'co-management for the working class' and 'broad consultation' with society on important issues. As a Polish analyst put it, these consultations usually degenerated into 'one-sided monologues' (Gulczyński 1980). However, in the 1970s political affairs were not of major concern to most Poles, who were largely uninformed and uninvolved in politics. A national OBOP poll in 1975 showed 70% of the respondents affirming that it was impossible to know what was happening in politics. Another 1977 survey of urban residents found quite low levels of participation in urban political and social institutions. In a hierarchy of eight values, 'participation of the citizen in deciding about societal affairs' ranked sixth, below concern for 'the economic development of society'. And while most people claimed to have voted in the last elections to the Sejm, only about a third properly indicated in which year they had occurred (the previous year) (Jasiewicz and Jasińska 1981, pp. 219–39).

Even by 1980, the issue of political participation was not very salient. In a survey on the importance of various public policy issues in 1980 (before August), 'guaranteeing citizens a growing say in decisions affecting them' ranked ninth out of ten issues. The others concerned more basic and mundane concerns over (in rank order) medical care, housing, full employment, care of the aged, pollution, crime, education, and equality. Only 'guarantee equal rights for men and women' was ranked lower than the participation issue (Siemieńska 1982). All of this shows a surprisingly low level of interest, knowledge, and participation in political affairs for a socialist society that is highly politicized and where the propaganda encourages and portrays a high degree of involvement. It suggests the regime had succeeded in diverting attention from the political sphere to the economic one.

1975–80: RETRENCHMENT AND FRUSTRATION

The economic advances of 1971–5 were possible only by heavy reliance on the Western countries. By 1975 serious imbalances plagued Poland's foreign trade. Poland was a net importer of foodstuffs, her foreign trade deficit was 7.5 billion złotys and her hard currency debt had reached $8 billion, from only $1.1 billion in 1971. Domestically, the economy had overheated as well. Between 1971 and 1975, real wages and investments had both increased at about twice the planned rate, which itself was quite high. More importantly, governmental food price subsidies had risen at an annual rate of 20–40% as a result of frozen retail prices and greatly increased procurement prices paid to farmers. By 1976, these subsidies had reached 100 billion złotys, nearly 8% of national income (Gitelman 1981, p. 147).

The government had insufficient resources to continue the rapid and multifarious growth strategy of the previous years. The 1975 draft for the next five year plan called for rates of growth in personal incomes, investments and industrial and agricultural production that were only about half of the rates actually achieved in the previous period. Another major feature of the new plan was the decision to rationalize the price structure of agricultural products. Food production and consumption had increased greatly in the years 1971–4, but bad harvests in both 1974 and 1975 had reduced the availability of some foods, especially meats. The problem was compounded by the fact that real incomes in Poland had grown much faster than agricultural production during this period, causing demand for food, especially meat, to exceed supply. The artificially low meat prices, frozen since 1971, put further pressure on supplies. All of these factors contributed to the public's negative assessment of the food supplies situation, mentioned above.

They also led the regime to increase retail food prices. While this may have been necessary, the government went about it in a clumsy way, without preparing the population. The price hikes, announced in June 1976, were sudden, drastic, and unexpected; they ranged from 50% for butter and 69% for meat products to 100% for sugar.

The workers reacted as before, with strikes, work stoppages, and protests.[2]

Perhaps this need not have occurred. In a survey of opinion on the price increase after the fact (July 1976), the Central Committee's research center (IPPML) found that 61% of the sample agreed that it was necessary to eliminate food price subsidies if the savings were assigned to wages, pensions and other benefits. Most (63%) however, thought that the increase should have been done in stages. The more aware people were of the economic situation, the more supportive they were of price increases. Fully a quarter of the sample did not even know there were government subsidies on food! And, as might be expected, those that did not were less supportive of price increases than those that did (34% compared to 69%) and were less likely to think the price increases would lead to improved market supplies (41% compared to 61%). As the author of the report on the results of the survey concluded, 'in that situation, the introduction in June of 1976 of large increases in food prices, along with an insignificant rise in wages, pensions and benefits, could not count on widespread acceptance from society' (Sufin 1981a, p. 12).

Fearing the scope of protest that led to Gomułka's downfall six years earlier, the Gierek regime rescinded the price increases on the very next day. It also initiated a number of meetings between workers and high-level Party leaders, during which it was promised that in the future, there would be 'consultations' between the authorities and the citizens before major policy changes. At the same time, though, there was a roundup of workers who had been involved in the most violent and disruptive protests.

These events had a dramatic impact on the evolution and institutionalization of the dissident movement in Poland. The lack of any input from non-elite groups on the price rise strengthened the determination and convictions of those who had argued for some decentralization of political authority. And the rapid retreat of the leadership in the face of protest highlighted the weakness of the regime and the potential strength of the working class. For the first time now, there emerged a realization of the common interests of the workers and the intellectuals in political reform. Many workers came to realize that economic improvements were impossible with-

---

[2] Alex Pravda (1981, p. 177) compares the Polish experience to the Hungarian one, where the authorities 'have taken great care to give considerable notice of impending price increases and to phase these over a longer period'.

out prior changes in the political structure. Intellectuals became increasingly aware that the power to force change could only be found in the working class; the intellectuals themselves, few in number and easily isolated from the masses, could not by themselves effect significant changes in society.

One result of this realization was the establishment in September 1976 of the Committee of Workers' Defense (KOR) by fifteen prominent intellectuals. The purpose of the new organization was 'to provide legal, financial and medical aid for the victims of [government] reprisals, since the trade unions, the social welfare agencies and official bodies whose duties should include the defence of workers' interests are unable or unwilling to do so' (*Dissent in Poland* 1977, p. 79). KOR was to play an important role in the development of the protest movement in the next several years. It provided that crucial link between the workers and intellectuals that had been missing in both 1968 and 1970. It acted as a disseminator of information and an agent for 'consciousness raising' among both workers and intellectuals. And it helped to provide the workers with an integrated ideology, both socialist and democratic, that was crucial later in the development of the workers' own representative organization (Montias 1980, p. 295).

The events of 1976 and the success of KOR (all of the June 1976 protestors had been released by the authorities by September 1977) led to an expansion of dissident groups and accelerated incidents of protest. The next several years saw the formation of the Movement for the Defense of Human and Civil Rights (ROPCiO), a Polish chapter of Amnesty International, the 'Flying University' of unofficial seminars and courses, the nationalist Confederation of Independent Poland (KPN), and an incipient Free Trade Union movement. The underground press also began to flourish in the latter 1970s, with appearance of such publications as KOR's *Biuletyn Informacyjny* and the fortnightly *Robotnik*, which by the summer of 1980 had reached a circulation of 20,000 copies.[3] These were accompanied by an increasing number of open letters of protest addressed to the Party leadership or the Sejm by various groups of intellectuals and even former political leaders. In October 1977, for example, fourteen former members of the Party's Central Committee (including former Party First Secretary Edward Ochab) addressed a

---

[3] For an annotated bibliography and discussion of these publications, see Preibisz (1982).

letter to Gierek calling for increased political and economic demo-cracy, changes in economic policy, and an expanded role for trade unions (Raina 1978, pp. 444–51). By 1979, even some current Party officials were calling for reform. Jerzy Wiatr, a Party member and influential sociologist at the University of Warsaw, wrote in the weekly *Polityka* that 'one can govern wisely only when one con-sults different alternative viewpoints on each prospective solution, before making a final decision, and only when one allows the sup-porters of different opinions to present their arguments' (cited in deWeydenthal 1979, p. 54).

Despite the mounting tide of protest and challenges to the regime in the late 1970s, there was virtually no reform of either the political system or the economy during this period. On the political side, in fact, there was a continuation of the process of centralization that had begun in 1972 with an expansion of the nomenklatura list, the elimination of intermediate territorial levels of administration, and the fusing of government and Party leadership positions at all levels (Bielasiak 1984). The first version of the newly revised Constitution, published in January 1976, identified the Polish United Workers' Party (PZPR) as 'the leading political force in society'. A storm of popular protests about this and other provisions of the new docu-ment led to the revision of this formula to the Party as 'a guiding political force in the building of socialism'. Even so, this explicit recognition of the role of the Party was more than had appeared in the previous 1952 Constitution.

Gierek did attempt some 'populist' style reforms in the late 1970s, such as assigning Central Committee 'lecturers' to major plants to consult directly with workers, and by convening a national meeting of the Conferences of Workers' Self-Management, the first such meeting in the twenty years of the Conferences' existence. But these efforts were simply extensions of the old 'transmission belt' ideas that did little to improve mass–elite communication or popular input into decision-making (Gitelman 1981, pp. 139–40).

The contrast between popular perceptions about political as opposed to economic improvement is evident by comparing Table 2.3 with earlier tables in this chapter. It is apparent from the second column, for example, how little confidence workers had in the very institutions that were supposed to represent them at the factory level. As we have seen above, in contrast, a large majority of those polled believed that both the national leadership and the economy had

Table 2.3. *Opinion on improvement of local political institutions since 1970*

Has activity improved?	Those responding yes (%) Members of Party factory committees	Others
Party factory committee	81.3	36.6
Factory council	49.0	39.8
Workers' council	38.2	28.9

Source: Sufin 1981b, p. 40.

improved considerably since 1970. In contrast, there was still little support for those local institutions where the voice of the workers was supposed to be heard. On the basis of polls in small and medium sized towns in the mid-1970s, Renata Siemieńska (1982) concludes that local leadership was considered by ordinary citizens to be inadequate, ineffective, and corrupt.

In comparing the first and the second columns, it is apparent how wide the gap was between the Party activists and the rest of the workers. This was particularly true on the activities of the Party committee itself. Members of the committees overwhelmingly believed they had improved; few non-members agreed. The same poll reveals that on most *other* issues, party activists and other workers were in substantial agreement. The activists were only slightly more positive in their assessment of conditions of work, productivity, etc. than were others; but on the political question of the role of the Party at the factory level, there were wide differences. These differences were to appear in dramatic form again in the 1980s.

The lack of political reform was accompanied by economic stagnation. Many economists, both Western and Polish, were arguing that economic reform was impossible until there was political reform. There could not be economic decentralization in the face of political centralization. In December 1976, Gierek had announced his 'new economic maneuver' to cope with the mounting economic difficulties. This amounted simply to a scaling back on investments and concentration on light industry, food production, and the agricultural sector. There was no commitment to any structural reforms in the economy. In fact, in 1976 and 1977 there was a further centralization of economic control, as many medium sized enterprises belonging to local authorities were transferred to industrial associations (*zjednoczenie*) and ministries (Tarkowski 1983).

The lack of structural economic reform in the 1970s was only partly due to the reluctance of the regime to initiate such changes. In the early 1970s, when the regime did have a certain amount of political capital with the population, it may have been possible to launch a reform program. During that period, however, with real incomes and consumption rising so rapidly, there was no particular impetus to make changes. By the latter 1970s, when it became clear that the earlier gains were not sustainable and that the standard of living was bound to decline, the regime had lost that capital. Given the lack of *political* legitimacy, the regime had come to depend on economic means to maintain support. When that tool was blunted as well, the authorities did not have the resources necessary to undertake a reform program. As Alex Pravda (1981, p. 164) aptly describes the situation:

although economic reform seemed to offer the population a great deal, widespread wariness of sacrificing security and stability for uncertain higher rewards made the majority skeptical about its advantages. The political opponents of reform, who saw the traditional social compact as part of the old centralized system, capitalized on such natural conservatism.

ON THE EVE OF AUGUST 1980

The late 1970s saw a continuous decline in economic growth. The rate of growth of national income, which had leaped from less than 3% in 1969 to almost 11% in 1973, dropped relentlessly from that year on. In 1978, the growth rate was only 3%, and 1979 saw a 2% *decline* in national income, the first decline since World War II. Industrial production had grown at the smallest rate ever, only about half of the planned rate. And agricultural output was down from the previous year, despite a planned 3% increase. With the country's hard currency debt at some $20 billion by 1980, Poland could no longer acquire the foreign credits necessary to sustain the level of imports of the early 1970s. A huge amount of machinery, including $660 million worth of imported machinery, was not being used because of lack of complementary machines or unfinished investment projects (Fallenbuchl 1982, p. 11). The Poles had also become heavily indebted to the Soviet Union. One Western economist suggests that in 1980 alone, Soviet 'hidden trade subsidies' to

Poland amounted to $2.4 billion or more (Vanous 1982, p. 86). There were also serious imbalances in the domestic economy. A major problem was that wages had grown much faster than the rest of the economy during the 1970s. Between 1971 and 1979, national income grew by 80%, and the personal wage fund by 161%. This was a particular problem in 1979 and 1980; in both those years the national income fell (by 2% and 5%, respectively) while the personal wage fund grew (by 9% and 12%). The result of this, though, was increases in prices and the cost of living (Krencik 1980). These distortions were accompanied by a steady decline in the productivity of labour in Poland. While labor productivity had grown at an average annual rate of 5.3% from 1970 to 1975, it began a sharp decline from that year, to only 2.5% in 1979. Furthermore, the increased government agricultural subsidies, in the face of relatively stable retail food prices, were swallowing up a quarter of the entire state budget by 1980. All of these problems led First Secretary Gierek, at the February 1980 Party Congress to call for 'a spirit of perseverence and sacrifice' by the population. Given the level of expectations engendered by the early 1970s, however, and the lack of reserves of political support for the regime, this appeal was not likely to strike a responsive chord.

Expectations and living conditions in 1980

The standard of living for Poles had increased dramatically during the 1970s. This was particularly true in the sensitive area of food consumption, as is evident from Table 2.4. There is no doubt that the variety of foods and the diet had improved significantly during the 1970s. Consumption of meat, always a sensitive political issue, had risen in a particularly dramatic fashion such that by 1980, per capita meat consumption was higher than that in Hungary, and similar to the figures for most West European states. Even for possession of many durable consumer goods, Poland was similar to the levels in Austria and Great Britain. As we have seen above, there were also real gains in wages during the decade.

But the improvements during the 1970s were not uniform. There were some groups that did not do as well, particularly during the latter half of the decade. For some income groups, wage increases after 1975 were less than the cost of living. While the average pension

Table 2.4. *Food and consumer goods, 1970 and 1980*

	Year	
	1970	1980
Per capita consumption of:		
Vegetables (kg)	111	101
Fruit (kg)	32.8	37.7
Meat and meat products (kg)	53.0	74.0
Fish and fish products (kg)	6.3	8.1
Milk (liters)	262	262
Eggs	186	223
Ownership per 100 households of:		
Televisions	71.6	106.9
Electric washing machines	78.9	107.3
Refrigerators	36.7	96.3
Vacuum cleaners	45.1	90.1
Automobiles	3.7*	20.0

* Estimate.
Source: *Rocznik Statystyczny 1981*, p. 142; and 1971, p. 580.

had more than doubled during the 1970s, it had lost ground in comparison to the average wage. And while Poles may have had more consumer and food products than their neighbors, they also had to spend a good deal more on the basic necessities: 35% of net earnings went for food and shelter compared to 28% in Czechoslovakia and Yugoslavia (Krejci 1982, p. 49).

Most people recognized that things had improved since 1970. When a sample of urban males was asked in 1980 if their 'material situation' had improved over the last ten years, 18% said there had been significant improvement and another 42% that the situation had improved somewhat. Only a quarter thought there had been no change, and 12% that things had worsened (*Łódź 1980*). Nevertheless, this was not quite the ringing endorsement the economy had received in the middle of the decade. Indeed, between 1978 and 1980 there was a very sharp decline in the percentage of those who rated the previous year as 'good' (see Table 2.5).

To a considerable extent, the declining sense of satisfaction was due to real slowdowns in the economy, but probably an even more important factor in the sharp declines noted in Table 2.5 was *perceptual*. While the rapid growth in the standard of living had not

Table 2.5. *The public mood, 1974–80 (%)*

year	Good	The previous year was: Neither good nor bad	Bad
1974	60	14	8
1975	81	9	2
1976	23	23	37
1977	43	33	15
1978	46	33	13
1979	32	39	21
1980	8	11	78

Source: OBOP data cited in Siemieńska (1982).

continued through the latter 1970s, there had not been a real decline in living standards for most families. One can see the increasingly negative assessments even in factors that could not have changed much. In the city of Łódź, for example, similar questions were asked in 1976 and 1980 about one's occupational position compared to one's father's; about one's position in society compared with other people; and about one's occupational position in comparison with other people. In reality, there could not have been much actual change in these relative positions over a four-year period; but in every case, the respondents were much less likely to rate themselves 'higher' on these dimensions in 1980 than they had been in 1976 (see Table 2.6). Again, this speaks to the issue of expectations and perceptions. The slowdown in the rise in the standard of living was sufficient to create a wide gap between popular expectations and the reality of Polish life at the end of the 1970s.[4] The problem was compounded by the regime's 'propaganda of success' which encouraged people to think that further and greater gains were forthcoming.

The issue of privileges and inequality

Popular frustrations with the standard of living were exacerbated by perceived growth of privileges and inequality during the 1970s. The

---

[4] James Davies (1962) asserts that 'revolutions are most likely to occur when a prolonged period of objective economic and social development is followed by a short period of sharp reversal'.

Table 2.6. *Perceptions of relative social and occupational position, 1976 and 1980 (%)*

Category	Percent believing position higher: 1976	1980
Position in society compared to other people	19.9	11.7
Occupational position compared to father at similar age	76.4	63.9
Occupational position compared to other people	33.8	24.4

Sources: Łódź 1976 and Łódź 1980.

issue of inequality, especially income inequality, had sharpened during the 1970s as a result of increases in the gap between high and low incomes. This was a result of the Gierek regime's efforts to add wage incentives to productivity and economic growth in the 1970s. The growth in the income gap occurred in the period from 1970 until 1977.[5] From 1978 to 1980 there was a reversal of the trend, narrowing the differences between high and low incomes. The ratio of the top to the bottom income deciles (in the socialized economy), for example, grew from 2.84 in 1970 to 3.06 in 1976, then fell back to 2.88 by 1980.

Paradoxically, the increasing public concern over inequality was manifested at the very time when income inequalities were being reduced. This reflects in part the lag of perceptions behind reality, but the concern over inequality was also connected to the increasingly widespread revulsion toward the high incomes and privileges of the political elite. These, by all accounts, were becoming much greater in the latter half of the decade. These issues will be discussed more fully in the next chapters.

There was some effort to address these concerns at the Party's Eighth Congress in February 1980. Gierek promised more attention to social problems, 'especially those closely associated with social inequality and with discord concerning the unjustified disparity in the material conditions of families'. The government promised to take steps towards reducing income differences by increasing the

[5] For a discussion of income differentials, see Mason (1983a); Beskid (1982); Krencik (1980) and Flakierski (1981).

minimum wage and by more attention to welfare benefits such as pensions and family allowances. These promises did not allay public concerns. As Polish sociologist Witold Morawski (1980) later noted:

> The Polish experiences of the seventies show that various attempts at building an affluent society can bring with them a socially unjust distribution of goods and privileges of power, wealth and prestige, which release social conflicts of an ever widening range. These conflicts were among the causes of the 1980 crisis in Poland.

CONCLUSIONS

The events of December 1970 had initiated yet another phase in the cycle of political, economic and social changes in Poland. Under pressure from the workers, the leadership was changed, and the new leaders promised to follow through with both economic and political improvements. Meaningful political reform, however, was deeply threatening to the entrenched apparatus, and to the whole concept of the leading role of the PZPR. This principle, in turn, was the *sine qua non* of political rule in Eastern Europe posed by the Soviet Union, as had been demonstrated in other countries in 1956 and 1968. Long-term economic improvement probably could have been generated by a decentralizing economic reform program, but this was unlikely to occur without prerequisite political reform. And other entrenched interests would be threatened by major changes in the economy.

Support and legitimacy was therefore purchased by short-term improvements in the economy, themselves made possible only by a kind of faustian bargain with the Western states. When repayment was due in the middle 1970s, the bubble of economic growth was burst. The rapid expansion and compression of the 1970s, though, had created a whole new set of social tensions, which were to break into the open in 1980. In the 1950s and 1960s, social and occupational mobility had provided an important release valve for social pressures. In the early 1970s, such mobility was less important, since all sections of society were moving ahead. When this dynamic economic growth came to a halt, mobility might have returned to its original role. But by that time, mobility had greatly slowed. Occupational and social advancement was much slower and more difficult than it had been in the 1960s. This particularly affected the

most dynamic and capable workers in society, who often found
blocked their opportunity for advancement.[6]

There were other sources of social tension as well. The economic
growth of the 1970s allowed increased scope for the acquisition of
wealth, and for corruption by those in positions of power. In the
latter part of the decade, as most people experienced a contraction in
their standard of living, the appearance (and even flaunting) of
wealth, greed, and privilege was particularly grating. One result of
this was a tendency by many to retreat into 'privatism'. As one
respondent in the report of the 'Experience and the Future' study
group described it: 'a citizen in our country is convinced that
improvement in his own and his family's living conditions depends
not on how industrial or agricultural production grows, but on how
he manages to arrange things for himself, how effectively he is able
to grease other people's palms ... and on his own moonlighting'
(*Poland Today*, pp. 99–100). This was bound to have a deleterious
effect on the social fabric.

The rapid expansion and contraction of the economy in the 1970s
had unleashed two sets of forces that combined in explosive mixture
in 1980. The economic gains of the early 1970s had created
expectations that were frustrated in the second half of the decade. At
the same time, the gains in the standard of living had set the stage
for a new set of non-economic demands.

---

[6] For a discussion of this phenomenon in the Soviet Union, see Pravda (1982) and
Parkin (1971), p. 50.

3

Values of Polish society on the eve of August

The social and economic changes in postwar Poland had allowed the emergence of a set of values that went beyond material needs. Most of the basic needs of society had been satisfied by the rapid growth in the economy and the standard of living. Just as the satisfaction of basic needs allows the individual to advance to a higher stage of moral development, the satisfaction of basic needs in Polish society had helped develop 'post-materialist' values in the population.[7] A March 1980 poll in Poland replicating studies done earlier in Western Europe showed that 'post-material values' (such as participation, harmony, and intellectual development) were regarded as more important in Poland than in most of the Western countries (Siemieńska 1982). Nevertheless, this orientation was not unanimous by any means: Poles were about equally divided on the materialist/post-materialist scale. For many Poles, the most important national goals remained economic ('material') ones. This was to be a source of division in Poland after the formation of Solidarity. Many of Solidarity's supporters believed the primary task of the new union was to secure better economic conditions. For others, particularly the young activists who took the helm of the union, the major goals were non-economic.

Up until the late 1970s, there had existed a 'social compact' between the rulers and the ruled in Poland, much like that in the other East European states. Alex Pravda (1981, p. 163) describes this compact as containing three major elements. First, the population expected certain social benefits from the government, including

[7] Ronald Inglehart (1977) describes this phenomenon of the move from materialist to post-materialist values in the Western industrial societies as *The Silent Revolution*.

job security, full employment, and a relatively equal wage distribution. Secondly, there were consumption expectations, including some improvement in the range and availability of goods and relatively stable prices. Thirdly, in return, the citizens accepted compliance with the political system, though not necessarily with a high degree of commitment.

The decade of the 1970s was destabilizing of both the normative structure of society and the social compact. The values of Polish society were shaken in a number of ways. The early 1970s, while promoting the kind of economic growth conducive to the development of post-materialist values, also created a highly consumer- and material-oriented society. This may have been a deliberate effort on the part of the regime to deflect interest away from the more dangerous political sphere. The result, as seen in Chapter 2, was greatly heightened expectations of further increases in the material standard of living. The point of comparison for most Poles had changed: no longer was success and improvement judged in comparison to the past; now Poland was being compared explicitly to the West and to Japan. The official propaganda stressed that Poland was embarked on an economic miracle that would make it the 'second Japan'. This required a deferral of those post-materialist values until Poland could reach the newly set material standards.

The later 1970s also affected societal values in another way. As the economy began to break down, and living standards started to decline, there was a breakdown in the system of norms and values in Polish society. As ordinary Poles perceived greed, corruption and privilege to be rampant in the ruling circles, they increasingly became more greedy and more concerned with personal needs, rather than those of the group or the society. The orientation towards concordance and harmony, or law and order, was replaced by a more primitive instrumental approach, towards satisfying one's own needs.[8]

Social and economic change in the 1970s also affected the social compact between the regime and the society. In the latter 1970s, Poles increasingly came to feel that the regime was no longer keeping its side of the bargain. Consumption was no longer increas-

---

[8] These orientations correspond to Kohlberg's various levels of normative development in individuals. Jasińska-Kania (1982) applies this framework to societal developments in Poland.

ing, and even the concepts of full employment and egalitarianism were being eroded. On the other hand, there was also during the 1970s an effort by some groups in society to rewrite the social compact to allow more opportunity for participation in decision-making. At first, these demands were put forward by intellectuals: writers, academics, economists, etc. After 1976, partly due to the influence of KOR, these ideas spread into the working class as well. With little positive response from the authorities, the workers decided to act on their own. The summer of 1980 was the first major manifestation of this.

There were a number of principles to which most Poles were committed; these included egalitarianism, socialism, democracy and Christianity. All of these, however, were in flux in the late 1970s. Below we will examine each of these in more detail.

EGALITARIANISM

Equality has long been a highly valued goal in Polish society. This value has been reinforced in socialist Poland both through regime propaganda and through individual experiences. Many people have experienced rapid social and economic mobility since the war and feel a sense of gratitude and commitment to the processes and the system that allowed this. The commitment to equality and the increasing levels of support for this value are evident from numerous public opinion surveys from the 1970s and early 1980s. Surveys conducted in six towns in 1966 and 1977, for example, show the principle of egalitarianism moving up from sixth to third place in a hierarchy of eight values (see Table 3.1).

This table illustrates an important difference between the values of the population and those of local leaders in these towns. In general, there is little correlation between the two, but the biggest difference is on the issue of equality, which is last in the hierarchy for local leaders in 1978. This may reflect their own following of the emphasis on efficiency and incentives by the national leadership. This difference in popular and leadership values was undoubtedly a further source of strain between the leadership, even at the local level, and the population.

By 1980, equality was near the top of the list of Polish values. A March 1980 survey (based on the Rokeach scale of values) found

Table 3.1. *Hierarchy of values by population and local leaders, 1966–78*
(ranks)

Values	Inhabitants of six towns		Local leaders	
	1966	1977	1966	1978
To keep public leaders honest and truthful	1	2	3	5
To avoid conflict and maintain good relations among people	2	1	4	6
To look for new solutions to problems rather than keep things the way they are	3	4–5	2	3
To work for economic development of society	4	4–5	1	1
To sacrifice own interests for those of others	5	8	8	7
To equalize differences based on economic and social discrimination	6	3	5	8
To promote citizen participation in community affairs	7	6	7	4
To give priority to natl. goals over local ones.	8	7	6	2

Source: Jerzy Wiatr, ed., *Władza Lokalna a Zaspokojanie Potrzeb* (Warsaw: 1981); as presented in Siemieńska 1982, p. 8.

equality ranked second, behind only the family (Siemieńska 1982). A September 1980 OBOP poll found that equality and justice were the most important social political values in the country. Equality was understood as socio-economic equality, equality of opportunity, equality before the law, and 'a just distribution of goods corresponding to the principle: "to each according to his work"' (cited in Koralewicz-Zębik 1982, p. 8, and Jasińska-Kania 1982). The national *Polacy '80* survey, conducted in the fall of 1980, also found widespread support for the study's 'egalitarian model', which included propositions on limiting wages for the highest wage earners (90% support), realizing a policy of full employment (77%) and insuring more or less equal incomes to every citizen (70%).[9] Equality was also ranked highly by young people. In a 1977 survey of 12,000 secondary school students, they were asked 'what characteristics should a good social system have?' The open-ended responses, grouped in thirteen categories, showed that 'equality of the citizen' was in first place, mentioned by 61% of the sample. This was followed by 'respect for civil rights' (56%), social justice (50%), care for the living conditions of citizens (36%) and democracy (25%) (Kawecki 1981, pp. 120ff.).

The growing support for egalitarianism in the 1970s was partly due to the growing perception of inequality in Polish society. In 1974, 61% of one survey defined existing differences among people in Poland as great or very great. By 1980, 85% thought so. In that year, 67% thought that inequality had grown in the previous ten years; only 6% thought it had diminished (Koralewicz-Zębik 1982).

When asked about the main sources of differences among people, the most frequent response was 'income'. In polls during the 1970s and 1980, income was consistently in first place, followed by 'position' and education. This is not to say, though, that Poles favored a general levelling of wages. There was some attraction for this idea in the late 1950s and early 1960s, but by the late 1970s, most Poles accepted some wage differentiation and the meritocratic criteria of education, qualifications, talent and the quantity and quality of work in the determination of wages. Nevertheless, the 'social minimum' must be met first, and this should take into account age, one's family situation and individual needs. The meritocratic principles must be applied only after the individual is assured of enough to satisfy the basic needs of himself and his family (Koralewicz-Zębik, p. 21).

Numerous studies from the late 1970s showed that Poles were only slightly less egalitarian on the issue of the highest wages. A majority of Poles favored an absolute ceiling on income (Siemieńska

[9] There were some problems with these results, however, in that there was even stronger support for most of the propositions in the 'non-egalitarian–effectiveness model'. While 70% favored 'more or less equal incomes to every citizen', for example, 97% supported 'compensation strictly according to the output and quality of work'. The authors of the study resolve this paradox by suggesting that the population accepts both an egalitarian order and effectiveness as part of a 'good' social order. There are however, some methodological problems with the data too, especially in the tendency of respondents to answer 'yes' to all questions, even contradictory ones (*Polacy '80*, pp. 106–9).

1982). The *Polacy '80* survey showed that 90% favored limiting the wages of the highest wage earners. The interest in limiting these high wages was an absolute one, and not simply a means to provide more for the poorer sectors of society. In the *Łódź 1980* survey of urban males, two-thirds would have limited the wages of the highest wage earners even if that did not contribute to raising the wages of those at the bottom! This suggests how deeply felt was the irritation with those who lived so well in a social system that professed to be egalitarian. In this case, as with most of the values cherished by Poles, people generally favored the official regime values, but believed the reality of Polish society did not match the ideology and rhetoric. On egalitarianism, in particular, people wanted the rich and powerful to play by the rules that they themselves had propagated.[10]

While incomes were the main perceived source of inequality, there were others as well, and perceptions of inequality in these other areas had also grown in the late 1970s. This was true even in the area of class differences, which the regime had had some success in minimizing in the years after the war. In a study done by Stefan Nowak in the early 1960s, for example, almost 60% thought that 'differences between people belonging to different social groups' were less than before the war. And 49% thought that these differences would decline even further. Half of the urban population favored 'a complete elimination of social differences in Poland'. But these expectations were frustrated by later experience. In repeated surveys done in the city of Łódź, there was a significant growth in the number of those perceiving inter-class conflict in Poland between 1965 and 1976 (Koralewicz-Zębik, pp. 6–14). This perception grew in the four years after 1976. In Lódź, the percentage of those believing that the city's population was divided into 'various groups, strata or social classes' grew from 73.3% to 79.9%. There was an even sharper growth in the number of those thinking there was 'dislike or mistrust' among those groups, from 41.7% to 55.9% (*Łódź 1976* and *Łódź 1980*). These perceptions again reflect the increasing tension and fragmentation in Polish society in 1980. The sense of community and trust, which had been quite strong in the country even during harder times, had begun to break down.

[10] These issues were not just reflected in popular views. The 'Experience and the Future' study group had raised the same concerns about minimum and maximum wages in its reports. See *Poland Today*, p. 144.

The popular views on inequality did not always coincide with those of the political elite, and this was another important source of dissension in society. As Table 3.1 shows, egalitarianism rose quickly in the hierarchy of values of citizens (from sixth to third), but it dropped just as fast among local leaders in those towns, from fifth to eighth (last) place. Similarly the egalitarian model was more strongly favored in 1980 by non-Party members than by Party people. This is somewhat surprising, given the regime's official propaganda favoring this value. It does reflect, however, the emphasis on consumption, efficiency, growth and incentives by the national leadership – values that often contradicted those of egalitarianism. Official propaganda trumpeted standards of living (cars, foreign travel, etc.) that were out of reach of most Poles, contributing to popular frustration and resentment (see Nowak 1980). So while egalitarianism was losing ground in both theory and practice at the national level, it was of increasing concern to the population.

CONCERN OVER PRIVILEGE

The issue of inequality was closely tied to that of privilege. In the late 1970s, 'position', contacts, privileges, and 'the elite model of the social structure' increasingly came to be seen as a major (and the most visible) source of inequality in Poland (Koralewicz-Zębik 1982).[11] As Marek Tarniewski (1982, p. 14) pointed out in an essay on 'equality and justice':

> those who talk about equality often have in mind the struggle with privileges or the limitation of privilege, especially privileges sanctioned through legal or quasi-legal arrangements. This refers then to equality before the law. This is the sense in Poland of the slogans of equality of access to leadership positions and the abolition of the institution of nomenklatura.

Nomenklatura is the system whereby the Party controls appointments to leadership and other sensitive positions in the state and other organizations. A Central Committee document defines nomenklatura as 'one of the basic tools that guarantee that only people who are ideologically reliable, who are highly qualified, and who act in the social, political, and cultural interests of the country, will be called upon to fill management positions' (cited in Smolar

---

[11] These results, in an official poll (OBOP), were embarrassing enough that the results have been very difficult to find, and have not been mentioned in any published sources in Poland.

1983, p. 43). The popular concern with political access and nomen-klatura had grown during the 1970s as the nomenklatura lists had grown. More and more positions were added to the lists, meaning that these jobs were essentially restricted to Party members. From the popular point of view, the use of nomenklatura eliminated considerations of competence, training or experience for important appointments, and led to an almost exclusive reliance on contacts and political 'reliability'. All of this simply contributed to the declining ability of the leadership to manage the economy. This then brought together the concerns over the standard of living and over egalitarianism. The privileged strata were feathering their own nests at the expense of the rest of the population.

The issue of privilege was not often discussed in the official media before 1980, and partly for that reason the rumor network elabo-rated and exaggerated the stories of privilege. After the Gdańsk events and the easing of censorship, the issue of privilege was covered in both the official press and the Solidarity press, and was raised in some of the public opinion polls. An October 1980 issue of *Literatura*, for example, discussed the worsening economic situation, and asserted that the imbalance in supply and demand was worsened by 'the granting of privileges to certain regions, profes-sions, echelons of the service hierarchy, and persons, all of which contributed to a climate of struggle for the satisfaction of one's own needs' (Gulczyński 1980). Other accounts focused on the abuse of authority and the excessive and ostentatious wealth accumulated by Gierek and his associates. The privileges granted to the militia and the army were a particular concern and were the subject of one of the twenty-one demands raised in Gdańsk in August 1980.

Even within the Party, there was concern over the issues of equality and privilege. In a report on the content of letters addressed to the Party's Central Committee after August 1980, there was considerable expression of concern over excessive wage dispropor-tions, unequal distribution of scarce goods and social services, and privileges connected with official positions (Sufin 1981a, pp. 220–1). As will be seen below, many of the perceptions and grievances of the population were shared by many members of the PZPR. This was to contribute to the ferment and reform that affected the grass-roots of the Party in 1981.

On the whole issue of egalitarianism, the regime was caught in somewhat of a bind. Even before the 1970s, the population had perceived a gap between the ideal and reality of an egalitarian socialist state. Most people supported a more egalitarian system, as the official ideology claimed to do, and therefore found non-egalitarian tendencies in high places to be particularly offensive. In the 1970s, with the emphasis in the economy shifting to productivity and efficiency, there was a necessary relaxation of the drive toward more equality, especially in wages. Most Polish managers viewed a widening of income differentials as necessary for improvements in productivity and output.

No doubt these tendencies did contribute to the economic growth of the early 1970s, and the accompanying improvements in the standard of living. Perhaps they were tolerated during those years for that reason, but with the slowdown in economic growth, the income differentials and privileges could no longer be tolerated. Indeed, there was a return to a more egalitarian wage structure after 1978, but this did little to blunt the criticism of the inequities and privileges that had mushroomed in the boom years of 1970–5.

DEMOCRACY AND PARTICIPATION

Democracy is defined and understood differently in the communist states that it is in the West. In Poland, the broader definition of the concept applied by official propaganda is generally accepted by the population, at least by the younger half of the population. In a survey of young people in 1978, only 27% identified democracy narrowly as concerning only relations between the citizen and the state; 41% defined a much broader sphere of activities including economic relationships, education and culture. Furthermore, 16% thought democracy was concerned *only* with economic relationships. In identifying the characteristics of democracy, the majority of young Poles mentioned only freedom of thought and belief, equality before the law, and the right to live in peace. The concepts of political participation and competition were far down the list, mentioned by fewer than a quarter of those surveyed (Olędzki 1981, pp. 248–9).

Given this broader definition of democracy, it is not surprising that most Poles believe that there is no existing system with those characteristics, though 38% of the population think Poland is a democratic country. Those who do not believe Poland is democratic mention the lack of freedom of speech, assembly and strikes (29%), limitations on freedom of religion (15%) and the lack of freedom of the press (13%). Again, specific freedoms seem more important than the participatory values; the lack of opposition parties and the lack of societal influence on the election of authorities were mentioned by only 10% each (Olędzki 1981, p. 253).

Young Poles also understand human rights in a broader sense than in the West, in line with official propaganda. When asked about the most important human rights, they most frequently mention the right to work (44.5%), the right to a life in peace, and the right to science. Freedom of speech is in fourth place (30.7%) in this hierarchy (Olędzki 1981, p. 255). Perhaps because of the lack of experience with competitive political institutions, Poles were vague on what kinds of institutions and political structure would best promote democracy. As Stefan Nowak wrote, 'people seem to see the need for "democratization" of the system without having a clear idea what democracy means in practice and how it should be realized' (Nowak 1980, p. 14). This problem is compounded by a rather strong strain of authoritarianism in Polish society, particularly in regard to political authorities, the law and bureaucracy (Miller, Słomczyński and Schoenberg 1981).[12] This characteristic was reflected in a number of polls both before and after August 1980 in which support for 'law and order' was often higher than that for expanded political participation. This posed a dilemma that was to plague Solidarity and contribute to its eventual defeat.

The issue of political participation was a particularly complex one. It was not a top priority among Poles in the 1970s. A number of studies in that decade showed that of thirteen goals and aspirations, 'the ability to influence the affairs of the nation and state' came in twelfth place, and *last* place among those under 24 years of age (Siemieńska 1982). Even at the community level, 'the promotion of citizen participation in community affairs' ranked very low in a hierarchy of values (see Table 3.1). Poles seemed much more concerned about 'keeping public leaders honest' than in actually engaging in community decision-making themselves.

Workers did, however, wish to contribute more to decision-making at the factory level, and were obviously frustrated at the lack of such influence. As is seen in Table 3.2, the overwhelming majority

---

[12] Kolankiewicz and Taras (1977, pp. 108–9) found in the political culture of Poland a combination of statism and individualism: 'The data suggest a tendency to value strong government and obedience as well as individual freedom.'

Table 3.2. *'Who should decide the most important matters of the shop?', by occupational group (%)*

Social-occupational group	Who should decide?	
	All groups	Techn-engineers
Director, main specialist	30.0	70.0
Section heads	31.6	60.5
Lower leadership	37.0	51.9
Engineers	40.0	50.0
Technicians	68.0	26.4
Skilled workers	86.3	9.2
Unskilled workers	84.9	9.8

Source: Drążkiewicz 1975, p. 17.

of workers wanted factory decision making to be made by 'all occupational groups', while the majority of the factory leaders wanted such decision-making to be restricted to the 'technical-engineering cadre'.

As with politics at the national level, workers were uncertain about the mechanisms to promote greater participation. Research in the early 1970s, for example, found little support for developing various forms of self-management (Kolankiewicz and Taras 1977, p. 107). By the end of 1980, though, there was more support for this idea. Fully 86% of the *Polacy '80* sample favored 'the introduction of full self-government by the staff in the management of the enterprise'. The strong interest in worker participation in factory governance reflects the frustration of workers' efforts in this direction. In both 1956 and 1970 they had been promised more genuine work councils and trade unions, but in neither case was there any long-term improvement. Perhaps the increased interest in participation at higher levels was bred of this frustration in the factory. As many intellectuals were beginning to argue in the late 1970s, genuine economic reform and decentralization could only come about after substantial changes in the system of governance.

Intellectuals had been arguing for some time for a more open political system, and one sees such appeals in numerous manifestos issued during the 1970s. The argument for broader participation and a more open political system was also a major theme in the various reports of the 'Experience and the Future' group (see *Poland Today*, pp. 115–16). After 1976, the arguments and influence of the intellectuals increasingly came to affect the workers and led many of them to the conclusion that genuine political reforms were necessary.

In polls done in the more open atmosphere at the end of 1980, the interest in democratic methods was solid, though not overwhelming. An OBOP poll found strong support for freedom to express an opinion (71%) and for society's influence on governmental decisions (61%), but these figures were lower than those for ensuring law and order in society (82%) and, in the top rank, equality and justice (90%) (Kurczewski 1981).

The *Polacy '80* survey also found strong support for the propositions of the study's 'polycentric model', varying from 79% to 92%, compared to support of only 25% to 49% for the counterpart propositions of the 'monocentric model'. The questions that were most strongly supported were for increased participation of non-Party people in governance (*decisively* supported by 72%) and for 'increased control by society over the authorities' (decisively supported by 70.8% and rather supported by another 21.6%). These *Polacy '80* data are somewhat disconcerting, both substantively and methodologically, in that while over 90% support increasing societal control over the authorities, more than half of the sample favored the opposite, increasing the authorities' control over society! In fact, over a quarter of those who *decisively* favored the former also decisively favored the latter. In part, this is a methodological problem (the way the questions were phrased) that plagued some of the questions on egalitarianism mentioned above; but it certainly also reflects both divisiveness and ambiguity in the political culture. While most Poles did want a more participatory system, many did not, and quite a few were divided on the issue. There has always been a strong 'law and order' element in Polish society, and many people wanted both law and order and a more pluralistic society. In the hectic days of 1980 and 1981, this was probably not possible.

The issue on which there was the most agreement in the area of democratic reform was on the role of the Party in Polish life. Western scholars have long identified the weakening role of communist parties in industrial societies. David Lane (1971, p. 135), for example, points out that 'a state socialist society is above all a technical-administrative society, where man's social position is increasingly determined by educational qualifications and technical-administrative performance'. Party functionaries did not fit into this scheme, since their skills were based on political qualities, such as cunning, demagogy, etc. Many Polish intellectuals were beginning to use these arguments in the 1970s for increased pluralization of the political system. Even a group of former members of the Central Committee and the Politburo issued an appeal for more democratization of intra-Party life and for a relaxation of 'administrative' decision-making by the Party. The Party, said the statement, cannot decree its own leading role (cited in Raina 1978, p. 447).

Popular dissatisfaction with the role of the Party is evident from the *Polacy '80* survey; 56% of the sample opposed 'strengthening the role of the party in the administration of power'. The continuing divisions on these issues in Polish society is apparent on this question too, however, as almost a third of the sample *supported* strengthening the role of the Party.

There appeared to be some doubt and confusion in the minds of many Poles about what democracy might entail, and how it would fit together with the stronger commitments to egalitarianism. The 1977 poll of the attitudes of young people, referred to earlier, showed only 25% selecting 'democracy' as a characteristic of a 'good social system' (Kawecki 1981, pp. 120ff.). Yet 56% selected 'respect for human rights' as an important characteristic, putting this in second place behind equality. Young people are more likely to have been effectively 'socialized' by the regime than older persons, and the socialization process would not have put much emphasis on the principles of democracy. Similarly, school children are more susceptible to and supportive of the official values promoted through the school systems, but one can assume that these values were similar for most Poles, a majority of whom were under the age of 30. Participatory democracy was not a widely held value by ordinary Poles in 1980. It was much more highly cherished by intellectuals. With the closer collaboration of intellectuals and workers after 1976, and an alternate form of political socialization occurring through the unofficial press in the latter 1970s, some of the ideas of democracy began to take hold among the workers. Even so, some of these political ideas were slow to germinate even in 1980. Only after August did the workers really begin to educate themselves in democracy, while at the same time trying to create an organization that would institutionalize it.

SOCIALISM

Most Poles accept the idea of socialism, even if the term itself is vaguely defined, as democracy is. Socialism, as typically defined in the West, is 'a doctrine that advocates economic collectivism through governmental or industrial group ownership of the means of production and distribution of goods. Its basic aims are to replace competition for profit with cooperation and social responsibility, and to secure a more equitable distribution of income and opportunity' (Plano 1976, p. 18). The basic concepts here are socialized industry, the idea of community, and equality.[13] Apart from this formal definition, as Walter Connor (1979, p. 227) points out, socialism as practiced in Eastern Europe, has also been 'about' growth and development. Even an eminent Polish sociologist agrees it is difficult to define socialism. Jan Szczepański (1979, p. 182) characterizes the 'socialist conditions of life' as including socialist means of production, a system of planning, the leading role of the party, a secular world view, and a just division of the national income. This definition is politically broader than the Western definition, including the leading role of the party and the secular worldview, but economically and socially more narrow, excluding the concepts of growth and of community. As we will see below, the popular conception and support for socialism in Poland more closely approximates the Western than the official Polish definition.

Even the 'Experience and the Future' study group, critical of many aspects of Polish society, acknowledged that 'the concept of socialism' is broadly accepted by society. The definition of this concept presented there, however, was quite broad indeed, including 'equality of opportunity, equality before the law, the principle of reward for work (and not on the basis of private connections), the right to work, the right to social help, equal and universal access to culture, the growth of self-management, the defense of popular initiative, the right to express one's own opinions and to criticize the authorities' (*Poland Today*, p. 116). As another respondent in the *Report* notes, though most people accept the socialist framework, 'the socialism that people see is compared to the socialism they want to see, and the discrepancy between reality and their standards is painful' (p. 59).

[13] Daniel Bell (1968) argues that 'the heart of socialism is to be found in the idea of community'.

Table 3.3. *Young people's assessment of socialism, 1977*
(%)

Response	Socialism in the world	Socialism in Poland
Decisively yes	31.0	30.1
Rather yes	47.2	38.8
Rather no	5.6	12.6
Decisively no	2.0	6.1
No opinion	13.7	11.5

Source: Kawecki 1982. p. 114.

Most of the available surveys on attitudes towards socialism are among young people. Table 3.3 shows the results of two questions posed to secondary school students in 1977: (1) 'would you like to see the world develop in the direction of socialism?'; and (2) 'do you agree that the good of Poland is irreversibly tied to the fate of socialism?'

Two-thirds or more of these students support the general idea of socialism. Of those who did not, the most frequently mentioned reason was the lack of congruence between 'theory and reality' under socialism.

Similar responses were obtained from a survey of university students in Kraków in 1974. Over 61% believed that Poland's future development was dependent on the development of socialism in the country. A further 24% thought this was not necessarily so, 'but that history has determined that Poland must develop under a socialist order'. Only 7% thought Poland would do better under some other system, but when asked about pride in various things, only 8.8% and 35.3%, respectively, were 'very proud' or 'sufficiently proud' of 'our social system and that element in it which we specifically term socialism' (cited in Simon 1981, p. 157). In another 1973 survey that asked young people 'of what may Poles be proud?', 'the socialist social order' was ranked twelfth of thirteen characteristics by students and eleventh of thirteen by young workers (Jerschina 1980, p. 278). As with democracy, there is a dichotomy between what is valued and what is perceived. While most Poles support the principles of socialism, they are skeptical that those values are being applied in the country. There is also apparent in these results a kind of grudging acceptance of Poland's ties with socialism and, by implication, with the Soviet Union. Even if support for the system is not overwhelming, there is a recognition that Poland must remain within the socialist camp, given its geopolitical position. The support for socialism does not translate into support for *Marxism*, though Szczepański's definition above seems to imply such an identity of concepts. In 1958, only 13% of Warsaw students identified themselves as Marxists; in 1978, 18% (cited in Jasińska-Kania 1982). Furthermore, many Poles, especially young ones, profess no strong political convictions at all, and claim little interest in politics. This rejection of the official ideology of Marxism and the official practice and institutions of politics indicates the limitations of political socialization in Poland. While most Poles seem to accept the general commitment to socialism, they are unhappy with the practice of politics in their society and with the way in which the regime defines the ideology.

On the specific principles of socialism (in the Western definition given above) there is also considerable support. Stefan Nowak (1981), in his survey of attitudes, has found widespread social acceptance of such changes as the nationalization of industry, agrarian reform, economic planning, and the transformation of the prewar class structure. However support for socialism is not by any means doctrinaire. Poles generally support the three sector version of the Polish economy, which allows for cooperative and private sectors of the economy, as well as nationalized industry. There is particularly strong support for private farms, especially by farmers (see Table 3.4).

Table 3.4. *Preference for various forms of agriculture, by society and by farmers, 1980 (%)*

Type of farm	Farmers	Society
Collective farms	8.8	11.0
State farms	7.0	9.5
Agricultural circles	34.6	38.3
Private farms	89.8	83.8

Note: Columns sum to more than 100% since respondents could give more than one response to question 'what kind of farms should be developed?'
Source: Polacy '80, p. 94.

Solidarity was later to make a major issue of the lack of investments in private agriculture which, it was claimed, was relatively more efficient than the state or collective farms.

Support for some private initiative in the economy, however, did not translate into acceptance of capitalism, either among the workers or within Solidarity. An article on 'Solidarity and Socialism' in the Solidarity newspaper *Jedność* (translated in Persky and Flam 1982, p. 127) rejected private ownership of the means of production, but also reinterpreted state ownership:

> The right to private property in the means of production was abolished in our country when production was put under state ownership. These facts are commonly accepted in Poland. The argument begins when official propaganda tells the entire nation that in Poland the means of production are socially owned. Theoretically, under socialism the means of production should be held in common ownership by those who actually use them, that is, the working class.

The idea of 'social ownership of the means of production' became an important slogan in Solidarity's efforts to redefine Polish socialism.

Most Poles believe that social inequalities are less than before the war and that socialism provides more opportunity for upward social mobility than does capitalism (Jasińska-Kania 1982). As seen above, there is deep and widespread support for most aspects of egalitarianism, and appreciation of the gains the regime has made in this area.

Even stronger levels of support are indicated for the spirit of community, what Daniel Bell (1968) has called 'the heart of socialism'. Among young people, where one might most expect an egocentric point of view, there is a surprisingly high commitment to the interests of the community. The following table presents the responses of high-school students to several questions which tapped social vs. individual concerns (see Table 3.5). In all of these responses, one sees a strong commitment to community interests and a willingness to subordinate individual ones for the community. When these students were asked what they would like to achieve in life, the most frequent type of response (with 61% grouped in this category) was 'interesting, *socially useful* work relevant to my qualifications' (stress added). When the researchers in this survey grouped the life goal responses on an egocentric, socio-centric continuum, they found 48% to be predominantly socio-centric, 19% bi-centric, and 28% egocentric (Kawecki 1981, p. 110). For adolescents,

Table 3.5. *Concern for community and self among young people, 1977 (%)*

Proposition	Agree	Disagree
1. One should always put the social interest ahead of one's own	73.9	19.3
2. One should first of all concern oneself with the good of oneself and one's family, and then the good of others	44.9	50.8
3. One should always feel responsible for the collective of which one is a member.	96.1	3.0
4. In life one should always follow the principle: everyone is responsible for himself.	30.6	66.3

Source: Kawecki 1981, p. 112.

a remarkably small proportion have an egocentric value system. A high proportion seem to have internalized the dedication to community interests that is an essential component of socialism.

The social consciousness and public spirit of Poles also surfaces in every-day situations. Poles, like most Slavs, will quickly and politely relinquish seats on public transportation to older people, invalids, pregnant women, and parents with small children. Such people are also allowed, and often even encouraged, to bypass queues (kolejki) at stores selling scarce items. There is, in fact, a rather elaborate code of line etiquette that determines who advances when. The attitudes of Poles toward queues and queuing regulations is revealing of more general values and the social consciousness. The rationing system, for example, is overwhelmingly supported by the population. It is accepted, however, not so much because of its practical effects (e.g. increasing supplies, shorter lines) but mainly for ethical reasons: it satisfies the popular feeling for justice in assuring a more equitable distribution of scarce goods. People generally favor providing more under rationing to those with the greatest need, but also less to those who have broken the rules of conduct (e.g. healthy people who are not working) or who don't need the rationed product (e.g. farmers for food). Furthermore, there is a preference for *central* control of rationing and queuing regulations, with minimal participation by people directly involved in the specific situation. This is seen as providing greater assurance of both fairness and of order (Fuszara, Jakubowska, and Kurczewski 1982). These attitudes on rationing and queuing provide insight into the Polish value system, writ small. They illustrate the Polish concern with egalitarianism, but not absolute equality, community spirit, and law and order. They illustrate these values in very concrete situations that Poles face every day.

RELIGIOUS VALUES

Many of these values find more systematic expression in the religious beliefs of Poles. The Roman Catholic faith is deeply rooted in Polish society, culture, and history. Its strength and support is particularly remarkable in a society where the official ideology is atheistic. Yet there are over 20,000 priests in Poland, providing about one priest per 1600 Catholics, close to the worldwide total of about one per 1400. A number of different surveys indicate that about 93% of Poles are 'believers', though not all of them are practicing Catholics (see Table 3.6).

High levels of religious belief are also found among young people, especially young workers (Jerschina 1980, p. 28). In the countryside, religious belief is almost universal, with only 1.8% claiming to be non-believers. The role of Catholicism in a communist country is made even more paradoxical by the fact that over 80% of *Party*

Table 3.6 *Religiosity of Poles, 1974 (%)*

Religiosity	Total sample	Residents of: Big cities	Countryside
Believing and systematically practicing	56.6	39.3	71.4
Believing but not systematically practicing	24.1	29.7	20.1
Believing but not practicing	11.4	17.9	5.6
Not believing	6.3	11.0	1.8

Source: Sufin 1981b, p. 54.

members claim to be believers, including almost 27% who are practicing Catholics (*Polacy '80*). This paradox may be explained in that most Poles see no important contradictions between science and religion. The 1977 survey of young people, for example, found that 71% believed religion and science to be compatible with each other. And though most believed in God, most also believed that one may find meaning in life independent of religion.

Since so many Poles are religious, it may not make much sense to discuss the attitudes of Catholics compared to non-Catholics. However, there are significant differences in many attitudes, and these do illustrate some of the value systems of the dominant political culture of the society. Religiosity, for example, is positively correlated with the principles of the 'egalitarian model' in the *Polacy '80* report. While only 50% of non-believers support more or less equal incomes for all citizens, fully 78% of practicing believers do.

Believers are also more likely to support the 'monocentric' power model than non-believers. As Table 3.7 illustrates, practicing believers are more likely than non-believers to favor greater control by the authorities over society, stronger central power, and stricter limitations on critics of the regime.

The only element of the monocentric model that believers support less than do non-believers is the question of strengthening the role of the Party. The greater support for strong central political institutions by those active in the Church is, as the authors of the *Polacy '80*

Table 3.7. *Religiosity and the monocentric model of power, 1980 (%)*

| Proposition | Percent of support among: | | |
	Practicing believers	Believers	Non-believers
Increasing control by authorities over society	56.4	50.0	42.9
Stronger central authority	48.4	41.0	39.0
Limiting dissemination of political criticism	28.0	—	21.6
Strengthening the role of the Party	34.7	38.1	49

Source: Polacy '80, pp. 116–18, 133.

survey point out, consistent with the authoritarian character of both institutions. As we will see below, this was later to pose some problems for Solidarity, as it became more closely associated with the Church, and the authoritarianism of the Church began to hamper the democratic activity of Solidarity.

On the other hand, the Catholicism of the Poles was one of the factors that led to the creation of Solidarity in the first place. As Father Józef Tischner, the Kraków theologian, has contended, 'the church educated the young Polish generation with three key concepts: human dignity, truth, and justice' (Darnton 1982, p. 108). Increasingly during the 1970s, young Poles especially found these values inconsistent with the society they inherited. With the election of Cardinal Wojtyła as Pope in 1978, there arose in Poland a new source of pride and unity. The Papal visit to Poland in June 1979 reinforced these tendencies, and instilled a new sense of hope and morale in society. The Pope's visit renewed the awareness of the Church as an alternate source of power and unity, independent from the Party and the state. The huge crowds that met the Pope created a sense of unity, strength, autonomy, and invincibility in the population that was to be a key factor in the evolution of the strikes the following summer.

CONCLUSIONS

Polish society in 1980 was strongly supportive of the principles of egalitarianism, democracy, socialism and religious faith. While each of these principles had something in common with official regime values, there were also some marked discrepancies. The regime professed to be supportive of egalitarianism and socialism, but most people perceived a wide gap between the profession and the practice of these principles in Polish society. The population was positively oriented towards socialism, but favored a more decentralized economic system than the one in place, allowing wider scope for workers participation in decision making at the factory level, and more room for private initiative and private enterprise, particularly in agriculture. While Catholic values were somewhat hierarchical and authoritarian, they were also strongly opposed to the dominant role of the PZPR in the society.

All of this should not suggest that these values were universally held or unchanging. On the contrary, during the 1970s, many of the traditional values of Polish society were challenged or undermined, and the divisions within the society grew sharper. Sociologist Bronisław Misztal (1983, p. 6) characterizes the period from 1976 to the summer of 1980 as one of 'dissatisfaction: the discovery of suffering and oppression'. He sees this period marked by three processes: the 'dusk of humanism'; increasing class antagonism; and blocked upward social mobility.

Each of these processes contributed to the tension in Polish society. The 'dusk of humanism' was caused by the increasingly materialist and consumer-oriented culture. As consumer goods became more difficult to acquire through normal consumer channels, corruption and bribery often became the means of exchange. The 'community spirit' gave way to a 'me-first' attitude and individualism, further straining the social fabric.

This process contributed to what Jadwiga Staniszkis (1981, p. 227) called 'the semi-feudalization of society' with different parts of society 'operating on the basis of different rules, status arrangements and special privileges'. This led to rapid increases in social stratification, with growing differences among regions, industrial branches, and social groups. The regime's attempts to implement economic reforms led to further dislocations and inequities. Thus, egalitarianism was also being eroded.

Tension and frustration was increased for those people outside the establishment who found their chances for upward social movement restricted. This was particularly the case for the young, who hoped to see the same kinds of social promotion that their parents experienced. But the reduced rate of economic growth in conjunction with the increasingly rigid status structure left little opportunity for this.

There was another shift occurring in the political culture; from 'subject' to 'participant' orientation. David Lane (1976, p. 78) summarizes this difference in the following way:

> The subject political culture involves a passive relationship to politics: an awareness of government and its activity but little participation in it; this culture involves an orientation to the output of a political system. In the participant culture, individuals have an active interest in government activity and are involved in policy-making. Here citizens have an orientation to both the input and the output of the system.

Most Poles would have been classified in the 'subject' category in the late 1970s. There was a fairly strong, though not dominant, 'monocentric' orientation in society, but there were an increasingly large number of participant-oriented groups as well. This orientation was largely confined to intellectuals at first, but gradually began to enter the working class. This was also bound to create conflict between those who desired a more pluralistic system and those who favored the more 'orderly' centralized system of rule.

When Poles were asked in early 1980 about the most important goals for the country, the most frequent responses related to the economy: putting the economy in order (53%) and maintaining high rates of economic growth (45%). In third place (39%) was 'giving people more say in how things are decided at work and in the community' (Siemieńska 1982). So while there was strong support for increased participation, it was viewed as less important than the standard of living. When these goals were to come into conflict, many Poles opted for the economic ones over the democratic ones.

There were other differences on egalitarianism versus democracy. Those with higher educational levels and occupational status tended to be more democratic and less egalitarian than others. So there was a division between intellectuals, more strongly favoring democracy, and the rest of society, more oriented toward egalitarianism. The one exception to this was skilled workers in industry, who exhibited strong support for both egalitarianism and democracy (Nowak 1980, p. 15). It was this group, the skilled workers in the dockyards and the mines, who initiated the strikes that led to the creation of Solidarity. As we will see in the next chapters, Solidarity managed to bridge many of these gaps, pressing for a society that was both more egalitarian *and* more pluralistic. This initial strength later became a source of weakness, though, as the union struggled to accommodate an enormous range of different, often conflicting, interests.

4

1980: causes and results

The unrest of 1980 was caused by a number of factors: blocked channels of political communication and lack of representative institutions; frustrated economic expectations; the annoyance over privileges and inequality; and the problems caused by the economic crisis. Many of these issues were addressed in Chapter 3, as aspects of the value systems in Poland. Here these issues will be related more directly to the events of 1980.

BLOCKED CHANNELS OF COMMUNICATION

Every political system, democratic or authoritarian, needs to maintain a system of communication between the leaders and the led. These communications need to operate both ways: the population needs to know what the government requires of them; and the government needs some measure of public actions and attitudes, even if it does not always act on the basis of this knowledge. In Poland, the Party, the trade unions, youth organizations, etc. have acted as 'transmission belts' for this two-way process. But by 1980, these institutions were increasingly ineffectual. They were largely unrepresentative of the population, especially of blue collar workers, impairing the 'upward' transmission of information. Partially because of this, they were even weak in transmitting information about the goals and policies of the regime to the population.

As a Solidarity leader in Wrocław said in September, 'it could no longer go on as it was; in essence nobody represented us, nobody stood for the interests of the workers'. While living standards, wages, market conditions, and meat prices may have sparked the protests, he said, the roots were much deeper than that (*Odra*, October 1980,

Table 4.1. *Solidarity and the management of power (%)*

Proposition	Solidarity members	Other unions	Non-union
Favor increased control of society over authorities	80	68	70
Favor increased role for Party in administration	32	50	34
Oppose decision-making by strong central authorities	59	48	56

Source: Polacy '80, pp. 114–18, 131–2.

p. 8). The inadequate representation of the workers was especially
evident in the Polish United Workers' Party. From 1958 to 1975,
there were more white collar than blue-collar workers in the Party.
This had been remedied somewhat in the late 1970s as a result of a
sustained drive by the Party to recruit more manual workers, but in
leadership positions, blue-collar workers were still underrepresented. These problems of Party representation are presented in
more detail in Chapter 6.

The lack of participation in the Party by workers was reflected in
a lack of trust in the institution. A May 1981 survey by the official
OBOP on trust in fifteen institutions in Poland showed the Party in
last place, with a positive rating by only 32% of the sample. Support
for the Party was particularly weak among young people (OBOP,
'Społeczne Zaufanie'). As might be expected, those who joined
Solidarity were even less supportive of the Party. The discomfiture
with the Party and its role in society, especially by those who joined
Solidarity, is evident from the *Polacy '80* survey conducted at the end
of 1980. Poles overwhelmingly wanted 'increased control of society
over the authorities'. Solidarity members in particular strongly
favored decentralization and democratization (see Table 4.1).

Solidarity members, more than non-ubion people or members of
the old 'branch' unions, favored more societal control and opposed
an increased role for the Party and the centralization of decision-
making. It is pertinent to note here also the 'conservative' orientation of members of the old unions. In virtually all of the questions
posed in the *Polacy '80* survey, these people were decidedly more

supportive of strong central controls and decidedly more hostile to Solidarity and the 'renewal' in Polish society.

Other representative institutions in Polish society were emasculated during the 1970s as a result of a process of centralization that was 'unknown even in the Stalin era', in the words of a Polish sociologist (Tarkowski 1983, p. 29). The local Peoples' Councils, billed as the basic and most representative agency of the government, had been reduced to 'agents for carrying out decisions of the higher tiers in the hierarchical administrative structure of the country' (Tarkowski 1981, p. 5). In the Peoples' Councils, as in the Party, manual workers were underrepresented. In 1969, only 15.4% of all counsellors were workers; even in *city* councils, workers constituted less than a third of all counsellors (Drążkiewicz 1975, p. 19).

The institution of workers' self-management had also become weakened as a consequence of the centralization of planning and management. Here too blue-collar workers were isolated from the decision-making process as the 'engineering-technical cadre' increasingly came to dominate workers' self-government bodies, as well as Party and other organs at the factory level. According to a 1979 survey of 164 workplaces, this skilled white-collar group was twice as likely to take an active part in these organizations as were workers (Sufin 1981a, pp. 98–100).

Before the advent of Solidarity, the labor unions had become increasingly less important and less popular after 1956. Even the official press admitted (after the imposition of martial law) that the old unions were ignored by decision-makers and that the authorities were 'changing the ideas of partnership into state paternalism' (*Rzeczpospolita*, 4/8/82). An early 1980 survey on worker attitudes towards the unions revealed that workers had relatively little contact with the union authorities, felt they had little influence in the unions, and did not expect much from them (Widera 1983). A similar poll conducted among shipyard workers showed that only 8.3% thought the trade unions represented employee interests. An overwhelming majority (70.4%) thought their influence in their workplants was negligible or nonexistent (Bucholc 1983). It was these workers who the next year demanded the creation of their own independent trade union.

Workers were not well represented in the leadership of the unions either. Workers constituted 61.7% of union membership, but were only 34.5% of the union's factory committees, and 28.8% of the chairmen of the factory committees (Drązkiewicz 1975, p. 14). As a number of Polish surveys had shown, during the 1970s there were very few organizations and societies that were designed mainly for workers; those that were tended to be dominated, at least in the leadership positions, by the 'professionalized activists' who were usually white-collar workers.

The petrification of all of these institutions, and the lack of effective means for the articulation of the interests of the workers was not healthy for Poland. As Sociologist Witold Morawski later pointed out, such a system is a *sine qua non* for social and economic development. It was even more damaging to the psyche and morale of the workers. As the deprivations and tensions continued to build, the workers had no effective way to express their concerns. In 1980, they resorted once again to the only tool that had worked in the past – the strike. The first and foremost demand of the workers was for an independent and self-governing trade union. The formation of Solidarity was an attempt to create an institution genuinely representative of the interests of the workers. As Morawski (1981, p. 6) put it:

The year 1980 was a turning point, in that for the first time in our postwar history it became possible to institutionalize a system for the articulation of interests and social values. The creation of independent trade unions and the right to strike are institutionalized guarantees that society has certain instruments of control over the center of power.

EQUALITY AND PRIVILEGE

As discussed in Chapter 3, egalitarianism is firmly rooted in Polish society. Equality is a widely held value, and the egalitarian policies of the regime were genuinely applauded, but increasingly during the 1970s, Poles perceived a disjunction between theory and reality in this area. By 1981, 86% of the population believed that the differences in income in the country were 'flagrant' and 67% thought the poor were treated unjustly in comparison to those with money (Kurczewski 1981). In the city of Łódź in 1980, 80% thought the city's population was divided into 'groups, strata or social classes' and 56% of those thought there was animosity or distrust among those groups (Łódź 1980).

All of this was especially galling because it did not accord with the officially propagated values of egalitarianism. The crisis in Poland stemmed not from the lack of acceptance of the fundamental values of the socialist regime, but from a demand for social institutions more in accord with the values of the Polish population (see Nowak 1981). The Solidarity movement had a strong egalitarian element, and the members of Solidarity were even more egalitarian in orientation than the population at large (*Polacy '80*, p. 130). The perception of inequality was closely tied to that of privilege. In 1980, in fact, privilege was seen as the main form of inequality. As Kurczewski (1981) notes of the OBOP survey data on the subject of inequality, 'the inequalities principally are in the existence of privileged social categories, distinguished by high incomes and state positions. It was not the high incomes themselves that people objected to, but the use of official positions or contacts to acquire luxuries and other scarce products.'

The concern with privilege was a long-standing one, but had grown during the 1970s. In 1970, the Szczecin strike committee had called for limitations on the earnings of Party and government employees and eliminating the price breaks in the special shops for the Army and the police. The reports of the 'Experience and the Future' group had also strongly emphasized the need to eliminate privileges for those in the power structure. By 1980, there was a sense that the gap had widened between the privileged elite and the rest of society.[14] Furthermore, people had broadened their definition of who constituted the privileged class. The ruling elite took the brunt of the criticism, but manual workers were angry as well about the privileges of white-collar management at a time when there was a contraction of the wages and standard of living of the manual workers. It was clear, Jean Woodall (1981, p. 44) contends, 'that the canons of social justice were not always observed in the distribution of housing, nursery places, holidays, etc. The more privileged white-collar workers tended to profit more from this than blue-collar workers.' In the Łódź study mentioned above, by far the most frequently mentioned division causing distrust in the city was between 'the working class and the intelligentsia'.

For most Poles, the most annoying repository of privilege was 'the

[14] Jacek Tarkowski (1981) points out one reason for this: the overcentralization of the political and economic system had led to an expansion of 'patron-client relationships' which both disrupted the economic system and broadened the opportunities for corruption.

establishment', which had created 'a whole system of privileges' for itself (Tymowski 1981b, p. 10). There were many examples of this that were revealed in the year following the Gdańsk accords. The most spectacular was the lifestyle of Maciej Szczepański, the director of Polish Radio and Television, who had managed to acquire almost 3 million złotys in office. Among his many indiscretions, he built a number of country homes and stocked them with Western pornographic films. While Szczepański's was a clear case of corruption, there were many features of the system of privilege that were institutionalized, and even legal. The office of the Council of Ministers in Warsaw, for example, set aside a half billion złotys for the distribution of housing to its employees for payments covering only 20% of the real worth of the property (Tymowski 1981c, p. 26).

The high visibility of these issues is evident in the demands of the coastal strike committees. In the interest of equality, the workers put forward a whole series of demands that would help the poor. This was especially true in Szczecin, where the demands included the establishment of a social minimum, the raising of pensions and family allowances, the extension of maternity leaves, and special attention to increasing wages for those with the lowest. The concern with privileges was demonstrated in the demands to liquidate 'commercial' meat prices and to limit sales in the hard currency PEWEX stores, to eliminate 'all the privileges of the party apparatus, police and internal security police', and to make appointments and promotions on the basis of qualifications rather than political views or party membership.

FRUSTRATED EXPECTATIONS

All of these concerns, with lack of representative institutions, with equality and privilege, came together in a popular mood of frustration. Frustration derives not from mean circumstances, but from unfulfilled expectations. As spartan as life was for Poles from 1950–75, there were some real accomplishments during this period. 'The strategy of imposed industrialization' pursued during this period brought Poland to tenth place in the world in industrial output; it helped eliminate structural unemployment; it allowed unprecedented mobility for workers and farmers; and it contributed to a steady improvement in the standard of living. There were negative consequences as well. The economy could not keep up with the growing material needs of society, leading to shortages. The growth strategy led to the growth and entrenchment of a highly bureaucratized and centralized administrative apparatus. And it reduced workers' self-management to the task of mobilization (Morawski 1980, pp. 8–11).

All of these trends fueled demands for a society more democratic and more egalitarian. Still, the major concern of most people in 1980 was material. The economic growth of the early 1970s had created material expectations that the economy could not fulfill in the latter half of the decade. In their identification of the major problems facing them, from the personal level to the national, Poles first mentioned material factors: in the family, housing and furnishings were the main problem; in the factory, wages; in the locality, consumer goods; and at the national level, the economy (*Polacy '80*, pp. 74–5).

This is not to say that the issues of political reform and equality were not important. They were viewed positively by most people, but the economic issues were the primary ones. The supporters of political change probably fell into two groups. White-collar workers, who were already the most privileged members of society, and who often felt threatened by the cries for egalitarianism, perceived economic and political reform as the primary needs of society. For most workers, though, these were less important than immediate material needs. To the extent that they did support such reform, it was as a means to a healthier, more efficient, and more productive economy.[15] Solidarity, by supporting all of these demands, brought these disparate groups together. As Deputy Prime Minister Rakowski later admitted, 'the protest against the deviation from socialism, aspirations for complete justice, active participation in decision-making on public matters, and respect for citizens' rights and dignity' all found expression during Solidarity's existence (*Trybuna Ludu*, 5/4/82). There were many different interests here, supported by many different groups. Solidarity was a huge coalition, encompassing almost the whole of Polish society. Managing such a coalition would prove a difficult task.

[15] The *Polacy '80* authors assert, on the other hand, that in November 1980, issues such as self-government and media access were seen as autonomous goals rather than a means to economic improvement. They do not, however, support this assertion with data from their surveys (pp. 74–5).

THE 1980 OUTBURST

The accumulated tensions in Polish society began to surface in the summer of 1980. As before, the spark that ignited the discontent was an announcement of meat price increases, implemented on July 1. The increases were modest compared to the price rises attempted in 1970 and 1976, but after several years of economic decline and rising frustrations, the effect on the workers was catalytic. Unlike 1970 and 1976, however, this time the workers did not take to the streets in protest demonstrations. Rather, they stayed in their factories and laid down their tools. At first, their demands were purely economic: wage increases to offset the price hikes. The Gierek regime, anxious to avoid a repeat of 1970, ordered factory managers to concede the wage issues. As the first strikers won their demands, the strike movement quickly spread. By the middle of July, 51 plants had won pay increases and another 17 were on strike.

As the strike movement widened, so did the scope of the demands. In each factory, strike committees would form and hammer out lists of demands. Besides the initial demands for higher wages, these lists typically came to include demands for higher family allowances (often 'on par with those for the army and the militia'), the abolition of 'commercial' shops (where scarce food was sold at higher prices) and a more equitable allocation of housing. In July, the most extensive strikes and the most comprehensive demands were in Lublin, a crucial rail link near the Soviet border. The Lublin FSC truck factory strike committee put forward a list of 35 demands including freedom of the press and more autonomous trade unions (Singer 1981, pp. 214–15). The Lublin workers settled for a wage increase, but the increasing political nature of the strikes was being noticed in Warsaw. The Warsaw regional Party Committee, meeting on August 12, conceded the justice of the workers' wage demands, admitted the need for better planning and management, and promised more consultation with workers. However, there were no promises of any political or structural changes.

On August 14, the Lenin shipyard in Gdańsk went on strike. Within a few days, most of the shipyards and dock workers in Gdańsk and Gdynia had joined them. On August 16, delegates from 388 enterprises met to form an 'Inter-Factory Strike Committee' (MKS). This was an entirely new situation, with workers from different factories joining together to press their demands. It would be much more difficult for the regime to isolate the workers and meet only minimal demands. The MKS put together a list of demands that eventually numbered 21 and which included in first place 'free trade unions independent from the party and employers as provided for by Convention 87 of the International Labor Organization'. The 21 Demands also included the right to strike, freedom of speech and press, the abolition of privileges for the police and security services, and more widespread information and discussion of the economic situation and economic reform. These political demands were considerably more sensitive than the strictly economic demands for wage increases and improvements in government social services.

Gierek, in a television address the next day, promised higher pay, an improvement in services, and a commission to look into the workers' grievances, but he did not address the political demands issuing from Gdańsk. Meanwhile, the strikes spread and intensified both in the Gdańsk–Gdynia area and, by the 19th, across to Szczecin. After some initial unsuccessful efforts to isolate the strikers and to divide them, Gierek sent Politburo members Mieczysław Jagielski and Kazimierz Barcikowski to Gdańsk and Szczecin, respectively, to try to reach some kind of agreement. The striking workers were subsequently joined by a number of intellectual 'experts', who eventually took over the workers' side of the negotiations with the government.[16]

The result was a startling victory for the workers. In Gdańsk, there was little actual bargaining between the two sides. Rather, as one observer noted, Jagielski 'conceded, explained, or denied'. The agreement 'represented the Central Committee's unconditional surrender' (Leszek Szymański 1982, p. 18). The government did accede on all of the 21 Demands, though the agreements exhibited governmental hedging or delay on many of the points. While the government agreed to the creation of new and autonomous unions, the MKS pledged that they were intended only 'to defend the social and material interests of the workers, and not to play the role of a political party'. Furthermore, they would be based on 'the socialist system that exists in Poland today' and would 'recognize the leading role of the PZPR in the state' and 'not oppose the existing system of international alliances'. On other issues too there were some compromises. The government did not pledge to end censorship but rather to restrict it to 'protect the

---

[16] For a transcript of the open negotiations, an account of the closed ones, and a text of the final Agreements, see Kemp-Welch (1983).

interests of the state'. On many of the economic demands, the government side simply pledged to address the problem or work on it without necessarily agreeing to the specific demand posed by the workers.

The vagueness of many of the points of the agreements was to become a problem during the next year, as Solidarity and the government argued about implementation of the accords. There were also other aspects of August that were to cause problems later on. Andrzej Tymowski (1981a), one of the MKS advisors in Szczecin, later contended that the demands of the workers were both contradictory and unrealistic. The workers demanded, and the government agreed to, conditions that the economy could not fulfill. The economic situation in August 1980 was much worse than it had been in October 1956 or December 1970. Because of the lack of adequate information, the workers did not realize just how bad the economy was. It was impossible, said Tymowski, to simultaneously shorten the work week, lower the retirement age, raise wages, and improve market supplies. It wasn't that these were inappropriate demands, but that it was not a very propitious time for their implementation.

Another Solidarity advisor, Jadwiga Staniszkis (1981, p. 212), has criticized the 'lack of democratic culture' in the workers' movement and 'the strong emphasis laid by workers on such elements as leadership, trust and mobilization'. The Szczecin workers, she asserts, were reluctant to pursue negotiations in the open, and thought it sufficient that they had their own independent organization that they could trust. This could easily lead to authoritarianism within the movement. The charismatic nature of the movement, and particularly of Wałęsa, was likely to reinforce this tendency. Later, as we will see, this became a major source of strain within Solidarity, as the union struggled with questions of organization, hierarchy, and leadership.

Another issue that appeared in August, and was never finally resolved, was the relationship between the workers and their intellectual advisors. The link between these two groups had been forged by KOR after 1976, and KOR had played a major role in communicating information about the strikes in July and August of 1980. Many of the KOR activists, including Jacek Kuroń, were arrested or detained during the coastal strikes, and were therefore unable to play a direct role in the negotiations; but other intellectuals came to Gdańsk and Szczecin from all over the country, and played a major part in negotiating the agreements between the workers and the government. In Gdańsk, the experts virtually took over the negotiating process. That the workers allowed this to happen reflected both the trust built up between workers and intellectuals since 1976, and the deference of the former to the latter, most of whom were university professors, the highest status occupation in Poland. In Szczecin, the reliance on experts was not as great, but there too, the hand of the experts was visible in the agreements. The Szczecin Accords included a provision, missing in the Gdańsk Agreements, for the government to establish a 'social minimum'. The constitution of a social minimum was one of the major interests of sociologist Andrzej Tymowski, one of the Szczecin experts.

The participation of the experts was very important for the workers in providing the legal and tactical advice leading to the Agreements and the establishment of Solidarity, but there were potential drawbacks as well. The concerns of the intellectuals were often quite different from those of the workers. While the primary interest of the workers was in the economic realm, the intellectuals focused more on long-term, structural, and political change. Probably such change was necessary before there could be substantial changes in the economy, but these two groups were pushing for major social, economic and political changes *all at once*. It was unlikely that all of these changes could be accomplished quickly. When it became apparent that this was so, the conflict of interests between these two groups was revived.

THE PUBLIC'S RESPONSE TO GDAŃSK

All of these potential problems, however, were swept away in the tide of popular exhilaration and excitement that greeted the Gdańsk Agreements. A survey conducted on September 1 showed that 89% of the population thought that the August strikes had been justified (Kurczewski 1981). The *Polacy '80* survey at the end of 1980 revealed that 91.7% of the population supported the Agreements signed after the strikes (60.1% of those *decisively*) and only 2% did not. This overwhelming support cut across every social and occupational category. Even 58% of *Party* members *decisively* supported the Gdańsk Agreements.

There were two points in the Agreements that were considered the most important: the freedom to form independent trade unions and the promise of a general wage increase. Ranked next in importance

were the other 'economic' issues concerning improved social services
and benefits, price stabilization, and work-free Saturdays. The
public expressed less interest in the reduction of censorship and the
regime's promise to keep the public more fully informed on important issues (Kurczewski 1981). While Poles supported a more open
political climate, the driving issues for the majority were economic
ones. The independent trade unions were seen as a tool to follow
through on the Agreements and to effect an improvement in the
economy.

There was also almost universal support for the formation of the
'Independent,   Self-governing   Trade   Union   "Solidarity"'
(Niezależny Samorządny Związek Zawodowy Solidarność). Ninety
percent favored the formation of free trade unions, and only 4%
were opposed. At the end of 1980, 63% intended to join the new
union, and only 19% did not. The growth in membership was
extraordinary. By the end of November 1980, 7.5 million people had
joined Solidarity – including over half of all workers in the socialized
sector of the economy. By mid-January 1981, another million had
been added to the rolls. Approximately a third of all Party members
also joined Solidarity in the early months. People joined Solidarity
for a variety of reasons, but the reasons most frequently listed first
by members were 'that thanks to Solidarity, Poland will be better'
(39.6%) and 'because it is an independent union' (22.4%) (OBS,
'Socjologiczne Badania').

The expectations for improvement in the economy are evident
from Table 4.2. These data are drawn from the monthly question
posed by OBOP about expected improvement in living conditions.

Table 4.2. *Expectations of improvements in standard of living,*
1980

Date	% Expecting improvement	% Describing economy as 'bad'
July	22	65
September 2	70	
Mid-September	59	86
October	43	96
November	38	92
December	47	

Source: OBOP data reported in Kurczewski 1981.

Table 4.3. *Most important matters to be settled, December 1980*
(%)

Issue	Total	Specialists
Standard of living	30.2	14.9
Law and order	19.5	18.2
Economic reform	13.3	30.5
Agricultural policy	7.6	6.2
Others	29.4	30.2

Source: Polacy '80, pp. 71–2.

In the days after the Gdańsk and Szczecin Accords, there was a dramatic rise in optimism about the economy. This was entirely separate from any actual improvement in the economy, as demonstrated in the second column of the table. Already within a few days, expectations began to fall somewhat, but during the rest of 1980, they remained much higher than they had been before the August events. People expected a great deal from Solidarity.

For most people, the most important national needs to be taken care of were economic ones (see Table 4.3).

This survey, conducted at the end of 1980, shows once again the concern for predominantly economic issues. While 'specialists' (typically those with higher or specialized education) were most interested in the more politicized issue of economic reform, this issue attracted little interest in the population at large. Rather, they wanted an improvement in the economic situation and, after a hectic summer and fall, a return to a more stable situation. Ordinary Poles were less likely than specialists to see the connection between economic reform and economic improvement.

The question on important problems was followed up by asking how each person's 'most important matter' might be dealt with. The responses are presented in Table 4.4. Here again, there is a surprising degree of support for a more orderly, disciplined, and peaceful society, and relatively few people primarily interested in the more political issues of participation, union activism, and censorship. This concern for 'law and order' can be explained in a number of ways. First, the supporters of this concept were as likely to apply it to the authorities as they were to society. It was not just a more stable social and economic situation that people wanted, though that was

Table 4.4. *What is necessary to solve problems? (%)*

Thriftiness and social discipline	26.2
Peace and order	22.2
Better work	16.0
Real participation of working people in government and self-government	10.3
Prohibiting personal gain derived from positions of responsibility	7.7
Strengthening the independent trade unions	5.8
Full information in the media about the real situation in the country	5.3
Greater trust in authorities by citizens	2.7
Greater trust in citizens by authorities	1.9
Other	1.9

Source: Polacy '80, pp. 47–8.

important, but also a *government* that was legally responsible and accountable. Many of those who supported 'law and order', for example, wanted brought to justice those who had abused their positions of authority. As one Polish analyst of another survey put it, people wanted 'value returned to law', with an independent judiciary, and the 'submission of the leadership apparatus to the courts' (Kurczewski 1981).

Secondly, the wish for a more stable situation derived from a sense of fatigue and fear of conflict in Polish society. Poles, after all, had had little experience with open political conflict, except in relatively violent form. As Jacek Maziarski wrote in January 1981, 'the presence of conflict ... still seems to many people hard to live with; there is a subconscious longing for the times when there was perhaps no freedom of discussion but when the nerves were not exposed to such tests'. The succession of strikes, demonstrations and invective since July had begun to wear on people by the end of the year. Almost half of the population (49%) were worried about 'the prospect of destabilization of and threat to the state'. Certainly some of these fears were also directed toward the Soviet Union, whose leaders had threatened Poland all through this period.

Finally, the interest in calm and stability was not viewed as incompatible with the process of 'renewal' which most people also favored. As we will see in more detail in a subsequent chapter, the supporters of 'law and order' more frequently favored decentralization of power and a more pluralist political system than the opposites. But the more *immediate* and pressing concern was with a more stable economic situation. Unlike many of the specialists and economists, much of the public thought economic stabilization should precede political reform.

The public was inclined to be trusting of both Solidarity and the regime in the early months after August. In a poll two weeks after the Gdańsk agreements, 28% thought that the agreements would be honored by the government, and another 52% thought they would be partially honored. Only 9% thought they would not be. There was impatience as well; 65% thought the implementation of the agreements was proceeding too slowly (Kurczewski 1981).

One Polish scholar characterizes the period from August through December 1980 as one marked by a series of 'wishful attitudes' in society: a belief in the omnipotence of the movement; the belief that the authorities had come to terms with society; and a belief in the possibility of overcoming the crisis through the kind of spontaneous mobilization that led to the creation of Solidarity in the first place (Misztal 1983, p. 11). All of these beliefs would be challenged in the following year, but even by November there was a small-scale retreat to pessimism. One sees this from Table 4.2 above. Another late November poll indicated that 40% of the population saw no important changes in Poland in recent months. Of those who thought that there had been changes, 19% thought the changes were only for the worse. A mere 12% perceived there to have been important changes for the better during this most revolutionary and tumultuous period in Poland's history.

THE REGIME'S RESPONSE TO GDAŃSK

Even before the Gdańsk agreements were initialed, there were signs of conciliation and change within the Party leadership. On August 18, in a national radio and television speech, Gierek promised an improvement in market supplies and social services, more authentic participation in public life, reform of the trade unions, and the appointment of a commission to look into the workers' grievances

(Robinson 1980, p. 12). The seriousness with which the Politburo viewed the continuing strikes on the coast was evident with the appointment on August 21 of Mieczysław Jagielski, a full Politburo member, as the chief negotiator with the striking workers. At the Central Committee's fourth plenum on August 25, there were major leadership changes of the offices or personalities most bitterly criticized by the workers. Among those removed were Jerzy Łukaszewicz, head of the Central Committee's ideological education department; Jan Szydlak, head of the Trade Union Council; Tadeusz Wrzaszczyk, chairman of the economic planning commission; and Maciej Szczepański, head of Polish Radio and Television. At the plenum, Gierek acknowledged the need for radical change and promised more democratic procedures for electing trade union officials (Robinson 1980, p. 16). The regime also eased somewhat the news blackout on the events on the coast. On August 27, Jagielski appeared on Gdańsk television and gave a frank report on the negotiating process. The same day, *Sztander Młodych* published the full list of the Gdańsk MKS demands, along with pictures from the Lenin shipyards.

Eventually, though, as the workers continued their demonstration of resolve, Gierek moved toward a more hard-line position. After the initialing of the Gdańsk Agreements, Gierek did not appear in public for several days. Finally, at a late night meeting of the Central Committee on September 5, Gierek was replaced as Party First Secretary by Stanisław Kania. Once again, the workers had brought down the leader of the Party.

The change in the top Party position led, as always, to major changes in both the leadership and in Party policy.[17] The next weeks and months saw an almost complete turnover in the membership of the Politburo and the Secretariat, and extensive changes in the regional Party leadership. One of the more remarkable changes was the elevation of a Catholic theologian and Znak Sejm representative to the position of Deputy Premier. Never before in Poland, or elsewhere in the Soviet bloc, had someone so closely affiliated with the Church been appointed to a ministerial position.

In the first months after August, the new Kania regime seemed genuinely committed to reform. In his first speech to the Central Committee, broadcast nationally, Kania pledged to honor the

[17] For a discussion of the impact of leadership succession on policy, see Bunce (1980), and Mason (1983a).

Agreements signed with the workers. He acknowledged legitimate grievances by the workers and conceded that the protests had been directed against deviation from socialist principles rather than socialism itself.

It had been much easier to sign the Agreements with the workers than it would be to carry them out. Some of the provisions of the Gdańsk and Szczecin accords could be effected quickly, and most of these were. On September 1, the texts of the Gdańsk Agreements were published in *Głos Wybrzeża*, a Gdańsk newspaper, and the following day in *Głos Pracy* and *Życie Warszawy*, in accordance with point 5 of the Gdańsk Agreements, and a similar provision in the Szczecin accords. On September 1, the government issued an order to the hard currency PEWEX shops throughout the country not to sell Polish production in short supply. This had been one of the elements of demand 11 in the Gdańsk Agreements, and was also one of the provisions of the Szczecin accords. And on September 2, the Prime Minister announced the establishment of a commission of party, government, management and worker representatives to oversee the implementation of the Szczecin Agreement, as provided in that Agreement. During September, the government completed a draft bill on price controls, approved increases in wages, pensions and family allowances, and raised some agricultural procurement prices, and allowed the radio broadcast of Roman Catholic masses. All of these were also elements of either the Szczecin or Gdańsk Agreements, or both.

Other points in the agreements were achieved somewhat later, often under continued pressure from Solidarity. In accord with the Szczecin accords, a government printing house published 50,000 copies of the Human Rights Convention and the Helsinki Final Act (to which Poland was a signatory). In response to point 10 of the Gdańsk accords, the Minister of Food Industry announced in November that Poland had virtually halted food exports. And in December, workers installed a plaque in Szczecin commemorating the workers killed in the 1970 demonstrations – this had been another of the Szczecin demands. Plans for meat rationing were announced in November, but were not fully implemented until 1981 because of public reservations about the plan.

On some of the bigger issues, there were more difficulties. The issue of wage increases was one of the thorniest. The Gdańsk Agreements specified that there would be 'gradual' wage increases for all workers, especially the lowest wage earners. It was agreed that these initial wage increases, to be negotiated in individual factories and branches, would be implemented by the end of September. The government would then develop by October 31 a program of pay increases to come into effect by the beginning of 1981. This was a difficult provision to monitor, since it involved no general national wage increases, but rather increases to be determined and negotiated on a factory-by-factory basis. Near the end of September, Solidarity's national leadership announced that the wage increase agreement had not been kept and called for a one-hour warning strike on October 3. Later the same day, the government announced that by the end of October, 8 of the 12 million public employees would have received raises. Solidarity was not assuaged and the strike went on. The wage issue remained a sore point through the rest of the year, with Solidarity contending that the wage raises had never been provided for all employees. The government made its case in a long article in *Trybuna Ludu* at the end of January 1981 on the 'realization' of the Szczecin agreements (*Trybuna Ludu*, January 30, 1981). The Council of Ministers had, on September 6, provided for additional funds for the wage fund. By the end of 1980, the planned wage fund of 914 billion złotys had been exceeded by 40 billion złotys. The average wage in the socialized sector was 24% higher in December 1980 than one year before. Twelve million workers had received pay increases. Furthermore, the wage fund was to increase by another 17% in 1981. Efforts to help those with the lowest incomes were made by raising the minimum wage to 2400 złotys monthly and increasing benefits for single-parent families, university students, and young marrieds. Perhaps these points did not precisely meet the arguments of Solidarity, but they do indicate some movement on the part of the regime, as well as the complexity of the issue.

Conflict also arose over the issue of work-free Saturdays. The government was reluctant to shorten the work-week at the very time that it was trying to boost production and wages. The government plan was finally announced in January 1981. During 1981 there would be 25 free Saturdays (every other week), then successively more free Saturdays each year until all were free in 1985. This scheme satisfied the formal agreement between the workers and the government at Gdańsk, though it did not meet the 'Addendum' to point 21, added by the MKS, for 'all Saturdays off every month'. It was not clear, however, whether this addendum was actually part of the Agreement. The Solidarity leadership criticized this government plan on the grounds that Solidarity was not consulted in its development. The issue of censorship was another divisive one. The Government had agreed at Gdańsk to have a new censorship law before the Sejm within three months. By the middle of November, there were already several draft proposals, including one by the Ministry of Justice and a second by 'an informal group of journalists and lawyers' (*Polityka*, November 15, 1980). The issue was a complex and sensitive one and partly because of this, the government missed the original deadline. It was July 1981 before the new censorship law was finally approved. In practice, though, censorship was radically reduced after the Gdańsk Agreements. The government had agreed to allow the union to publish uncensored material 'for internal use only', and such materials were published all over the country. Even the official press had become much more lively and open. Rakowski's *Polityka* became so popular that its unofficial price was sometimes a hundred times the cover price.

The most important and divisive issue of all was 'the establishment and functioning of independent, self-governing trade unions' – the first of the 21 Gdańsk demands. Solidarity chapters were springing up spontaneously all around the country in September and October. However when the Gdańsk chapter of Solidarity submitted its statutes to a Warsaw court for registration, the application was temporarily denied. The court insisted on a number of changes, including a specific reference in the statute to the leading role of the PZPR. The next six weeks were tense and dangerous. Solidarity at first threatened to strike, and then called for a general strike on November 12 if the Supreme Court did not approve the union. Kania and Premier Pińkowski flew to Moscow to consult with Brezhnev. In the end, the Supreme Court ruled that the charter did not have to include the reference to the Party. Rather, it was agreed that the Statute would contain an addendum which included that part of the Gdańsk agreements specifying that the new unions would 'recognize the leading role of the PZPR in the state'.[18] The registration crisis was defused.

Solidarity supporters later claimed that the government had not

[18] An excellent discussion of the registration crisis is provided in Ascherson (1981), pp. 195–9.

fulfilled a single one of the original 21 demands. This seems an unfairly harsh criticism. The government did move toward fulfilment of almost all of the 21 points in the agreement. In several cases, the actual points in the agreement itself did not fully meet the original demands of the workers, but it was the *Agreements* that the regime was bound to, not the original demands. On this count, the government did fairly well, at least in the last quarter of 1980. The lack of fulfilment was often in timing rather than process. For example, the regime did not meet the three-month deadline for the censorship law, as specified in the Gdańsk Agreements, but eventually the Sejm did approve such a law, the most liberal in the Soviet bloc. Solidarity supporters also asserted that the regime came through on agreements only under continued pressure from the union. This is largely true, though not surprising. The nature of the political process in any country is managed conflict, pressure, and compromise. Solidarity won its very existence through such measures. The regime subsequently used them in trying to protect its interests. The new union could not expect the government to concede these epic changes without a fight. The problem was that neither Solidarity nor the regime was accustomed to political bargaining and compromise. Both needed more time to adjust to the new environment. Unfortunately martial law put an end to the development of that relationship.

CONCLUSIONS

The protests of the summer of 1980 were sparked by economic problems, though there were many other issues at stake: the failure of the regime to live up to its own ideals of egalitarianism and democracy, and to follow through on promises it had made to the workers several times before. During the early 1970s, Poles had lived well and had traveled extensively in the West. They came to expect further improvements both from the record of accomplishments in Poland from 1970 to 1975, and from the increasingly appropriate comparison of living standards with Western Europe.[19]

In August 1980, the workers got the government to agree to some major changes. This had happened before, in both 1956 and 1970,

---

[19] Andrzej Tymowski (1981a) points out that it is no accident that the major strikes were in the port cities, where sailors and dockworkers have the most continuing and direct contacts with foreigners.

and both times the regime had gradually whittled the reforms down to nothing. The creation of Solidarity was an ingenious method to insure the regime's compliance with the agreements. Solidarity provided an institutionalized mechanism to monitor the Agreements. As Witold Morawski (1981, p. 5) wrote, 'the creation of independent labor unions and the right to strike are institutionalized guarantees that society has certain instruments of control over the centers of power'.

The workers' initial political demands were rather modest, as indicated in Morawski's mention of 'certain instruments of control'. In 1980, at least, there was no great interest in sweeping political reforms. The 21 Demands had no direct political components, and in the final agreements, the workers pledged themselves to limit their activities to the economic realm and renounce the role of a political party. The workers did feel that they should have a greater voice in production at the factory level, and in consumption at the national level; the regime conceded this. On the other hand, there was little of the 'liberal political culture' in the workers' movement (Staniszkis 1981, p. 212). While there were such elements in the strike movement, these were largely grafted onto the workers by the intellectuals, where there *was* strong sentiment for a more pluralist political system. These ideas would take some time to root and mature in the working class.

Many of the phenomena described above are typical of revolutionary movements. There were a number of aspects of the Polish workers' movement in 1980 that were unique. First, this was the first case where the working class had united, as a class, against a communist government. This was a paradox for Marxist–Leninist ideologists, since the socialist state was supposed to represent the interests of the workers. How was one to explain a workers' revolt in a workers' state? From the beginning of the strikes until well after the imposition of martial law, official spokesmen recognized the grievances of the workers as legitimate, and attributed Poland's problems to a lack of adherence to true socialist norms.

Still the paradox remained. Contrary to the official view, the events of 1980 could be viewed as a second stage in the development of a communist state. The first stage had created the economic base that Marx posited as necessary for material abundance under communism. It had also created a society that was literate, healthy, and secure. But in a kind of dialectical way, these accomplishments had created the pre-conditions for a fundamental transformation in the system. The population was no longer willing to accept the rules of the system uncritically. They wanted more of a voice, even if not necessarily a governing one. This was particularly true in the economic sphere. In the earlier stage, the state had assumed control of the means of production. Now the workers wanted more direct influence, demanding 'social control' of the means of production and, perhaps more importantly, of the means of consumption (Woodall 1981, p. 39).

Finally, Solidarity itself was unique simply by virtue of its size and comprehensiveness. There had been protest movements and groups of various sizes and strengths in different communist countries, but there had never been an organization as large and as popular as Solidarity, in Poland or elsewhere in the bloc. This was, for the movement, both its strength and its weakness. Its size assured that the government and the Party would take it seriously; but it also meant that it would be stupendously difficult to organize, manage and direct. Most people joined Solidarity before it had even developed a coherent program. During 1981, the union was simultaneously enrolling members, hammering out an organizational structure, developing a program, and pushing the government on a number of specific policy issues. As Solidarity advisor Andrzej Tymowski (1981b, pp. 11–12) warned in mid-1981, the union needed to set a hierarchy of needs and demands and to develop long-term plans for change, and not simply demand everything 'here and now'. Given Solidarity's multiplicity of goals and constituencies, and its desire to remain representative of Polish society at large, it was difficult to follow this advice. In the next chapter, we will see how Solidarity reacted to these challenges during 1981.

5

The rise and fall of Solidarity

Solidarity's membership grew phenomenally in the months following the Gdańsk agreements. By mid September, over 3 million workers from 3500 factories had joined the union or were about to. By the end of October, membership was estimated at seven million. And by the beginning of 1981, membership had peaked at 8 million or more. Most of the membership growth was in these last months of 1980. The *Polacy '80* and *Polacy '81* surveys conducted at the end of 1980 and the end of 1981 show roughly the same percentage of the sample professing membership in Solidarity: 36–37%. This would indicate a national membership of about 9.4 million, an astounding figure for any organization. Approximately 60% of the non-farm workforce belonged to Solidarity.

Most of the initial joiners were blue-collar workers in the major cities, but after the turn of the year, membership began to spread to all sectors of society. Intelligentsia and white-collar workers began joining in greater numbers in 1981. With the registration of 'Rural Solidarity' in May 1981, membership expanded in the countryside, though Solidarity was never as strong there as in the cities. Shortly thereafter, the 'third sector' of the economy, the craftsmen and service workers, applied for registration of their own division of Solidarity.

As indicated in Table 5.1, a majority of virtually every non-farm occupational group belonged to Solidarity. Solidarity was strongest in that part of the workforce most treasured by the regime, skilled industrial workers. It was this group that started and managed the strikes in the mines and dockyards in the summer, and they who

Table 5.1. *Solidarity membership by occupation (%)*

Occupation	Percent belonging to: Solidarity	Branch unions
Skilled workers in heavy industry	86.7	3.3
Skilled workers in light industry	74.1	10.2
Foremen	73.5	14.2
Skilled and semi-skilled workers	69.0	15.0
Doctors, others with higher education	68.2	4.5
'Middle cadre'	66.7	16.7
Unskilled and agricultural workers	55.4	14.9
Office workers and administration	51.7	22.4
'Higher cadre', specialists, engineers	51.7	31.0
Teachers	47.5	2.5
Craftsmen	14.3	4.8
Farmers and families	12.7	1.5
Retirees	12.5	12.7

Source: Polacy '81, pp. 186–7.

became the dominant force in the union.[20] By the end of 1981, membership in that category was almost universal. The only 'weaknesses' in Solidarity's representation was among farmers and farm workers, pensioners and other unemployed persons (6–11%).

Solidarity was also well-represented in some highly sensitive areas. The head of Polish Radio and Television asserted that over 40% of all journalists and 60% of all television technical crews belonged to Solidarity (cited in Starski 1982, p. 148). Of even more concern to the regime was the large number of Party members who joined Solidarity. It was said in Poland that about a million Party members had joined the union, out of a total of about three million members. This figure is supported by the *Polacy '80* survey, which shows fully 35% of Party members belonging to Solidarity. This dual membership in the PZPR and Solidarity was particularly strong in elite and leadership positions in society. For example, of Party members who were specialists with a higher education or in

---

[20] Jean Woodall (1981, p. 45) has suggested that it is these skilled industrial workers who have the most revolutionary potential in society, having displaced the traditional industrial working class in this role.

the 'leadership cadre', 55% also belonged to Solidarity; and of skilled workers who were Party members, 76% were in the union (*Polacy '81*, p. 190). The fact that a majority of the 'leadership cadre' was also in Solidarity suggests that there was not a strong division between Party members and Solidarity, or even between Party activists and Solidarity. The dividing line was higher up, between the Party elite and the rest of society. The alignment of many Party members with the union, and the ferment and reform at the grassroots in the Party during 1981, suggest that the division was quite sharp even within the Party, between the top and the bottom of the structure.

As noted in Chapter 4, Poles were attracted to Solidarity for many different reasons: the hope that Solidarity could achieve an improvement in the standard of living for workers; the frustration with the gap between propaganda and the realities of Polish life; the increasing annoyance with the manifestations of privilege in Poland; and Solidarity's promise of being an institution genuinely representative of the workers. The most important reasons for the unrest, and for joining Solidarity, seem to have been economic, however, rather than political.

There is evidence for this in the results of an October 1981 survey of 1000 Solidarity members on the reasons for their joining the union. Respondents were asked to select their primary motive for joining from a list of ten, then indicate others that were also factors. The top three choices in both the primary and the secondary list, were as follows: 'because, thanks to Solidarity, it will be better in Poland'; 'because it is an independent, self-governing trade union'; and 'because it is an organization that will guarantee the independence of Poland' (see Table 5.2).

The imprecise nature of these responses makes it somewhat difficult to assess the relative weight of economic, political and ideological motivations of the members of Solidarity. But the first two reasons, mentioned by a majority of those polled, are less 'political' than some of the others. The 'political' factors, openly offered in some of the responses and covertly in others (e.g. 'independence of Poland') were of secondary importance to most members. A breakdown of these responses by period of entry into Solidarity shows that those who joined early on were more likely to mention the political factors (such as 'independence') than were those who joined in early or late 1981. As Solidarity grew, the political issues became less important.

Table 5.2 *Reasons for joining Solidarity (%)*

Reason	% citing as:	
	Main reason	One reason
Thanks to Solidarity things will be better	39.6	81.1
Independent self-governing union	22.4	75 *
Independence of country	7.2	54.2*
Honest organization, honest people	5.8	45.8
Better program than Party	5.1	46.1
Solidarity cooperates with Church	2.5	45.5*
Solidarity is a major force	1.8	25.8
Real possibility for action	2.1	39.1
Majority of society belongs	1.8	25.8

*These figures are not clear in the source.
Source: OBS, 'Sprawy Podstawowe' and 'Socjologiczne Badania' (10/81).

This is a natural tendency in social movements of any kind. The initial strikes were stimulated and led by 'radicals' who were willing to take risks. With the signature of the Gdańsk Agreements, and even more so after the registration of Solidarity, the risks diminished. A broader range of people, including many conservative and cautious types, then felt more comfortable in joining the organization. Many more older than younger people, for example, joined 'because a majority of society belongs'.

The table above is also indicative of the wide diversity within Solidarity. There were many different reasons for joining the union, even by single individuals. At least a quarter of the sample identified with each one of the nine motives. On many of the motives, the responses were highly differentiated. Older people were more likely to have joined because Solidarity was an independent trade union. Young people more often than older mentioned 'political' motives. And practicing Catholics were much more likely than non-believers to mention Solidarity's cooperation with the Church (OBS, 'Sprawy Podstawowe').

Encompassing almost the whole nation, Solidarity was an incredibly broad coalition of forces. Managing this coalition would be a difficult task. In the early stages of Solidarity's growth, this problem was mitigated and obscured somewhat by the flush and excitement of power, success and energy. Bronislaw Misztal (1983) describes Poland between August and December 1980 as 'society as a crowd' and from December to March as an 'excited crowd'. The charismatic leadership of Lech Wałęsa helped to sustain this excitement, but sooner or later, the momentum generated by excitement and charisma would wane. After that, some organizational and doctrinal unity would be necessary to sustain the movement.

SOLIDARITY'S ORGANIZATION

The organization of Solidarity was all the more difficult because of the spontaneous circumstances in which the union emerged. As strikes spread throughout the country in the summer of 1980, each enterprise would constitute its own 'independent, self-governing trade union' (NSZZ), some of which did not at first affiliate with Solidarity. In the first weeks, the national organization was nominally under the leadership of the Gdańsk Interfactory Strike Committee. Only after the first meeting of Solidarity representatives from around the country on September 17 was the 'National Coordinating Committee' (KKP) formed.

From this point on, there was continuing discussion, debate, and conflict over the organizational structure of the union. The 'regional' structure of Solidarity was the necessary outcome of the genesis of the movement. It allowed for a large amount of local and factory-level input into decision-making, and was an appropriate structure for dealing with the authorities at the regional (województwo) level. The decentralized organization matched the participatory and democratic spirit of the movement.

On the other hand, a decentralized organization weakened the ability of the central leadership to deal with the authorities at the national level. It also conflicted with the charismatic style of leadership, which to a considerable extent held together the sprawling union. Already by the end of 1980, as Staniszkis (1981, p. 225) observed, tension had developed between the national leadership and the local activists, 'with the latter pushing for more open operations and for institutionalized guarantees of control from below, and the former unwilling to give up the charismatic features of its position'. During 1981, this split was widened by increasingly different perceptions of Solidarity's situation. The local leaders, isolated from the process of negotiations, adopted a 'plot vision of society and politics' which thrived on and contributed to the rumor network. The national leadership was not as inclined to accept the conspiracy theories, and found more room for compromise and agreement with the authorities (Misztal 1983). The problems of organization were compounded as Solidarity grew and became more complex. While Solidarity was first and mostly structured on the regional basis, a number of 'branch' structures, organized by profession or industry, also began to appear. Solidarity steelworkers, for example, formed a 'steel industry committee' made up of representatives from the whole country. And a 'science commission' attached to Solidarity designed an organizational chart that had an 'All-Poland Coordinating Commission for Science' (Ogólnopolska Komisja Porozumiawawcza Nauki) parallel in the hierarchy with the regional offices of Solidarity. The administration of Solidarity was complicated even further by the many organizations that were affiliated with or cooperated with the union in various ways, including Rural Solidarity, the Independent Student Union, the Rural Youth Union (all organized in early 1981), the Organizing Committee for Social Justice (Komitet Organizacyjny Praworządności Społecznej), founded in November 1980 to provide legal aid for the 'repressed', and long-standing organizations such as KSS-KOR.

Solidarity's national leadership had to cope with these organizational issues at the same time that it was faced with a host of substantive ones. Immediately after the signature of the Gdańsk Agreements, the union began its long struggle to pressure the regime to fulfill each of the points. The issues of wage increases, legal registration of the union, and free Saturdays absorbed much of the union's energies up through January 1981. These were concrete and specific promises made by the regime in the Agreements. Later, a broader interpretation of the Agreements led to other demands and more conflict: over a farmers' union, self-management, and access for Solidarity to the mass media. Solidarity organizations from the factory to the national level produced and distributed hundreds of unofficial 'bulletins' and other publications and, beginning in April, its own legal national weekly, *Tygodnik Solidarność*, with a circulation of 500,000 copies. By February 1981, Solidarity had also become involved in 'normal' union activities by developing a social fund 'to improve the health conditions of working people and to insure a social minimum for working people and their families' ('Informator Biuletynu'). This itself was an enormous undertaking; most *governments* have difficulty achieving such goals. All of these developments, and the rapid growth in membership, had occurred before the union had developed a formal statement of purpose; Solidarity's formal program was not finally approved until October 1981.

All of these activities, occurring so quickly and spontaneously, were a strain on the organization and leadership of the union. By April 1981, many of the organizational and administrative concerns of Solidarity had been superseded by internal factional problems. What sparked these problems was the resolution of the March Bydgoszcz incident. On March 19, 200 police had forcefully broken up a sit-in strike by farmers demanding the registration of Rural Solidarity. Twenty-seven people were injured, including Jan Rulewski, a member of Solidarity's National Commission. Solidarity planned for a national strike on March 31 if the government did not investigate the incident and punish those responsible for the beatings. When Wałęsa reached an accord and called off the strike on March 30, many of his colleagues were furious. Andrzej Gwiazda, Vice-Chairman of the National Commission, sent an open letter to Wałęsa, criticizing him for this failure to consult with the Commission on the issue. Such 'autocratic decisions', he said, were undermining democracy in the union. He offered his resignation. Gwiazda was persuaded to stay on, but there were other losses. Karol Modzelewski resigned as Solidarity's spokesman, marking the increasing tension between Solidarity worker-activists and their intellectual advisors. And Anna Walentynowicz was dismissed from the Solidarity Presidium of the Lenin Shipyards because of her opposition to Wałęsa's actions. Walentynowicz was a national symbol of the movement; the dockyard strikes in August 1980 had been sparked by the dismissal of Pani Anya by the management.

The bitterness in the wake of Bydgoszcz gradually diminished, but the divisions within Solidarity did not. The existing disagreements between the regions and the center were exacerbated by the divisions between the radicals and the moderates. After March, the position of the moderates and intellectuals within the movement was weakened. The 'prophetic function of leadership' was strengthened, and was accompanied by closer ties with the clergy and the church bureaucracy. These ties had drawbacks as well as strengths though. It made it even more difficult for many intellectuals to associate with the movement and, even more so, for Solidarity to continue attracting support from the existing power structure (Misztal 1983, p. 15).

SOLIDARITY'S POLICIES AS A REFLECTION OF PUBLIC
OPINION

Apart from the task of fulfilling the worker–government accords of August 1980, Solidarity had no overall plan of action until the spring of 1981. At the end of February, Solidarity's National Commission approved for public discussion a draft outline of Solidarity's program for the future, which had been prepared by Solidarity's advisory Center for Social and Labor Union Tasks. The final 'Program' of Solidarity was hammered out at the union's first Congress in October, and appeared as a special supplement in *Tygodnik Solidarność*.[21] Both of these documents, as well as most of Solidarity's activities during 1981, very much reflect the popular mood and societal values, as presented in Chapter 3. The draft program postulated as the four main sources of inspiration for the movement 'the nation's best traditions, Christianity's ethical principles, democracy's political mandate, and socialist social thought'. This statement incorporated all of the dominant values in Polish society: nationalism, Christianity, democracy, egalitarianism, and socialism.

There was particular stress in this draft program on egalitarianism. In part, this was to make up for some perceived lacunae in the demands of August 1980. As Andrzej Tymowski (1981a) later argued, the 1980 demands had included few provisions for pensioners, for the liquidation of privileges, for the reduction of the gaps in incomes, and for expanding social services. The demands, said Tymowski, issued mostly from younger workers and spoke mostly to their needs. There were few long-term demands either at Szczecin or Gdańsk. Solidarity's preliminary program, on the other hand, contained numerous references to the need for 'social equality', 'social justice', the principle of a social minimum, the definition of a *maximum* income level, and the reduction of privileges. While the draft recognized the necessity for income differentiation based on quality, quantity, and difficulty of work, 'the principle of meeting the social minimum has precedence' over the rule of 'to each according to his work'. In fact, the draft renounced demands for new wage

---

[21] The draft program did not appear in the press in full until the April 14 issue of *Głos Pracy*. It is translated in Radio Free Europe *Reports*, July 22, 1981. The final program appeared in *Tygodnik Solidarność*, October 16, 1981; translated, among other places, in the quarterly *World Affairs*, vol. 145, no. 1 (Summer 1982), pp. 25–61.

increases in favor of expanded pensions, disability payments, family allowances, etc. to meet the needs of those who are worst off. All of these provisions were in accord with the popular support for egalitarianism; they may even have been somewhat ahead of the popular mood.

On economic issues, the draft program also emphasized the necessity of protecting the poor and weak. The draft did not really take a stand on the *form* the economy should take; i.e. on the mixture of capitalism and socialism. As noted above, the governing principles of the union included socialist *social thought*, not necessarily socialist economics. Solidarity did support a greater role for the market and for competition, for workers' self-management, and for greater decentralization of planning and production; but whatever economic reforms were adopted, the government should 'give priority to the economically weaker groups'.

Egalitarianism was also evident in Solidarity's final October program, though perhaps not so strongly stated. As in the preliminary program, there were numerous references to the need to support and protect the poorest and weakest groups in society. And the idea of a 'social minimum' was restated, though in more limited form as 'the guiding principle of *incomes* policy' (stress added). Egalitarianism and protection of the poor remained the cornerstone of socialist thought for Solidarity.

The term 'socialism' was not used at all in the Solidarity Program, even to describe social policy, but there was no overall rejection of socialism as an economic system. As Solidarity advisor Bronisław Geremek contended, 'the new model of relations between the state and society as proposed by Solidarity is a socialist model' (*Kurier Polski*, November 27, 1981). There was no particular desire or program to return to a capitalist economy. The one major exception to this was agriculture. The Solidarity Program had little to say about agriculture *per se*, but Solidarity publications, and later Rural Solidarity, were active in calling for more support for the private sector in agriculture. This was as much a practical matter as an ideological one. As Solidarity often pointed out, private farms were at least as productive as socialized ones, yet they were allowed only about half the fertilizer and a quarter of the investments per hectare given to the socialized sector (Czuma 1981). Solidarity wanted simply a more equitable distribution of resources for private agriculture.

'Democracy's political mandate' was another key element of the preliminary program, and this also very much reflected the public mood. Solidarity was cautious in its demands in this direction, however. There was no appeal for free elections or a multi-party system. Rather, the draft program called for the right to form independent associations, the curbing of censorship, judicial independence, restrictions on nomenklatura, and expansion of civil liberties.

The union's October program was much more direct and far-reaching in its demands for democracy. 'The state should serve man and not rule over him', said the program. Solidarity's objective was 'a self-governing republic'. In pursuit of this, the union demanded 'democratic reform and self-management at every administrative level', from the factory to the national government. All enterprises, while remaining socialized, should be controlled by an elected workers' council and run by a director appointed by the council. Local communities should be run by 'territorial self-government groups which are legally, organizationally and financially independent'. These groups should be chosen in free elections among 'various programs and various candidates'. Self-government at the national level would be assured by restoring the authority of the Sejm (Parliament) and by amending election rules to allow all political parties and organizations to nominate candidates. 'Government should serve society as a whole', the program asserted; 'it cannot do this if it is confined to a single political party'.

All of these points in the program were consistent with the popular support for democracy within the socialist framework. Most Poles favoured an expansion of democratic participation, particularly at the workplace, while recognizing the parameters for political reform: the maintenance of a role (if not *the* role) of the PZPR, the preservation of socialism, and the insurance of civil ties with the Soviet Union.

Christianity, another major component of the Polish value system, was also an element of Solidarity's program, albeit not a strongly stated one. The relationship between the union and the Church was always somewhat uneasy. Wałęsa himself had strong ties with the Church, and often stressed this in symbolic ways. He signed the Gdańsk Agreements with a large pen commemorating the Pope's 1979 visit to Poland. And he often wore, even after the dissolution of Solidarity, a 'Mother of Poland' pin with the image of the Black Madonna. On the other hand, many of Solidarity's intellectual advisors were not practicing Catholics, and were uncomfortable with Solidarity's association with an institution that was in many respects both conservative and authoritarian. Solidarity's preliminary program, then, referred only to Christianity's *ethical principles* as a source of inspiration and further hedged by promising to 'never give up the lay nature of our organization'.

The head of the drafting commission for the final Solidarity program was Bronisław Geremek, an historian who was also a member of KIK, the lay Club of Catholic Intellectuals. Tadeusz Mazowiecki, also of KIK, and other Catholic intellectuals were also on the commission. Despite the role of these people, the references to Christianity in the final program were mostly indirect. Only in the introductory statement did the program explicitly mention 'the values of Christian ethics'. Interestingly, though, it also acknowledged the importance of Pope John Paul II's encyclical 'On Human Labor'. This encyclical had appeared in the interim since the preliminary program. In his encyclical, the Pope criticized both capitalism and Marxism, but he asserted that labor had priority over capital, that private property was subject to the demands of the common good, and that social welfare benefits such as unemployment benefits, pensions, and health care were matters of justice, not just of charity. This commitment to the individual, and particularly to the poor and disadvantaged, was prominent in the Solidarity program, as noted above. The Program, like the Encyclical, also called for greater involvement by the worker in the determination of his living and working conditions and environment. The Encyclical provided some common ground between Christianity and socialism, and it was this area that was stressed in Solidarity's Program.

Both the preliminary and final programs also stressed the importance of *national* values, culture, and history. In the preliminary program, national values are recognized as 'a valuable and vital part of our collective consciousness' and 'a platform for social integration and generosity'. The protests of 1980 were partly a reaction against efforts 'to eliminate our national values from our social consciousness'. The final Program uses similar language, but also mentions specifically the importance of 'consolidating national and state sovereignty'. All of this is a thinly disguised protest against the restrictions on Polish sovereignty posed by the Soviet Union, and the distortions of Polish history in official versions of that subject.

One of the most remarkable features of the Solidarity era was the vigor with which Poles attempted to reopen chapters of Polish history. The year 1981 saw a plethora of frank 'revisionist' histories, in both films and print, of Polish relations with Russia and the Soviet Union, of World War II, and of the national disturbances in 1956, 1968, 1970, 1976, and 1980. Some of these explicitly and sarcastically contrasted the official version with the popular one. The Solidarity newspaper *Jedność*, for example, in an anniversary article on 'Poland, June 1956', included pictures of workers carrying signs saying 'we demand bread'. Underneath the picture was a caption in quotation marks: 'enemy agents succeed in provoking street demonstrations'. Historical precedents were even tied subtlely into the Solidarity Program. The Program drew on a slogan used by students in the 1968 demonstrations, for example, in saying that 'history teaches us that without freedom there is no bread'.

Solidarity's programmatic ideas on equality, socialism, democracy, Christianity and nationalism accurately reflected the dominant values in Polish society. The values were not static, though, and neither was Solidarity's plan for action. The final program was more radically democratic, and somewhat less egalitarian, than the preliminary program.[22] To some extent, the differences were due to differences in the groups who drafted the preliminary program and the final one, but a more important factor was the changes in the political and economic environment between the spring and fall of 1981. During that time, the economic situation in Poland had worsened rather than improved. The gains in wages, etc., achieved with the Gdańsk Agreements had not led to any improvement in the standard of living, as prices had also increased, and consumer supplies had become even worse. This had a number of effects on public opinion. Support for egalitarianism eroded somewhat as people became increasingly concerned with their own welfare in difficult circumstances. It was also becoming apparent that the government had only so many resources, and improvements of social services cut into wages and consumer goods. A second change was a growing conviction that economic improvement could only come about with more extensive changes in the political system. The establishment of the independent self-governing trade union Solidarity was not enough. Self-government had to be extended

---

[22] On the differences in the two versions of the program, see Mason (1984).

throughout the society. Such changes, however, were even more threatening to the ruling elite than the events of 1980.

THE PUBLIC'S ATTITUDES TOWARDS SOLIDARITY

August 1980 created a sense of euphoria in Poland. The workers had created an institution that was genuinely their own. The government had caved in under overwhelming pressure from the population. Many people felt that the workers' movement, manifested through Solidarity, was invincible. These feelings were typical for members of a new and dynamic organization. They were critical in helping Solidarity struggle through its formative months, but they could not last forever. Eventually, some disillusionment would set in.

In the early 'post-August' period, support for Solidarity was overwhelming and uncompromising. The *Polacy '80* survey at the end of that year showed that 91.7% of the population supported the Gdańsk Agreements of the previous August, with 60% expressing 'decisive' support. Almost 90% expressed support for the activities of Solidarity at the national level. Over 89% believed that Solidarity better defended the workers' interests than did the old unions. During 1981 Solidarity, along with the Roman Catholic Church, was the most trusted institution in Poland. In similar polls on confidence in fifteen institutions, conducted by OBOP in May and by Solidarity in October, Solidarity was rated positively by over 90% of the respondents (see Table 5.3).

These polls indicate both the strength and permanence of popular support for Solidarity. only the Church and, in the OBOP poll, the Army comes close to the confidence engendered by Solidarity. When these responses are broken down into more detailed categories (decisive support, etc.), Solidarity emerges in an even stronger position, especially in the Solidarity poll.

Because of the spontaneous development and sheer size of Solidarity, there was no consensus on just what Solidarity was (see Table 5.4). This table reveals some of the divisions and uncertainty within Solidarity by the fall of 1981. Solidarity *members* were most likely to characterize Solidarity as a labor union, but the union's activists were more likely to view Solidarity broadly, as a social movement. Given the opportunity for multiple choices in this survey, 40% or more of the sample identified Solidarity as a union, a social movement, an organization of Poles, and 'social self-government'. Those

Table 5.3. *Trust in institutions, May and October 1981*
(% expressing trust)

Institution	Population (May)	Solidarity (October)
Catholic Church	94	94
Solidarity	91	95
Army	89	69
Sejm	82	50
Council of State	73	29
Supreme Control Council (NIK)	69	35
Government	69	21
Procuracy	60	24
Courts	59	28
Branch Unions	56	21
Democ. Party (SD)	53	28
Natl. Unity Front	50	19
United Peasant Party (ZSL)	46	22
Militia	42	22
PZPR	32	7

Sources: OBOP, 'Społeczne Zaufanie', May 1981; OBS, 'Komunikat', October 1981.

Table 5.4. *What is Solidarity?* *(multiple responses, %)*

	Solidarity members 1st place	All	Congress delegates 1st place	All
Labor union	48	86	18	69
Social movement	20	60	59	92
Organization of Poles	19	59	18	58
Social self-government	5	46	0	23
Political party	1	16	0	0

Sources: OBS, 'Sprawy Podstawowe'; 'Socjologiczne Badania', October 1981.

with a higher education were twice as likely as others to view Solidarity broadly, as a social movement. On the other hand, qualified workers were more likely than other groups (especially white-collar people) to view Solidarity as strictly a labor union. There were some built-in differences and conflicts here as well.

It is clear that Solidarity was many things to many people. One should also note here the category of 'political party'. While *none* of the 271 Congress delegates identified Solidarity this way, 16% of the members thought this was one of the characteristics of the movement. As we will see below, this 'radical' group within Solidarity was never very large (less than one third of the membership), but it did pose some problems for the union, both in terms of internal divisions and of Solidarity's image.

The scope of Solidarity's activities became somewhat of a problem by the spring of 1981. The union was confronted with organizational overload. It was struggling both with the regime and with its own identity. While battling with the government over censorship, media access, rural Solidarity and the strike, Solidarity was simultaneously working out its own organizational structure, program and leadership. It was taking on an established bureaucracy and party before it had fully matured itself.

Recognizing a problem with the scope of the union's activities, Solidarity conducted a poll among its members on what kind of activities the union should be pursuing. The questionnaire listed ten activities and asked the respondents if, on each of them, Solidarity should have a decisive voice, an advisory one, or no role at all. The results are presented in Table 5.5. The small percentages in the third column indicate that most Solidarity members thought the union should have *some say* in virtually all areas from factory to the national level. On the other hand, there were only three areas in which the majority believed Solidarity should have a decisive role, and all of these related to strictly labor union affairs. There was also a considerable division in Solidarity's membership on the issue of the scope of the union's activities. While two-thirds favored a decisive role in only these labor union areas, a third or more favored a decisive role for Solidarity in *all ten* areas. The argument for a broad role for Solidarity was made by a number of speakers at a July Solidarity Conference on the union's program:

There are voices saying that Solidarity should limit itself to purely trade union activities ... such a limitation, especially now, is not possible. The defense of workers' interests in our conditions is effective only if it is conducted by a genuinely independent movement. Achieving and maintaining that independence is dependent on the introduction of changes in the

Table 5.5. *What activities should Solidarity be involved in?* (%)

Concerns	Decisive voice	Advisory voice	No voice
Improving living conditions	84.3	13.7	0.0
Improving working conditions	65.3	32.5	0.1
Assessment of factory leadership	65.3	29.2	1.0
Assessment of state and party leaders	47.5	36.4	5.6
Formation of political consciousness	46.2	41.6	5.0
Reform of state functioning	40.9	50.6	1.6
Division of the national income	40.7	53.4	1.3
Appointing factory leadership	38.8	53.4	2.7
Governing of the region	32.5	58.9	3.2
Appointments in state administration	31.5	55.7	6.5

Source: Krasko (1981), p. 187.

environment and thus a change in social-economic conditions. ... In this situation it [Solidarity] must undertake activity going beyond the sphere of the immediate defense of the workers; it must be a wider social movement, which in our conditions always has a political meaning (Bielski 1981, p. 6).

Comparing the results of Table 5.5 with those in Table 5.4, it appears there was both division and confusion about Solidarity's role. Very few members of Solidarity identified the union as a 'political party', but a sizable minority advocated a range of activities for Solidarity that were more appropriate for a political party than for a labor union. This may simply reflect the lack of experience with participatory governance. From the perspective of most Poles, the only significant political party was the PZPR, whose range of activities was all-encompassing. To demand less than this, then, may have been seen as less than political. From the Party's point of view, however, for Solidarity to have acquired a decisive voice in regional government and administrative appointments would have made the organization most definitely 'political'. In another context or another country, the views of a minority might not have been so important. In this case, only 30–40% advocated this comprehensive role for Solidarity. In Poland, though, it *was* important for two reasons. First, because of the extremely democratic political culture of the movement, it was considered important not to alienate any group or faction. When Solidarity Congress delegates were asked 'what should Solidarity be?' the most frequent response (by 80%) was 'democratic' (OBS, 'Socjologiczne Badania'). Solidarity's strength, its very existence, was due to its democratic and representative nature, but in an organization almost as large as the society itself, it was impossible to fairly represent all groups and views. This was a major paradox for the union. Second, the regime tended to put undue emphasis on the policies and statements of the radicals within the movement. In part this was for propagandistic purposes. It is easier to discredit an opposition force if it can be portrayed as destabilizing and extreme. In addition, the *regime* did not understand the processes of debate and compromise characteristic of a participatory democracy. When a public statement is made by a member of the Party's Politburo or Central Committee, it reflects the official line. This was not the case with Solidarity, where factional disputes were out in the open, and where the center had considerable difficulty coordinating and restraining actions in the regions. The Party leadership was, no doubt, genuinely worried about the statements and actions of the 'minority' within Solidarity.

Most members of Solidarity had little interest in depriving the Party of its political role, or even in effecting major changes in the political system. For most Solidarity members, the most important matters were economic ones. In a fall 1981 poll of 1000 Solidarity members, in fact, the pollsters did not even ask about the importance of wage increases and market supplies, assuming everyone would rank these as highly important. The ranking, by perceived importance, of 19 other issues, is revealing of the interests and priorities of Polish workers (see Table 5.6). It is apparent from this poll, as with others mentioned above, that economic issues, and the very survival of the state, were of greater interest and importance to Solidarity members than were issues of political reform. Poles also wanted more open information, particularly about Poland's his-

Table 5.6. *Importance of various issues for Solidarity members (%)*

Issue	(1) Of primary importance	(2) Very imp.	(3) 1 & 2
1. Reform of economy	43.1	36.9	80.0
2. Sovereignty of country	43.6	35.7	79.3
3. Knowledge of true history of Poland	32.0	45.0	77.0
4. Caring for wronged social & occupational groups	28.9	47.5	76.4
5. Increased openness of information; limitation on censorship	31.8	43.2	75.0
6. Protection against unemployment	26.3	46.1	72.4
7. Raising morality of society	26.5	40.0	66.5
8. Respect for Poles in world	19.3	47.1	66.4
9. Self-government in workplace	21.1	43.7	64.8
10. Civil rights	24.2	39.2	63.4
11. Fostering authentic leaders	24.8	35.8	62.6
12. Freeing Poland from political influence of other states	28.1	33.9	62.0
13. Unmasking incompetence & dishonesty among party & political leaders	22.5	39.5	62.0
14. Safety and hygiene at work	17.8	43.2	61.0
15. Deferring repayment of Western loans	17.7	39.1	56.8
16. Teaching people the necessity for firm demands toward the authorities	10.5	35.5	46.0
17. Depriving the Party leadership of feeling of political monopoly	16.0	29.8	45.8
18. Elevating a broad range of workers to factory leadership positions	8.7	35.5	44.2
19. Investigation of voice of people outside Warsaw region	9.9	33.8	43.7

Source: OBS, 'Sprawy Podstawowe', 1981, p. 1.

tory but less than a quarter of this sample identified as 'of primary importance' the 'democratic' issues of self-government, civil rights, and limitations on the role of the Party. While these were viewed as important issues by most people, they were not of *primary* importance.

Through the difficult months of the spring and summer of 1981, Solidarity members were generally supportive of the policy-line, achievements, and tactics of the national leadership, and particularly of Lech Wałęsa. An acid test of Wałęsa's authority occurred with

Table 5.7. *Assessment of tactics of Solidarity, May 1981 (%)*

Subject of negotiations	Sol. did all that was possible	Sol. should have been more active
Access to mass media	44.6	52.1
Trade union law	59.2	31.8
Censorship law	36.1	52.4
Right to form Rural Solidarity	66.6	20.3

Source: Krasko 1981, p. 169.

the Bydgoszcz events in March 1981. When Wałęsa reached an agreement with Deputy Prime Minister Rakowski and called off the planned general strike, there was a great deal of protest from other national and regional solidarity leaders, who felt Wałęsa had conceded too much. The public, however, supported Wałęsa's decision. Polls by the official OBOP and by Solidarity's OBS showed about 90% supporting the decision to call off the strike (Kania 1981 and OBS, 'Decyzje'). A Solidarity poll shortly thereafter showed that large majorities accepted all five points of the agreement (assessment of the Bydgoszcz events; guarantees for the activities of Solidarity, compensation for strikers; right of farmers to form Rural Solidarity; freedom to express views contrary to official ones (Krasko 1981, p. 167).

On most issues, Solidarity members thought the union was doing all that it could (see Table 5.7).

There is an interesting dichotomy here. On the more substantive issues of a trade union law and the registration of Rural Solidarity, the union's members seemed satisfied with the progress made. On the issues of censorship and the mass media, however, most Solidarity members were for a more activist approach than the leadership had been following.

The issue of censorship and media access was an important and sensitive one. The Gdańsk Agreements had included promises for a new censorship law within three months and for the mass media to reflect 'a plurality of ideas, views and opinions'. The official position of Solidarity's National Coordinating Commission was that 'the mass media are societal property' and that Solidarity demanded 'appropriate participation in the system of social control of radio and television'. While the censorship law was long delayed, and not finally approved until July, Solidarity did achieve some access to the mass media. In early 1981, the union began publishing the regional weekly *Jedność* (Unity) and editing a column in *Dziennik Bałtycki*, the local Gdańsk daily. In April, Solidarity got its own national weekly publication, *Tygodnik Solidarność*, with a circulation of 500,000. Solidarity–government negotiations in April and May finally led to an agreement that Solidarity would be given 30 minutes once a week on national television, 15 minutes a week on local television, an hour a week on national radio and 20 minutes a week on local radio. The union would also be allowed to have its own radio and television studios. This was a major breakthrough for Solidarity. In light of the popular distrust of the official media, and the extensive rumor network in Poland during 1981, it was vital for there to be some other sources of information that people could trust. Most Solidarity members relied on Solidarity bulletins and flyers as their major source of information (see Table 5.8). Given the irregular nature of these publications, and their local origins, they were not the best source of information about national events.

The popular lack of trust in the official media, especially the press, was even admitted by the Party press. The Party monthly *Życie Partii* reported the results of a May OBOP poll on trust in media, with Solidarity in first place (trusted by 86%), followed by Polish radio (72%), television (71%), foreign radio (63%) and the press in last place (61%) (*Życie Partii*, 9/16/81).

The lack of movement by the regime in fulfilling its promises for media access simply intensified popular feelings on this issue. A late 1980 poll showed 82% of the population supporting Solidarity's access to the public mass media. By the end of 1981, 90% of the population, and 96.4% of Solidarity members, favored such access (*Polacy '81*). The issue of media access had become a vital one by that time, as the battle for the minds and allegiance of Poles was increasingly waged in the media. The regime's propaganda attempted to divide and discredit Solidarity. Those who had access to Solidarity materials, particularly those in the big factories, received balancing information and opinion from the union. Others, especially in the countryside, were more dependent on the official media. Solidarity's access to radio and television would have remedied this problem. This is precisely why the regime was so recalcitrant.

Table 5.8. Sources of information for Solidarity members (%)

Source	Main source	Use	Do not use
Polish mass media (press, radio, tv)	19.6	67.2	32.8
Information put out by union (bulletins, leaflets)	42.0	86.8	13.2
Meetings of the union	4.2	47.3	52.7
Private conversations	3.6	64.2	35.8
Foreign mass media (RFE, BBC, foreign periodicals)	8.8	54.2	45.9

Source: Krasko (1981), p. 171.

While Solidarity's leaders were supported on most of the major issues facing the union, there was not such unanimity on the union's tactics, and in particular on the strike weapon. Indeed, this seemed to be the single most divisive issue among Solidarity members and within the population.

This had not always been the case. The strikes of the summer of 1980 had been enormously popular and had, after all, led to the creation of Solidarity. The right to strike was incorporated in the Gdańsk Agreements. In a poll taken at the beginning of September 1980, 89% thought that the strikes had been justified. After that point, though, support for Solidarity's strikes slowly diminished. Already by October 1980, only 67% of a poll supported the one hour warning strike at the beginning of the month (Kurczewski 1981). It was clear too that support for the strikes was not as strong outside the cities. While 72% of workers supported the warning strike, only 56% of farmers did so. When Wałęsa called off a general strike over the Bydgoszcz events at the end of March, 94% of a national sample and 90% of a Solidarity poll approved the decision (Kania 1981). By the spring of 1981, there were increasingly evident divisions even within Solidarity about the usefulness of the strike tool and its effect on the economy. As is evident from Table 5.9, a substantial minority expressed reservations about the use of strikes, especially the general strike.

While most Solidarity members support all of these tactics, the lowest level of support appears for the general strike, and a quarter of the sample was undecided on this issue. There are also some reservations about the warning strikes. This same survey asked

Table 5.9. *Assessment of Solidarity's tactics, May 1981 (%)*

Form of pressure	Used too rarely	Just right	Used too often	No opinion
Negotiation, persuasion	29.7	53.4	4.3	13.1
Information action (leaflets, posters, etc.)	17.0	67.0	9.3	6.6
Preparation for strike	8.8	70.9	15.2	5.0
Warning strike	9.1	67.5	17.3	6.1
General strike	12.2	50.9	11.9	24.9
Boycott government decisions	15.1	59.0	7.5	18.4

Source: Krasko (1981), p. 173.

union members how Solidarity should move toward realization of the agreements signed with the government so far. By far the most popular tactic, supported by 85% of those polled, was 'informing society about progress in the fulfillment of the agreements, pointing out what and who is interfering with the process'. Over 60% favored avoiding strikes, while attempting to improve the productivity and organization of labor. Compared with these approaches, only 44% favored the more hard-line tactic of 'constant pressure on the government with the threat of strikes' if the agreements were not carried out. Thirty-seven percent favored seeking out people in the state and Party leadership for cooperative action. All in all, by May 1981, there was a decidedly conciliatory attitude on the part of most Solidarity members. The strike should be used when necessary, but in a more restrained fashion.

As 1981 wore on, the economic situation became worse and worse. The government claimed that the continuing strikes were a primary cause of the economic difficulties. Indeed, Solidarity's national leadership recognized the problem too. At the beginning of the year, the National Coordinating Commission had attempted to exert some control over the strikes. It appealed to local and regional chapters to abstain from strikes except as an immediate response to local administrative pressure or intimidation. Nevertheless, 'unauthorized' strikes continued through the year, and intensified in the summer, as food shortages became more serious. Finally, during a one-hour general strike on October 28, Wałęsa called for an end to that form of protest which, he said, simply hurt the workers. The next strike, he said, should be an 'active one'. 'We'll work to our own instructions and distribute what we produce ourselves. That way it will go to where it's most needed ... to hurt them, not us' (*Washington Post*, October 29, 1981).

The same week Solidarity's OBS conducted a poll on whether recent protest strikes organized by Solidarity were necessary. Only 11% thought that all the strikes had been necessary and another 41% thought the majority had been; but 34% thought a majority or all of the strikes could have been avoided. The Sejm was then considering a bill that would temporarily suspend the right to strike. When asked what the response of the union should be if the bill was passed, only 28% of Solidarity's members favored a general strike. Twenty-two percent suggested protest without a general strike, and another 35% were against any form of protest action (OBS, 'Komunikat', November 1981).

At the end of 1981, support for strike action was even weaker in the general population. The *Polacy '81* survey asked people which kind of protest acts they supported. On the issue of strikes, the sample was clearly divided: 46.3% supported strikes as a form of protest, while 47.9% were opposed to this form of protest.

In fact, there was substantial sentiment in favor of an outright ban on strikes; 46.2% of the sample favored such a ban, while 49% were opposed to such an idea. Solidarity supporters, of course, were much more in opposition to a strike ban, but even 37% of them favored such a ban by this time. Solidarity's own poll of its members' attitude toward the Central Committee's resolution on a temporary suspension of the right to strike found 24% approving and 63% opposing the resolution (OBS, 'Komunikat').

The issue of the strike, then, was a deeply divisive one in Poland on the eve of martial law. Roughly half of the population and two-thirds of Solidarity members still supported the strike apparently believing it to be the only effective means for the union to pressure the government. On the other hand, half of the population and a strong minority of Solidarity's members were opposed to the strike, even to the extent of banning it until the economy could be stabilized.

SUPPORT FOR SOLIDARITY'S LEADERSHIP

The declining support for the strike is reflected in some drop in support for Solidarity's leaders and the activities of the union at the national level. Support for the leadership remained strong through the end of 1981, though there were signs of disaffection. A series of OBOP polls from the end of the year showed a decline in those expressing trust in the 'leadership of Solidarity' from 74% in September of 1981 to 58% in November (OBOP, 'Napięcia Społeczne'). The data from OBOP may be suspect on this issue, though there is evidence of declining support for the union and its leadership in other polls as well, including those of Solidarity. In an October Solidarity poll on whether the national leadership of Solidarity had made any major mistakes in the previous few weeks, 51% said no. But 17% said yes, and 30% had no opinion (OBS, 'Członkowie Związku'). The level of support for the leadership on this issue is a far cry from the virtually unanimous support expressed for the union and its leaders a year before. For those saying there had been major mistakes, about a quarter each thought the leadership had been too hardline, or too compromising. When asked whether confidence in Solidarity's leaders had grown in recent weeks, roughly one third each thought it had, there had been no change, or that it had declined. It is clear, though, that the increasing disillusionment with the leadership was not for uniform reasons. When asked how they would assess the position of Solidarity during the latest (October) negotiations with the government, 52% thought it was just as it should be, 16% believed it was too 'soft' and 11% believed it was too hardline and radical. On how the union should behave in *future* negotiations, 36% opted for a more hardline position and 17% for a more compromising stance (OBS, 'Komunikat').

All of these results, on Solidarity's activities, positions, and leadership, attest to the deep divisions within Solidarity, and in popular attitudes towards Solidarity. On almost every issue, a broad middle group supported the activities of the union; but there were sizable minorities putting pressure on the union to be both more radical and more moderate. There was a growing awareness among Solidarity members of the existence and problem of factionalism within the movement. When asked about possible 'threats' to the union in May 1981, the most frequent response was 'internal quarrels' (Krasko 1981, p. 182). When the delegates to Solidarity's national Congress were asked if there were divisions in Solidarity, the most frequently perceived division (by 77.5% of the polled delegates) was that between radicals and moderates (OBS, 'Socjologiczne Badania').

Table 5.10. *Support for the activities of Solidarity at the national level, December 1980 and December 1981 (%)*

	12/80	12/81
Decisively support	57.9	33.2
Rather support	31.2	37.7
Rather not support	3.3	9.2
Decisively not support	1.2	4.7
Difficult to say	5.6	15.2

Source: Polacy '81, p. 117.

All of these factors contributed to a general erosion of support for Solidarity during 1981 (see Table 5.10).

By the end of 1981, support for Solidarity was still quite high, but it was not the universal and uncritical support that it had enjoyed in its early months. Already by the spring of 1981 there was some disappointment with the achievements of Solidarity. When asked if the union 'is currently fulfilling your expectations', 45.5% responded 'completely' and 48.9% 'to a certain extent'. But when asked if *in the future* one's expectations for the union would be realized, 48.5% said 'completely', but only 27.2% 'to a certain extent'. Almost 23% responded with 'it is difficult to say' (Krasko 1981, pp. 164, 185). There are many explanations for the decline in confidence in Solidarity: the increasing awareness that Solidarity could not solve all the problems Poland faced, particularly when confronted with an intransigent government; the increasing differentiation and fragmentation of Solidarity, as it grew and diversified its activities; the declining 'charisma' of the organization and its leaders as Solidarity became involved in the grimy details of economic recovery; and the continuing decline of the economy, creating an increased desire for calm and stability in the marketplace and the society.

DIVISIONS WITHIN SOLIDARITY

By the end of 1981, Solidarity's monolithic form was increasingly jeopardized. There had always been differences within the movement, of course, but these had largely been papered over in the exciting and heady months at the end of 1980 and early 1981. As Solidarity's momentum slowed somewhat in the face of obstacles posed by the regime, many of these differences began to emerge.

Even at the end of 1980, the authors of the *Polacy '80* survey had detected two main 'syndromes of views'. The first group tended to support egalitarianism, a monocentric political order, and a substantial role for the Church in public life. Typically, these views were supported by those with low levels of education, by workers and farmers, those living in small cities and towns, people in lower leadership positions, and religious believers. The second orientation was non-egalitarian and pluralistic and favored limiting the role of the Church to religious matters. These views were typically supported by those with a higher education, 'specialists' in the workforce, those in higher leadership positions, non-believers, and residents of large cities (*Polacy '80*, p. 134). Solidarity was a bridge between these two groups and two points of view, supporting at the same time egalitarianism and political pluralism and maintaining strong links with the Church.

These divisions began to appear on specific policy issues almost from the beginning of Solidarity. On how to divide the wage increases specified in the Gdańsk Agreements, for example, those with an elementary education or less were much more likely (32.5%) than those with a higher education (17.5%) to favor assigning the increases 'only to those earning the least'. One sees similar differences in the views of unskilled workers compared to specialists (*Polacy '80*, p. 85).

One of the major cleavages to emerge during 1981 was between residents of the cities and farmers. At first there was a high degree of solidarity between urban and rural residents. Farmers were almost as supportive of the Gdańsk Agreements and the constitution of Solidarity as were people in the cities. Reciprocating, urban residents strongly favored the establishment of a Solidarity for farmers in 1980. During 1981, tensions grew between the countryside and the city. In the cities, food supplies became increasingly problematic, such that by the summer and fall of 1981, there were major urban demonstrations complaining of the lack of food. The most dramatic of these was the August mass transit strike in Warsaw, when hundreds of buses and trams were stalled bumper-to-bumper in a fifty-hour confrontation with the police. The problem of shortages was compounded by summer price increases which were meant to offset increased purchase prices paid to farmers. By the end of 1981, the overwhelming majority of urban residents thought that life was much better in the countryside than in the cities. This

Table 5.11. *Who lives better, in country or city? 1980 and 1981, (%)*

| Who lives better? | Opinion of residents of: | | | |
| | Cities | | Countryside | |
	1980	1981	1980	1981
People in cities	36.8	4.1	52.2	14.9
People in country	35.7	72.4	20.3	53.1
No difference	20.2	16.1	17.9	21.5
Hard to say	7.3	7.4	9.6	10.5

Source: Polacy '81, p. 94.

Table 5.12. *Opinion on establishment of Rural Solidarity, 1980 and 1981 (%)*

Do (did) you favor?	1980 Overall	1981 Overall	1981 Urban	1981 Rural
Decisively so	62.9	30.3	20.0	43.2
Rather so	24.7	29.2	27.1	30.7
Rather not	4.2	11.4	15.5	6.1
Decisively not	1.4	7.6	11.7	3.3

Source: Polacy '81, p. 123.

marked a sharp turnaround in views over the course of the year (see Table 5.11).

The registration of Rural Solidarity in May had increased the bargaining power of farmers and contributed to the improved economic position of farmers, as the regime increased purchase prices, boosted agricultural investments, and extended social benefits into the countryside. By the end of 1981, Poles were much less convinced that the establishment of Rural Solidarity had been a good idea (see Table 5.12).

Though almost 63% had decisively supported the establishment of a rural trade union in December 1980, by the end of 1981, only 30% felt that strongly that it had been a good idea to constitute Rural Solidarity. In the cities, less than a majority 'decisively' or 'rather' supported the farmers' union. The rapid decline in solidarity between the cities and the countryside is not, perhaps, so surprising.

There had always been considerable tension between these two groups. The excitement and success of Solidarity had temporarily overcome these differences, but as the economy continued to deteriorate, these old tensions began to resurface.

The tensions and divisions within the Solidarity membership were reflected in differences among the union's leadership. As seen above, from the poll of Congress delegates, Solidarity activists had a broader and more activist vision of the union's role than did the membership at large. Many more of the delegates than national members indicated 'political' motives for joining Solidarity. Of the delegates, 26.5% indicated their primary motive for joining was 'to insure the independence of Poland'; only 7.2% of the national membership indicated this as the primary motive. That such a sizable minority had political aspirations for the union was bound to lead to internal conflict between these 'radicals' and the moderates, who saw a more limited, trade union role for Solidarity. When the Congress delegates were asked if there were divisions within Solidarity, 78% identified the division between radicals and moderates. Half or more also mentioned the division between workers and intelligentsia and between delegates from large and small regions (OBS, 'Socjologiczne Badania').

Already by early 1981, some Solidarity actions were taking on a political coloration, especially at the regional level. In January 1981, for example, the Solidarity regional committee in Bielsko-Biała directed a two-week strike over charges by Solidarity of incompetence and corruption by local party and state administrators. As a result of an agreement reached between Solidarity and a government commission, many of those officials were removed from office. Similar strikes demanding changes in government personnel were held in other regions. The Party leadership tried to deflect these actions by threats, and accused Solidarity of behaving like a political party, but in the end, often relented by removing the most offensive bureaucrats.

The Bydgoszcz affair in March marked the most bitter and dangerous confrontation of the year between Solidarity and the government. What had begun as a protest against police brutality led to a whole series of unrelated demands by Solidarity's National Commission. The government should not only investigate the incident and punish those responsible for the violence, but it should also guarantee freedom from persecution for Solidarity members, allow the establishment of Rural Solidarity, and deliver on Solidarity's previous demands for freeing political prisoners, allowing Solidarity access to the official media, and accommodating Solidarity's demands for strike pay. 'Linking' demands in this way made it more difficult for the regime to accede, and less likely that Solidarity would get what it wanted on the issue at hand. Nevertheless in most cases, as for the Bydgoszcz incident, some kind of compromise agreement usually emerged, usually by virtue of an accommodating position adopted by moderates on each side. In the case of the Bydgoszcz agreements, Wałęsa reached an accord with Deputy Premier Rakowski, despite bitter opposition from some of the more radical leaders of the movement.

By April 1981, Wałęsa was trying to curb the confrontational elements within Solidarity. 'There are people', he said, 'who always want to battle ... but both society and the union have had enough of confrontation ... it is necessary to change our modus operandi' (*Tygodnik Solidarność*, no. 2, 1981).

The splits within Solidarity were both exploited and exacerbated by the regime's propaganda. In a speech to the Sejm in June, Premier Jaruzelski claimed that the government wanted to 'help' Solidarity 'cleanse itself of hostile, anarchistic, and adventuristic elements ... that have been placed in leading positions at many levels of the trade union'. These elements, he claimed, were pushing the union in an anti-socialist direction (Radio Free Europe Research, *Polish Situation Report* – hereafter RFER – June 19, 1981). This kind of language simply contributed to the siege mentality within the independent labor movement, making it that much more recalcitrant on *its* side of the negotiations.

By the fall of 1981, perhaps because of the seriousness of the economic crisis, moderate voices were heard on both sides of the political fence. In September Politburo member Olszowski invited 'all patriotic forces', including Solidarity to participate in the Front of National Unity. This was an opportunity for Solidarity to achieve a formal role in decision-making (or at least in consultation), but many union activists viewed the offer simply as an effort by the regime to coopt the union. The next month, Deputy Prime Minister Rakowski proposed a mutual Solidarity–government commission on the food crisis, but Solidarity again invoked the linkage principle by refusing to participate unless the union would be allowed first to present its views on television.

On Solidarity's side, Wałęsa was steering the movement in a more moderate direction as well. In September, he agreed to accept the Sejm version, rather than the Solidarity one, on the new legislation for employee self-management. Under the Sejm version, the government would retain the right to nominate managers of defense and other key industries. The workers would have the initiative in all other cases. At Solidarity's October Congress, Wałęsa easily defeated his challengers in being reelected as Chairman of Solidarity's National Commission (KKP). Furthermore, the new KKP Presidium elected at the Congress consisted almost entirely of Wałęsa supporters, indicating popular support for the leader's moderate course. Wałęsa's most important critics and challengers, including Andrzej Gwiazda (Solidarity's co-founder from Gdańsk), Jan Rulewski (Bydgoszcz regional chairman), and Karol Modzelewski (former Solidarity press spokesman) did not get seats on the Presidium.

The chances for compromise seemed even greater after the first meeting of the 'Big Three' of Wałęsa, Jaruzelski and Archbishop Glemp on November 4. The regime continued to push for a 'historic compromise' toward a 'Front of National Accord'. Solidarity's KKP issued a statement saying it was prepared to make concessions and compromises for the good of the nation. However, in the face of the conciliatory stance by Solidarity's national leadership, the divisions between the radicals and moderates, and between the center and the regions, continued to plague the organization. The national leadership was unable to mute the inflammatory voices or restrain the strike initiatives of the regional organizations. This was Solidarity's democratic dilemma. Its very *raison d'être* was based on its democratic organization, decentralized structure, and tolerance of dissenting views; but in the face of a powerful adversary, Solidarity needed central guidance and controls to see the union through a difficult period. The inflammatory voices only provided a pretext for the regime to crack down.

These radical voices continued during the very time that government–Solidarity negotiations were ongoing. A November issue of *Tygodnik Solidarność*, for example, claimed that 'the existing political institutions . . . cannot fulfill their tasks . . . we think that we should start building an accord not from the roof down, but from the foundation up' (cited in Leszek Szymański 1982). At the same time that Wałęsa was calling for an end to strikes, work stoppages and strikes were occurring all over the country, and by November had shut down even many of the universities. Wałęsa and the national leadership had lost control of the union, at a time when hard-liners were coming to the fore in the Party leadership. It was in this tense atmosphere that Solidarity's National leadership met with the regional leaders in Radom on December 3. The gulf between the moderates and the radicals became dramatically evident at this forum. The regime, however, focused its attention only on the statements of the latter, and used these as a justification for the crackdown that occurred ten days later.

CONCLUSIONS

Solidarity's size and scope was both its strength and its weakness. The almost universal appeal of the independent union, and its huge membership, forced the regime's leadership to accommodate Solidarity and some of its demands. The broad-based nature of Solidarity's program imbued the union with an aura of authority and universalism both within Poland and without. Precisely because of these factors, Solidarity acquired a myth of omnipotence and invincibility. It tried to achieve everything at once. When Solidarity ran into obstacles, the myths began to disintegrate, and the movement to fragment. The exhilaration born of Solidarity's early successes gave way to apathy and fatigue. The regime capitalized on all of this and moved in for the kill.

Even some of the original Gdańsk demands which were eventually fulfilled were in some respects counterproductive. As Solidarity advisor Andrzej Tymowski pointed out in November 1981, the wage increases won in August had increased spendable income without a corresponding increase in production or productivity, leading to inflation and market disequilibria. Similarly, the contraction of working hours (through free Saturdays, etc.) led to a reduction in output, and the earlier retirement ages to an expansion in the government's social fund. Neither the government nor the economy could afford these changes.

These systemic problems were probably less important for the union than its own internal ones. Solidarity emerged so suddenly and grew so fast that it did not have time to develop its structure, program, and policies in any orderly way. Rather, it had to do all of these things at once. By the spring of 1981, Solidarity was struggling to get access to the funds and buildings of the old unions, to gain access to the mass media, to support the creation of a rural union, and to get the government to follow through on the Gdańsk Agreements. All of this was happening at the same time that the union was attempting to work out its own internal organization, settle upon some kind of programmatic guidelines, and establish specific policies for the union itself (membership, dues, social fund, etc.) and for the country as a whole. Not yet fully established, Solidarity was suffering from organizational overload.

The myth of invincibility also led Solidarity into some dangerous areas. Having forced the government to concede on *all* of its 21 demands at Gdańsk, the workers' movement believed it could win concessions in other areas as well. During 1981, Solidarity inserted itself into discussions of the control of the media, the role of the communist party, the selection and dismissal of government and party officials, the reform of the economy, and the electoral procedures for the Sejm, peoples' councils, and other state institutions. Solidarity claimed that it would stay out of politics, and most of its members favored a quite narrow range of activities for the union. At the same time, the union often put forward demands which, as Bronisław Misztal (1983) has put it, if granted 'would amount to the abdication of those in power'. The absence of any Soviet intervention in Poland had created a myth of external autonomy and invincibility as well, and led Solidarity into dangerous political waters in the foreign affairs arena. The most blatant example of this was the expression of support for workers' movements elsewhere in the Soviet bloc adopted at Solidarity's Congress:

As the first independent union of Eastern Europe we deeply feel a sense of community and, contrary to the slanders spread in your country, we are the authentic representatives of the working class in Poland. We support those of you who have decided to enter the difficult road of struggle for free and independent unions. We trust that our representatives can meet soon to exchange experiences.

This message simply added to Soviet aggravation, leading the Soviet news agency TASS to claim that the Gdańsk assembly had been turned into 'an anti-socialist and anti-Soviet orgy' (Ruane 1982, p. 233). The extensiveness and insistence of Solidarity's demands led Andrzej Tymowski (1981b, p. 12) to express a warning which, in retrospect, was tragically prescient: 'we have accomplished too much that, wanting to achieve even more, we risk losing everything'.

The myth of invincibility was compounded by the myth of unity. As seen above, Solidarity was overwhelmingly supported by the population, especially in its early months. This unity, however, had been forged more from negative feelings than from positive ones; it was directed against the existing power structure and resulted from the lack of alternative channels for expressions of dissatisfaction and dissent. Once the forum for the articulation of interests had been forged with the creation of Solidarity, this broad coalition began to disintegrate. Different groups had different, often conflicting, interests and priorities. As one Solidarity observer noted in the spring of 1981:

The Solidarity movement at this moment has neither a defined ideology nor a worldview, bringing together believers, non-believers, Piłsudskiites, Dmowskiites, people of every possible hue and people without a defined political view. It is necessary first of all to develop an introduction, not a range of choices (Paczkowski 1981).

In developing its program, Solidarity attempted not to alienate any of these groups in its coalition. In doing so, it was unable to narrow the options and focus its direction. It was still trying to do everything at once. The normal divisions and conflicts within Polish society began to emerge within Solidarity. The divisions weakened the organization, as did the increasingly troublesome economic and political environment. As it became clear that Solidarity could not quickly accomplish all it had set out to do, many of the union's lukewarm supporters began to drift away. Others became annoyed with the intransigence of one side or the other. Polish society was unaccustomed to sharpness of political debate, both within Solidarity and without, engendered by the more open political atmosphere. The higher level of tension even induced increased physiological problems in the population. As Jacek Maziarski (1981) noted as early as March:

our society is not yet used to living with publicized open conflicts, because until now they were kept secret and pushed under the surface. Over the years, we have gotten used to a fictitious vision of public life devoid of differing positions and conflicts. ... Under our conditions, lacking developed institutional mechanisms, each mention of a difference of position produces a nervous atmosphere and occasionally is received as a threat to the stability of the state.

Solidarity was developing as an appropriate 'institutional mechanism' for the expression of different interests, but it was not given the chance.

6

The Party and 'renewal'

The Polish United Workers' Party (PZPR) is 'the leading political force in society' according to the country's Constitution. The Party Statutes adopted in 1959 defined the Party as 'the vanguard of the working class, the highest form of its organization, the guiding force of the socialist revolution'. Yet by 1980, the Party had virtually collapsed as an institution representative of the interests of the workers. The weakness of the Party was at least partly responsible for both the development of Solidarity in the summer of 1980 and for the imposition of martial law in December of 1981. The lack of trust in the Party and its authoritarian and unrepresentative character led the workers to demand an institution more responsive to their own needs. But the growth of Solidarity during 1981, and the continuing disintegration and fragmentation of the Party led the military to preempt the Party's leading role in 1982.

The collapse of the Party in 1980 and 1981 was due to a number of factors. The Party leadership bore the burden of the economic failures of the late 1970s and the consequent decline in the standard of living. The Party itself had grown rapidly in size during that period, though the influence of ordinary Party members and local Party organizations declined in the face of increasing centralizing tendencies in the latter half of the decade. This led to problems of morale even within the Party, and the growth of horizontal barriers between the mass Party membership and its leadership. In the population at large, there was increasing annoyance and disgust at the failure of the Party to rectify the economic situation and to allow a more honest and open discussion of Poland's problems. This was compounded by the widespread perception that the elite was increasingly looking after only its own interests, with an expansion of benefits and privileges accruing to those in power.

By the spring of 1981, though, the 'renewal' movement that was sweeping the country began to penetrate even the Party, which embarked on its own reforms and house-cleaning. Much of this initiative came from the bottom ranks of the Party, and some of it was resisted at the top. But the changes that did occur were genuine enough to worry the Soviet party leadership, which issued a number of warnings to its Polish counterpart. As the Party became less hierarchical and less disciplined, as Party members continued to join Solidarity, and as Solidarity continued to mount its challenge to the monocentric nature of the Polish political system, the Jaruzelski regime apparently feared a total collapse of the Party. The vacuum created by such an event could have been filled only by Solidarity or the Army.

THE PARTY BEFORE 1980

The Party's problems did not begin in 1980, of course. The organization had always had difficulties in establishing its legitimacy in Polish society, and in keeping the membership both representative and 'elite'. The disturbances of 1970 had challenged the Party, and the new Gierek leadership initiated a purge of the membership, followed by an expansion of the Party's rolls. The broadening of the membership was meant to improve the Party's representation and contacts in society. At the same time, the Party was reorganized in the mid-1970s to enhance its 'control' function. One result of this was the merging of party and state offices at all levels. After 1973, for example, the first secretaries of each province, district and city were to become the chairmen of the corresponding people's council. The tendency of the Gierek regime to consolidate and centralize decision-making meant a loss of authority even for the Party organizations at the local and regional levels. As a Polish sociologist noted, while the significance of the peoples' councils and local party committees had never been very great, their significance 'fell almost to zero' in the latter 1970s (Tarkowski 1983).

The riots of the summer of 1976 demonstrated once again the lack of institutionalized mechanisms for the expression of workers' grievances. In the absence of any trusted official channel of discontent, the workers took to the streets. One of the regime's responses to these events was a sustained campaign to increase the number of workers and young people in the Party. Once again, the regime hoped that by reaching into these disaffected populations, the Party could neutralize some of the dissent. Indeed, in numerical terms at least, the Party experienced some success in this campaign. By the end of 1979, members and candidates of the Party constituted almost 12% of the adult population, and over 20% of those employed in the socialized economy. These were the highest such percentages in the Party's history. This expansion had managed to increase the representation of young people, women, and workers in the Party's ranks, making it as representative in these categories as it had ever been. Workers, for example, constituted 46.2% of the Party in 1979, compared to 41.8% in 1975.

Despite these improvements, the Party was still highly unrepresentative of the population in several basic respects. While there were more blue-collar workers as Party members, for example, this group was still not well represented in Party leadership positions. Though blue-collar workers made up almost half of the Party, they held only 10% of the central party leadership positions, and were only 3% of the discussants at Central Committee plenary sessions (Kolankiewicz 1982, p. 59). The Party also remained highly unrepresentative of the peasantry which made up about one-third of the workforce, but less than 10% of the Party. This fact was of less interest to urban residents than the perception, largely based on fact, that the Party was dominated by highly educated white-collar workers with high incomes. Official Party statistics showed that 12% of Party members had a higher education, compared to just 7% of the workforce. But a sample of working males in the city of Łódź showed that 30% of the Party members had a higher education; compared to 11% of non-Party members. In fact, over *half* of those with a complete higher education were Party members (*Łódź '80*). While the Party did consider it important to attract the 'best' people to the organization, including the best educated, this kind of differentiation was bound to be grating to the less educated blue-collar workers.

Another source of differentiation, though one undoubtedly linked to the educational and class factors, was in income. A recalculation of figures from a Party sponsored survey shows that Party members are almost twice as likely to be in the top of five income brackets, and less than half as likely to be in the lowest, as is evident from Table 6.1.

Table 6.1. *Party membership and income*

Annual income* (złotys)	% at each income level Party members	Non-members
under 12,000	5.8	13.9
12,000–18,000	17.6	26.3
18,000–30,000	47.4	41.8
30,000–42,000	20.0	13.0
over 42,000	9.1	4.9

*Annual household income per person.
Source: Recalculations from Beskid and Sufin (1981), pp. 567–70.

Furthermore, Party membership is a major determinant of income *aspirations*, even when controlling for the effect of education and income (Szafnicki and Mach 1982).

The expansion and diversification of the Party did not, then, solve the problems of credibility and representation for the regime. The Party still did not have firm roots either in the working class or the peasantry. If anything, the expansion of the Party simply fortified the popular image of the Party as being made up of 'opportunists'. Furthermore, the failure of the regime to allow decentralization of power and decision-making even within the Party hindered the development of confidence in the Party by society, and of morale within the organization. The public assessment of the Party remained highly negative.

POPULAR ASSESSMENT OF THE PARTY

The Party had never been very popular in Poland, but the lack of confidence in the organization was never publicly affirmed until the spring of 1981, when the press briefly referred to an official public opinion poll on confidence in institutions (see Table 5.3). Of fifteen such institutions, including the government, the militia, and the old trade unions, the Polish United Workers' Party ranked dead last. While this poll showed 32% of the population expressing confidence in the Party, a similar survey conducted by Solidarity among its own members in November 1981 also showed the Party in last place, but with only a 7% confidence rating. This very low level of support for the 'leading' organization in the society was derived from a number of complaints Poles had with the Party and with those in power.

These included a widespread feeling that those in policy-making and managerial positions were incompetent; that they abused their positions of power by attaching extravagant privileges to their positions; that the Party and the elite closed off access to decision-making for non-party people and ruled by compulsion rather than consensus; and that the Party had forsaken its own stated ideals of socialism and egalitarianism. These were wide-ranging issues, and brought into question the very role of the Party in Polish society.

Incompetence

The sense of the Party's and leadership's incompetence was not always as strong as it was by 1980. During the first half of the 1970s, for example, there were some positive evaluations of the Gierek leadership. An official poll from 1975 showed that almost 85% of the people believed that 'in the last several years society had confidence in the leadership of the country' (Sufin 1981a, p. 21). Over 90% of this sample believed the developments in the country since 1970 had been 'quick', and the most frequently mentioned reason for these developments was 'the new leadership of the Party and the country'. Even making exception for the official nature of this poll and the more stifled atmosphere in which it was conducted, the results are markedly different from the 1981 questions on trust in the government and the party mentioned above. This decline in confidence in the late 1970s was due in large part to the decline in the economy and the standard of living during that period, and the simultaneous burgeoning of Poland's foreign debt. Many Poles wondered where the money had gone, and assumed that it was either wasted or appropriated by the elite. This contributed to the widespread belief and discussion of incompetence in the economic and political leadership. A poll conducted among a small (330) sample of men in Warsaw in the summer of 1979, for example, showed that only 20% thought 'ability' had a decisive role in helping people reach high positions in Polish society. As the researchers pointed out, a similar question asked in the United States showed 70% assigning a decisive role to ability (Gadomska 1981).

Privilege

The popular perception of incompetence in the Party and the country's leadership was aggravated by widespread feelings that the elite was unjustly benefiting from its positions in power. The issue of privilege was always a sensitive one in Poland, a society that highly values the principle of egalitarianism. Unequal distribution of wealth and power is seen as contradictory with the basic principles of socialist society. These issues had always been discussed in Poland, though largely in private. In 1979–81, however, they were treated more directly and openly in both the official and unofficial press, contributing to popular frustration.

In the unofficial 'Report on the State of the Republic' by the 'Experience and the Future' study group, the issues which most clearly stood out in their description of society were 'the social structure, its hierarchical character, antiegalitarian tendencies, and the emergence of a system of privileges that conflicts with the sense of social justice so deeply rooted, thanks to socialist ideology, in our society' (*Poland Today*, p. 57). There was a widespread perception in Polish society at the end of the 1970s that social inequalities had increased over the past decade. But as one analyst of some official (OBOP) public opinion data pointed out, 'the present egalitarianism' was not directed against the differences in earnings as such, but 'mainly against the economic position and life style of the leadership apparatus'. Most people, he pointed out, believe:

it is unfair that high positions are linked with privileges and they demand that incomes be reduced, and that availability of goods in short supply, such as housing and automobiles, access to special shops, private clubs, clinics, etc. to persons in high positions, be restricted (Kurczewski 1981).

All of these issues and complaints were to become strong elements in Solidarity's appeal and Solidarity's program. In the preliminary program for Solidarity ('Directions of Solidarity') drawn up by a group of the organization's advisors in the spring of 1981, there were demands both for restrictions of privileges on the elite, and for the costs of economic recovery and reform to be borne 'particularly by people enjoying privileges linked with the exercise of power'. The restrictions on privileges were especially directed at those in 'the power apparatus' and were aimed at limitations on apartments, office automobiles, special health services, and revelation of their incomes and properties.

It should be noted here that the concern over privilege was *not* directed at the Party membership at large, but rather at those in positions of power. In fact, there was considerable concern over elite privilege even *within* the Party. A Party report on letters addressed to the Central Committee by rank-and-file Party members mentioned numerous letters advocating 'the liquidation of commercial stores and other special stores' and 'stores in the militia, the army and the committees of the PZPR' (Sufin 1981b, p. 221). The last reference to the committees of the Party suggests that the concern with privilege was not just in the central apparatus of power, but at lower levels as well. Here, as elsewhere, we see that the divisions in Polish society in 1980–1 were not so much between Party and non-Party people, but rather between those in positions of power (at all levels) and the rest of society, Party and non-Party alike.

The role of the Party

While the issues of competence and privilege were sensitive and inflammatory ones, questions about the role of the PZPR in Polish society were potentially much more dangerous and destabilizing. The issues raised in this context included overcentralization of power and lack of democracy within the Party and the excessive control and dominance of the Party in societal decision-making.

These kinds of criticism were voiced both by the public and by rank-and-file party members during 1980 and 1981. Kurczewski's (1981) analysis of an official 1980 OBOP poll concluded that the leadership be rotated and that 'the principles of selection and promotion be democratized' within the Party. The 'Experience and the Future' group also argued for limiting the terms of office of the top leadership levels of the Party (*Poland Today*, p. 173).

Perhaps the most systematic criticism of Party organization and leadership came from within the Party. In a series of letters addressed to the Central Committee after August 1980, the most frequent suggestion was for a limitation on terms of office for Party authorities. The writers also called for more and better information within the Party, secret elections, changes in Party nominating procedures, and open sessions of the Central Committee and lower level committees (Sufin 1981b, pp. 209–30).

These criticisms were accompanied by complaints of the increasing centralization of power in the hands of the central Party apparatus. This centralization took two forms: the arrogation of decision-making authority by the Party from the state and other institutions; and the concentration of power within the Party from the periphery to the center. Solidarity, in its Program, asserted that the method of governing based on the domination of the central party–state institutions 'had led the country to ruin'.

Many of these issues were summed up in a set of recommendations issued to the Party's Central Committee by a group of experts attached to the Party's Institute of the Basic Problems of Marxism-Leninism. Their report, delivered in October 1980, defined the main characteristic of the crisis as a lack of confidence in the governing of society and suggested a number of changes, including: decentralization of state and party authority; greater intra-party democracy and egalitarianism; the widening of 'social participation' in decision-making and increased autonomy for other institutions; and an improvement of Party electoral procedures, including the naming of two candidates for each leadership position (Sufin 1981b). Many of these changes were made in the Party during 1981, as will be seen below.

Many of these criticisms of the Party were, of course, a reflection of a deeper sense that the population had little opportunity to voice their opinions or participate in decision-making. The popular sense of alienation from politics had increased dramatically during the latter 1970s. In 1976, among a sample of males in the city of Łódź, only 41% cited the degree of 'participation in governing' as a source of tension and conflict in society. By 1980, fully 80% thought so (*Łódź 1976*; *Łódź 1980*). Solidarity's preliminary program hammered at the idea that the loss of democratic institutions was the root cause of the crisis: 'the bureaucratic system of governing the state and managing the economy has helped establish a closed group of rulers who are not subject to control by the governed' ('Directions of Solidarity').

The popular frustration with the role of the Party and the centralization of power came out into the open during 1980 and 1981 and was revealed in the *Polacy '80* and *Polacy '81* surveys. In the former, conducted at the end of 1980, over 92% agreed with the proposition that there should be 'increased control of society over the authorities'. That this was not to be accomplished through the Party was evident from another question about 'strengthening the role of the Party in the administration of power'. In 1980 only 33% agreed with this proposition and 56% disagreed. By the end of 1981, only 20% favored strengthening the Party. When the question was phrased in the obverse in 1981, on *limiting* the role of the Party, 60% favored this idea, while only 20% opposed it. Even 46% of *Party*

Table 6.2. *Desired types of government power in public opinion*

Role of Party	Degree of centralization	
	'strong, centralized'	'decentralized'
With leading role	13.7%	10.8%
Without leading role	19.1%	33.6%

Source: Polacy '81, p. 207.

members favored limiting the role of the Party. In trying to get at the types of authority relationships desired by the population, the *Polacy '81* researchers asked if the respondents favored a centralized or decentralized system, with or without the Party playing a leading role. Four statements, reflecting the four possibilities, were posed to the respondents. The results are presented in Table 6.2.

There was obviously a considerable division on both dimensions, though by far the largest proportion favored a decentralized system without the leading role of the Party, and 'based on the participation of various social forces', as the statement was phrased. There was stronger support for a decentralized system (44.4%) than a centralized one (32.8%); but the really astounding result of this question was on the leading role of the Party. Only 24.5% favored such a role, while a clear majority (52.7%) opted for a system without the leading role of the Party. This testifies to the thoroughgoing disillusionment of Polish society with the PZPR. In Poland, as in all communist states, the leading role of the Party has been the *sine qua non* of the political system. This formula is incorporated in the Polish Constitution, and even in the 1980 Gdańsk Agreements. It was the basis on which the Soviet Union intervened in both Hungary in 1956 and Czechoslovakia in 1968. Yet by the end of 1981, the Polish Party was so discredited that the majority of Poles was apparently willing to revise that fundamental component of the political system.

This frustration with the PZPR, however, did not translate into a wish to constitute any *new* political parties. In the *Polacy '81* survey only 25% favored constituting some 'new political parties besides the PZPR, the Social Democratic Party and the United Peasant Party' (these are the two satellite parties of the PZPR, which are allied with the Party in the Front of National Unity and which have some seats in the Polish parliament, but with minimal independent political influence). Opposition to the creation of a new political party was fairly uniform across the political spectrum. Seventy-seven percent of Party members were opposed to the idea (though 24% favored it!), as were 69% of Solidarity members. There was also little support for the proposition that Solidarity should create a political party to operate alongside the union. Only 20% of the overall sample, and 23% of Solidarity members, favored this idea.

Poles, therefore, did not favor the elimination of the PZPR, or even its replacement by other parties. They wanted a more pluralistic society, in which 'society exercises more control over the authorities', and in which there is more room for political participation and political maneuver by other groups, including the existing non-communist parties and the trade unions. As Solidarity's *Program* put it: 'the state must serve man, and not rule over him; the state organization must serve society and should not be identified with a single political party'. Poles opposed the monopolistic control of power by the Party, not the Party itself.[23]

THE PARTY ADAPTS

The political crisis of 1980 was due, in large measure, to the failure of the Party to adapt to the changes that had occurred in Polish society in the previous two decades. As we saw in Chapter 3, most Poles accepted the principal features of a socialist society but wanted a more open political system. Solidarity helped focus and institutionalize these demands and forced the Party to react. Throughout 1981, the Party was on the defensive, as more and more of its prerogatives, authority, and membership slipped away. The regime could have reacted to Solidarity's challenge in one of two ways: by adapting itself to the changed environment, or by crushing the challenger. During most of Solidarity's sixteen months, the Party adapted. When these changes proved to be insufficient to the task, the regime had to resort to force. But by that time, the Party could not manage even that task, and the Army had to intervene.

[23] The pseudonymous Jan Powiorski (1983, p. 126), in analyzing the data on the creation of new political parties, argues that Poles 'are simply incapable of imagining a concrete new form of political system (and a party system)'. He attributes this to the effectiveness of years of official 'anti-education', and illustrates this point with data from the *Polacy '81* survey which shows that support for the creation of new political parties rises with the educational level of the respondents.

The adaptation took two forms: initiated from below by the rank-and-file membership; and from above by the Party leadership. The former was a largely spontaneous phenomenon that was as much a part of the 'renewal' process as was the workers' movement. It was manifested in dramatic changes in Party membership, in the formation of unofficial organizational structures, and in challenges to the concept of democratic centralism.

Changes in Party membership

The increasingly vigorous and open challenges to the Party could not help but affect the members of that besieged organization. Between the end of 1980 and the end of 1981, over 400,000 members left the Party. This was by far the largest one-year defection in the Party's history and, at 13% of the Party's total membership, was the largest percentage decline except for the year 1958 (Mason 1982, p. 139). In February 1982, the official press admitted that the Party had lost almost a half million members since *July 1981*. It is evident that most of those who left were workers since the working class component of the Party had declined from 46.2% at the end of 1979 to 42.7% in early 1982 (*Rzeczpospolita*, September 2, 1982).

Many of those who left the Party joined Solidarity, but there were probably even more Party members who stayed in the Party *and* joined Solidarity. In two separate survey research polls at the end of 1980 (*Polacy '80* and *Łódź 1980*) 35% of Party members admitted to membership in Solidarity. This is close to the percentage of the general population in Solidarity (37%). An even greater number of Party members supported Solidarity, even if they did not join the organization. In the *Polacy '80* survey, 45% of Party members expressed 'decisive support' for the activities of Solidarity.

This dual membership in Solidarity and the Party was especially prevalent among skilled blue- and white-collar workers, as is apparent from Table 6.3. As the table shows, at the end of 1981, three-quarters of all skilled workers, Party and non-Party alike, belonged to Solidarity. There were also extremely high rates of Solidarity membership among specialists and the 'leadership cadre' including most Party members in these categories.

There are several possible explanations of why so many Party members, particularly those in prestige and leadership positions, would join Solidarity. First of all, the appeal of Solidarity was so

Table 6.3. *Party members in Solidarity, by occupational groups (%)*

Occupational groups	% in Solidarity among:	
	Party members	Non-members
Specialists with higher education and leadership cadre	55.0	69.5
Middle cadre and specialists	64.7	71.8
Office workers and administration	33.3	61.2
Skilled workers	76.0	77.6
Farmers and farm workers	15.8	20.0

Source: Polacy '81, p. 190.

widespread that it cut across the lines of the 'establishment' to include many supporters of the regime. Most rank-and-file Party members supported the existence and goals of Solidarity and saw in it, perhaps, a potential means to loosen the hierarchical controls within the Party. As Solidarity advisor Jadwiga Staniszkis (1981, p. 229) has pointed out, the anti-hierarchical, anti-institutional and egalitarian attitudes of Solidarity found support in the Party as well, and fostered genuine common interests between the 'renewal' movement in the Party and Solidarity's membership.

Secondly, it might be expected that Party members would be attracted to Solidarity simply because of their political activism. Party members are joiners and activists, and are more likely to have definite opinions on public issues. Solidarity provided a new channel for their activities, and potentially a more fruitful one. That PZPR members played an activist and leadership role in Solidarity is evident from data on Party membership among the factory commissions of Solidarity. In five of the six reported voivodships (regions), Party members constituted at least 20% of the Solidarity factory commissions (*Informator*).

The overlapping membership of Solidarity and the Party extended to the very top structures of both the Party and of Solidarity. At the Party's Ninth Congress in July 1981, 20% of the Congress delegates were also Solidarity members. The Congress even put a Solidarity member, Zofia Grzyb, on the Party's ruling Politburo. Similarly, there were Party members in *Solidarity's* leading bodies. About 6% of the delegates to Solidarity's autumn Congress were members of the PZPR (Misztal and Misztal, 1984). Several members of Solidarity's national commission were former or present Party members. The best known of these was Bogdan Lis, one of the leaders of the strike in Gdańsk in 1980, who had been a member of the Party since 1975. The changes in the Party also affected the professional apparatus. In the eighteen months after August 1980, 53% of the professional Party workers left the organization. In the preliminary elections leading up to the Ninth Congress, there was 'an almost complete turnover in the leadership cadre of the Party'. Eighty percent of the regional party committees were new, as were 65% of the village, town and factory committees, and 50% of the first secretaries of the primary party organizations (*Rzeczpospolita*, February 25, 1982). According to the Polish Press Agency, many of these newly elected local leaders were 'young people, not infrequently with short party membership records'. This 'renewal' and rejuvenation of the Party did raise the possibility of changes in *policy* as well, and perhaps of a more accommodating stance towards Solidarity. It also raised the hackles of concern and fear in the Soviet Union, that the Polish Party might be losing its 'leading role'.

Emergence of alternative Party structures

Another form of adaptation by the Party's rank-and-file was the 'horizontalist' movement. The impetus for this came from the city of Toruń, where the August 1980 strikes had been led by a Party member, Zbigniew Iwanów. After the strike was ended, Iwanów was elected first secretary of his factory Party organization. As Iwanów later said, 'the union was a safeguard for the people. But we owed it to ourselves to seek safeguards within the party, because the party had already suffered too many crises and one more might be deadly.' Iwanów and his Party colleagues in the Towimor ship machinery plant sought out contact with like-minded members of other primary party organizations. To formalize these contacts, they established an inter-factory Party consultative commission, modeled on the summer's inter-factory strike commissions. The consultative commission provided horizontal links among basic party organizations in violation of the statutory principle of exclusively vertical linkages between the basic organizations and the high level party bodies (Persky 1981, pp. 155–6).

In Toruń, some 7000 of 17,000 Party members eventually became affiliated with the consultative commission. The phenomenon also spread to seventeen other provinces. Many of these forums became a virtual alternative Party leadership in their regions. Many of the demands for Party reform, and for the convening of the extraordinary (Ninth) Party Congress, originated from these 'horizontalist' structures. In April, the horizontalists held an extraordinary meeting of their own in Toruń, bringing together 750 delegates from basic party organizations in 14 of the country's 49 voivodships. The conference, organized by the rank-and-file without previous sanction by higher authorities, discussed ways to improve the quality of Party work, to further democratize the Party, and to develop the service component of Party activity.

The response of the Party hierarchy to these developments was mixed. At first, horizontalism was opposed by the Party leadership. Later, as a prominent Party academic put it, it was 'recognized as legitimate as long as it restrained itself from creating an alternative power structure' (Wiatr 1981, p. 815). The Party *de facto* recognized the April Toruń conference by sending three Central Committee members as observers.

Horizontalism did generate opposition from other quarters, however. Soon after the Toruń forum, the Soviet news agency TASS accused the 'so-called horizontal structures' of being fronts for 'revisionist forces in the Party' who were demanding 'reform of the PZPR, the renunciation of its present organizational structure and the creation of various forums outside the statutes which would take the place of the leading organs of the Party' (cited in Ruane 1982, p. 152). In June, when the Soviet Central Committee sent a strongly worded warning to its Polish counterpart, it complained that the horizontalist structures were 'a tool for dismantling the Party' during the preparations for the forthcoming Party Congress. Similar criticisms were voiced by a number of conservative Party forums that emerged in Katowice, Poznań and elsewhere in the spring and summer.

The horizontalist movement was an encouraging sign of vitality at the grass-roots of the Party. In promoting more open discussion and decentralization the movement promised the kind of revitalization necessary for the Party to recover a sense of legitimacy. The movement was an important stimulus to the electoral reform that had such an impact on the Ninth Party Congress. On the other hand, as Jerzy Wiatr (1981, p. 815) has pointed out, it 'lacked unity of command as well as a coherent political programme', that would have allowed it to prevail in the long run. It was threatening to the established structure and hierarchy of the Party and, for that reason, to the Soviet Union. And it led to divisions within the Party as conservative groups emerged to challenge the reformers. All of these factors contributed, paradoxically, to the further weakening of the Party.

Party members and society

As a result of this ferment at the grass-roots of the Party, by the end of 1981 there were not major differences in outlook between members of the PZPR and the rest of society. Most of the views of society reflected in public opinion polls were similar to those held by members of the Party. Table 6.4, drawn from the *Polacy '81* survey, shows the responses to selected questions by Party membership.

On some of the major issues of 1981, a majority of Party members agreed with the majority view of non-Party members. It is clear from these data that Party members were by no means hard line on these issues. Fully 80%, for example, favored Solidarity's access to radio and television, one of the most controversial and divisive issues of 1981.

On other issues too, one sees a remarkable degree of support for Solidarity's actions and programs from the Party membership. Only

Table 6.4. *Public opinion of Party and non-Party members on major issues in 1981 (%)*

Issue	Party	Non-Party
Support guaranteeing Solidarity access to mass media	79.8	93.5
Support limiting the role of the Party in the administration of power	46.0	62.0
Support for the development of private agriculture	56.2	74.9
Oppose temporary increase in the powers of the Militia and the security forces	53.5	64.5

Source: Polacy '81, pp. 133ff.

Table 6.5. *Opinion on responsibility for crisis, by Party membership (%)*

Who's responsible?	Party	Non-Party
Government	25.5	41.7
Solidarity	8.7	2.4
Both	47.1	38.9
Someone else	4.4	6.1
Difficult to say	14.6	10.9

Source: Polacy '81, p. 112.

21% of Party members 'decisively opposed' strikes as a form of protest (compared to 13% of non-Party members). When asked about participation in acts of protest, party members *more* frequently admitted to such acts (21.6%) than did the overall sample (18.4%). When asked who was responsible for the governmental and political crisis, Party members rarely blamed Solidarity (see Table 6.5), though they were also less likely than non-Party members to assign primary responsibility to the government.

Furthermore, they overwhelmingly opposed hardline emergency measures to cope with the crisis at the end of 1981 (*Polacy '81*).

DIRECTED REFORM

Not all of the Party reforms came from the bottom ranks, however. The Party leadership also recognized the weakness of the Party, and the necessity for change. Stanisław Kania acknowledged this need soon after he replaced Gierek as Party First Secretary in September: 'what is a thousand times more important is what has to be changed within ourselves, how the authorities must change, how the methods of ruling and governing must change, how the methods with which the Party exercises its leading role must change. This is a fundamental topic for discussion' (cited in Ruane 1982, p. 41). Some of the changes initiated by the Party were largely cosmetic, but were an attempt to clean up the popular image of the Party. Other changes affected the very structure and organization of the Party.

In an effort to improve its image, the Party made substantial efforts to clean house during 1981, and to meet the criticisms of corruption, illegality, and privilege within the organization. The popular perception of the Party as being corrupt led the Central Committee to adopt a resolution in March 1981 which instructed 'central and local party auditing commissions to accelerate work on the definition of political responsibility of party members guilty of violations of law and of moral principles' and called on state and judicial organs to do likewise. The Party also proceeded to conduct 'individual talks' with Party members and to dismiss many from the rolls of the Party. Compared to the mass voluntary defections from Party ranks during 1981, however, the number of those purged was relatively small.

There were also efforts to defuse accusations that Party officials received extraordinarily high pay and fringe benefits. The Party monthly contended that Party salaries were lower than for equivalent positions in the state administration and economy, and that 'Party workers may not have any other sources of income, and do not receive any bonuses or periodic awards' (*Życie Partii*, April 1981). In an attempt to alleviate concerns about apparatchiki salaries, the article listed the wages for members of the Politburo and Secretaries of the Central Committee (25,930 złotys) and for other Party professionals down to the district level. The Politburo salary figure, if it can be believed, is 3.5 times the average national wage, which is within the maximum wage differential that most Poles accept. To blunt criticisms of privilege, Kania annulled a 1972 decree that had given special pension rights to the Party-government elite.

Another major accommodation the Party had made with society was in its attitude toward believers within Party ranks. Officially, of course, the 'scientific' and atheistic worldview of Marxist–Leninist party would be inconsistent with religious belief. In practice, that inconsistency has been overlooked in a society that is overwhelmingly Catholic. Public opinion polls from 1980 and 1981 showed that even most Party members professed religious belief. The Party finally came to officially recognize this when the Ninth Congress Program acknowledged that 'religious believers can join the party if they wish to and be politically active in keeping with its program'. This stand was reaffirmed, though modified somewhat, in an article on 'Believers in the Party' in *Życie Partii* (February 9, 1981). The article asserted that the PZPR was primarily a political party and not connected with people's world view (this a remarkable statement in itself). Believers could join the Party and the Party recognized religion as a private matter, but the Party should strive to change the worldview of believer-members in the direction of materialism.

Changes in Party rules and procedures

The Party leadership also allowed substantive reforms that profoundly affected the composition and operation of the organization. Party positions. The leadership of the Party, he said, must be 1980, when he called for 'free election of Party authorities' and for 'complete freedom to put forward and to discuss candidates' for Party positions. The leadership of the Party, he said, must be governed by 'the real will of the majority' (cited in Ruane 1982, p. 58). As a result of this high-level support, there was considerable change in the behavior of the Party's leading bodies even before the changes were formalized. Central Committee plena were much more frequent after August 1980 than before, and the debates were far more lively and open. At the March 1981 Plenum, for example, many CC delegates criticized the Party hierarchy for being cut off from the lower echelons and slow to act on the process of 'renewal'. Politburo member Barcikowski, speaking at the plenum, identified the main cause of the 1980 disturbances as 'the inadequacy of intra-party democracy, of rank and file criticism and control, in distortions in the system of electing the leadership and a faulty cadres policy' (cited in Sanford 1982, p. 48). During 1981, there was a wide-ranging debate within the Party and its meetings about the very nature of the Party and its 'leading role' in Polish society.

Much of the criticism of the Party generated both from the top and the bottom of the structure, was incorporated in the new Party election rules passed by the Central Committee in April. Delegates to the Congress were to be elected at provincial, plant, university and military party conferences. Nominations would be made by special electoral commissions. A crucial difference in the new rules was that there could be an unlimited number of nominations from the floor of the conferences and that the election would be by secret ballot. In the past, the maximum number of nominations permitted from the floor was 15% of the available seats. The 'provisional' electoral rules adopted in December of 1980 had allowed for 50%, but in response to widespread criticism of the limitation, it was dropped altogether.

In fact, the provision for unlimited nominations had *already* been adopted by some regional and local Party organizations. These changes in electoral procedures were formalized in the new Party statutes adopted at the Ninth Congress in July. The statutes also incorporated a number of other democratizing changes. Party elections at all levels, even for first secretaries and executive bodies, were to be by secret vote with multiple candidates. Party officials were limited to two five-year terms in office, and could not hold simultaneously more than two executive positions. Executive organs were subordinated to elected ones. At the top level, the Central Committee could annul decisions of the Politburo, and could convene special sessions of the Committee upon petition of one-third of the membership. Since the CC also elects the Politburo and the Secretariat, this meant that the Committee had the formal power, on its own initiative, to convene and replace the Party's executive bodies.

Leadership changes

Even before the Ninth Congress, there had been considerable turnover in the top leadership positions. Since August 1980 there had been two changes in Prime Minister (Babiuch to Pińkowski to Jaruzelski) and a change in First Secretary (Gierek to Kania). Only five of the nineteen members of Gierek's Politburo survived until July 1981.

The new Party electoral rules, in combination with the ferment of renewal in the organization, led to further and unprecedented turnover in the leadership of the Party at all levels. The Congress pre-elections began in May at the enterprise level, where about half of all the newly elected first secretaries held that post for the first time. Given the Party's method of indirect election, whereby lower elected bodies elect representatives to the next highest, the substantial turnover at the bottom resulted in even greater turnover at successively higher levels.

When the delegates to the Congress finally convened in Warsaw in July, 91% were there for the first time. Most of them were local leaders rather than nationally recognized figures; of 1964 delegates, 568 were secretaries of basic party organizations. The average age of the delegates was 40.

The turnover was just as sharp in the Central Committee elected by the Congress. Only 8% of the old CC were elected to the new one. This was the most substantial-turnover of a central committee ever in the Soviet bloc. Even members of the reigning Politburo were denied automatic election; only four of the sixteen received seats on the Central Committee. The central apparatus of both the Party and the government was largely eliminated from the CC, constituting only 1.5% and 2.5%, respectively, of the Committee (compared to 16% and 19% in 1980) (Misztal and Misztal 1984, p. 8). Few of the top regional leaders were elected to the CC either. Only nine provincial first secretaries won seats, compared to 25 at the Eighth Congress. The first secretaries of some of the major cities, including Gdańsk, Warsaw, Katowice, Poznań, Kraków and Lublin, were not represented on the CC. Only one category of the previous CC managed to survive in the new one: 80% of the generals and admirals held on to their seats. This was because the military was the one institution where there had been minimal personnel changes since August (Wiatr 1981, pp. 821–2).

There was also unprecedented change in the newly elected executive organs. Of the 16 full and candidate members of the Politburo, only four were reelected. Only three of eight CC secretaries were reelected. Yet this was no insurgency voting by the Central Committee. The CC elected those candidates recommended by Kania. All of the candidates nominated from the floor for these positions were defeated. The new Politburo (15 full members including Kania) contained four workers who remained in their jobs, including one Solidarity member, and three university professors. Of the fifteen, six had not previously held any top political positions, and three others had never held any national political post (Wiatr 1981, pp. 823–4).

In a new statutory procedure, the Congress, rather than the Central Committee as before, elected the Party's First Secretary from candidates nominated by the CC. The election was secret and contested, the first of its kind in the communist world. Kania was reelected with 1311 votes to 568 for Barcikowski.

CONSEQUENCES OF LEADERSHIP CHANGES

The personnel changes at the Ninth Congress were unprecedented for Poland, or for any communist country. The electoral procedures were themselves an indication of how far the Party had adapted itself to the changed circumstances. In the elections for members of the Central Committee, the Politburo and Secretariat, and for First Secretary, there were open nominations, multiple candidacies, and secret balloting. The Congress had achieved one of its main objectives, to elect a new leadership that could carry forward the process of democratization and reform.

Indeed, many aspects of the 'renewal' were formalized by the regime in the subsequent months. At the end of July, the new liberalized censorship law was approved. In September the Sejm passed the economic reform bill, providing for a more decentralized system of planning and production. The same month, it passed the Law on Workers' Self-Management, allowing workers in most factories to elect their own directors.

However, these reform measures were simply ratifications of policies developed before the Congress. In many respects, the Party after the Congress was even weaker than it had been before. While it certainly was a more democratic, reform-minded, and representative institution, it was also much less able to cope with the challenges from Solidarity on one side and the hardliners (and Moscow) on the other.

The new Party leadership, at both the regional and national levels, consisted largely of amateur politicians, or bureaucrats with little political experience. Since September 1980 almost all of the 49 provincial first party secretaries had been changed. Most of those who did keep their seats were not elected to the Central Committee, depriving them of a major voice in national policy. Two examples here, constituting major losses for the reform movement, were Tadeusz Fiszbach of Gdańsk and Krystyn Dąbrowa of Kraków.

The Politburo was a bigger problem. While the new Party executive was the most 'representative' it had ever been, it was also the least experienced. Most of the major political figures had been excluded from the Politburo. Half of the new members, representing no central political institutions, remained in their provinces and did not have frequent contact with the central political bodies. As Jerzy Wiatr (1981, p. 824) described it, 'never before was the Political Bureau so strongly decentralized'.

Precisely because of the lack of political experience at the top, the Party was less able to influence the course of events in Poland. It was increasingly less capable of dealing with the challenges from Solidarity, particularly the regional chapters, in a firm but conciliatory manner. Even more damaging, the newly elected Party leadership was incapable of restraining the Party's bureaucratic apparatus, which had remained largely unchanged through 1981. The appointed bureaucrats had the most to lose from the process of renewal, democratization, and decentralization, and were consequently more strongly opposed to all of this. Without a strong countervailing force in the Central Committee and the Politburo, the apparatus increasingly adopted an obdurate position toward both Solidarity and the reform element within the Party.

As a Polish observer described the situation in mid-1981, most Party members had 'joined with the rest of the community and supported Solidarity in its disputes with the party apparatus. The crisis moved away from the area of a conflict between the community and the party to that of a conflict between the party membership and their leaders and the bureaucratic apparatus' (Szczypiorski 1982, p. 134). The Party had joined the process of renewal, but the process was being blocked at the top.

In October, Kania was replaced as First Party Secretary by Premier General Jaruzelski, marking a further diminution of authority for the Party. Even Lech Wałęsa recognized the dangers posed by the weakening of the Party. In an interview with Western reporters just before martial law, he pledged to help the Party if it started to discredit itself or collapse:

There are no other realities here. We cannot overthrow the party. We cannot take the power away from it. We have to preserve it. At the same time, tame it and let it eat with us, so that it will relish what we create (*Washington Post*, October 1, 1982).

But it was too late even for Wałęsa to help the Party. In the face of accelerating demands from Solidarity and the accelerating disintegration of the Party, Jaruzelski was faced with considerable pressure from hardliners in the bureaucracy. There is even some speculation that the apparatchiks attempted to seize power for themselves in both March and December, and that Jaruzelski took measures to neutralize the apparatus just before the declaration of martial law (Spielman 1983, p. 32). With the invocation of martial law, Jaruzelski claimed that the army had taken control to reestablish order and stability and to prevent the total collapse of the Party which he said was threatened with 'physical liquidation'.

This may have been hyperbole, but the Party was in serious trouble. Besides the weakening of the organization mentioned above, there were also problems of internal divisions within the organization. Such divisions existed from the very beginning of Solidarity, and became both more open and formalized in the spring of 1981. Just as the Bydgoszcz incident had divided Solidarity, it also contributed to tensions within the PZPR. At the March 29 meeting of the Central Committee, there was open criticism of the Party's indecisive actions and the erosion of its authority and power. On the other hand, other Committee members faulted the Party for rejecting the grass roots initiatives in the Party that was part of the process of renewal. Stefan Bratkowski, the leader of the journalists' union, addressed an angry open letter to the plenum, accusing the hardliners in the Party of trying to provoke societal behavior that would justify the use of force. 'Our hardliners stand for no program except that of confrontation and disinformation', he charged (Ruane 1982, p. 143).

When the reformists in the Party began to consolidate their position through the horizontalist movement, the conservatives prepared platforms for a counterattack. In May 1981, *Trybuna Ludu* published the summary of a resolution adopted by a Party group that called itself the 'Katowice Discussion Forum' which claimed to be attached to the provincial Party committee. The statement accused the Party of committing basic errors under the influence of 'right wing opportunism and bourgeois liberalism'. The forum accused the Party's leadership of passivity in the face of a potential revisionist coup in the Party, and of failure to counter the horizontalist movement (Ruane 1982, p. 170).

While the Party's Politburo criticized the Katowice Forum, there was obviously considerable support for its point of view, as similar discussion groups emerged in Poznań and other cities. The conservatives also won powerful support from outside Poland with the June letter from the Soviet to the Polish Central Committee. The so-called 'Brezhnev letter' criticized the Polish Party leadership and reformist tendencies in the Party, in harsh language:

Continued concessions to anti-socialist forces and their demands have led to a situation in which the PZPR has been falling back step by step under pressure of internal counter-revolution, supported by imperialist foreign centers of subversion (Ruane 1982, p. 180).

The Moscow letter fortified the hardliners, who took the offensive once again at the emergency meeting of the Central Committee called to discuss the letter. Kania, while pledging to continue the 'socialist renewal', admitted that most of the accusations of the Brezhnev letter were 'fully justified'.

The hardliners and the Soviets continued to express their concerns through the Party elections and Congress of the summer, and the Solidarity Congress in the fall. With the removal of Kania as Party First Secretary on October 18, the hardline viewpoint became more prevalent. The Central Committee accused Solidarity of breaking the social contract and said that, if necessary, the government would use its constitutional rights to defend the vital interests of the nation and the state.

These splits within the Party simply made it even less able to handle the challenges from the outside. In November, there were even some attempts to expel party organizations from workplaces. At a machinery factory in Żywiec, the local Solidarity branch passed a resolution demanding that the enterprise cease financing the activities of the factory party organization. Ten days later, the workers's council there passed a resolution calling for the Party organization to vacate the premises of the factory. The official press claimed that such attempts to remove the Party from industrial enterprises had been mounted in 21 of the 49 voivodships (RFER December 15, 1981).

The threat to the Party was probably exaggerated by the official press, but in the tense atmosphere at the end of 1981, these incidents were of grave concern to the Party leadership. Both the Secretariat and the Central Committee addressed this problem at the end of November. The Secretariat issued a statement condemning 'the witchhunt against Party members, the attempts to force the Party committees out of the factories'. At the meeting of the Central Committee on November 27, Jaruzelski warned against 'pressure or threats of force to remove the Party'. 'The Party', he said, 'cannot be removed by force. There may be force to meet force.' There were two paths for Poland, said the General: national accord or confrontation. In a dark warning of what was to come two weeks later, he hinted that the latter could well lead to 'a type of state of emergency' (Ruane 1982, pp. 264–7). It is clear that the threat to the very existence of the Party, however unreal, was the catalyst for the declaration of martial law.

CONCLUSIONS: PARTY AND SOCIETY

The events of 1980–1 marked a fundamental turning point both for Poland and the other European communist states. For the first time in the postwar history of this region, virtually the entire population united in a demand for a qualitative transformation of the system. The core demand was for a widening of the base for participation in economic and political decision-making and restrictions on the decision-making prerogatives of the Party elite. Support for these demands was widespread even within the Party membership, which also suffered from the centralization of power.

Poland was moving from a 'subject political culture' to a 'participant' one. Solidarity was the main instrument for this movement, and the Central Party bureaucracy was the main obstacle. While many elected Party posts fell into the hands of reformers during 1981, the largely appointed central apparatus remained intact. It was this group that was most threatened by the challenges posed by society through Solidarity. As George Kolankiewicz (1981, p. 375) has pointed out, 'democratic elections and statutory changes in the party are little more than the first steps in rolling back the power of this "bureaucracy."' A principled and independent party 'sufficiently strong to act as an arbiter' was as threatening to the bureaucracy as was Solidarity.

Solidarity tried, but could not, reform the Polish political system from the 'outside'. For such reform, it was necessary to penetrate and reform the Party. There was a considerable amount of success in this regard. Many Party members joined and sympathized with Solidarity. The grass roots of the Party initiated significant changes in the rules, structure, membership, and leadership of the organization. Even the central Party leadership tried to accommodate to the new environment, by encouraging lower-level initiatives, democratization, and decentralization. By the end of 1981, the ongoing process of renewal caught on two horns of a dilemma: the reform was too slow for many members of Solidarity, and two fast for the Party bureaucracy (and the Soviets). Many members of Solidarity felt that the union had become too compromising and that the only way to move ahead was to continue the pressure on the Party and government. This group constituted only about a third of Solidarity's membership (and leadership) but it was a vocal minority. The regime targeted its criticisms on these 'radicals' and identified them as the dominant force within the movement. It was the appeals of this group for new Sejm elections and a referendum on the Party that triggered the declaration of martial law.

Many Poles were equally unsatisfied with the pace of change within the Party. As Szczypiorski (1982, p. 146) puts it, 'for Poles of the 1970s, the present party would have been the realization of their most ardent aspirations'; but for Poles in late 1981, 'the party is still not democratic enough, not sufficiently humble, too sure of itself, too ready to usurp power and therefore untrustworthy'.

On the other side, the Party apparatus felt its position was dire, and this perception was fortified by the continuing demands of the more radical Solidarity supporters. The regime had defined the process of renewal differently than Solidarity. For them, renewal 'was a process of social adjustment articulated and implemented "from above" by the regime' (Bielasiak 1984, p. 23). This, however, conflicted with what was happening both in society and in the Party itself, where most of the changes were generated from below. The Party leadership was put in an unusual and uncomfortable position: for the first time in its history, the PZPR was not the primary agent for initiating social and economic reforms.

The Party had undergone the most substantial changes in its history, indeed in the history of any communist party. Yet the population remained critical of the Party's concentration of power and privilege. From the other direction, the Soviet leadership was issuing dark warnings about the necessity of maintaining the leading role of the Party. The imposition of martial law probably reflected a combination of interests in the elite to maintain itself in power and to avoid the possibility of Soviet intervention.

During 1981, the Polish United Workers' Party had become less hierarchical, more representative, more democratic, and more reformist. It affected significant changes in its own membership, leadership, organization, and processes. But the Party, like Solidarity, exceeded the boundaries of the possible in the Poland of 1981. The changes that occurred in the Party threatened its 'leading role', the *sine qua non* of communist rule in Eastern Europe. While most Party members were willing to adapt the Party to Solidarity's Poland, much of the entrenched Party and government apparatus was not. And those elements found powerful support both within the country and without. Contrary to the expectations of most Poles, the democratization of the Party was not a sufficient guarantee of the process of renewal.

7

Solidarity and the regime at the end of 1981

By the end of 1981, Poland was divided and tired. The exhilaration of 1980 had been replaced by fatigue and frustration a year later. The causes for this were numerous and cumulative. The solidarity of the summer of 1980 had given way to bitterness and divisiveness within the movement. The sense of strength and power bred of the movement's unanimity had frittered away in the face of the obstinacy of the regime and the union's lack of progress in critical areas. Finally, and most importantly, the economy and standard of living had deteriorated even further during 1981, frustrating the main expectation that accompanied Solidarity's formation.

THE ECONOMY AT THE END OF 1981

Solidarity's most important promise was to bring a measure of efficiency to the economy that would allow improvements in consumption and the standard of living. It was perhaps too much to expect that major improvements could be accomplished within one year, but few. people expected that the economy would get even worse. Nevertheless, already by the middle of 1981 there were clear indications of the worsening situation. In his report to the June 12 session of the Sejm, Premier Jaruzelski noted declines in industrial production, coal extraction, retail market supply and livestock production, all during a time when disposable income was up by 20%. Meat procurement for 1981 was expected to be 500,000 tons lower than the previous year (RFER, 6/19/81). Part of the problem, at least, was the contraction of the work week after the introduction of 'free Saturdays'; according to one report even absenteeism on

Mondays increased (from 12 to 20%) after the elongation of the weekend (*Christian Science Monitor*, June 23, 1981).

By the summer of 1981, Poles suffered from widespread shortages of milk, butter, bread, meat, sugar and coffee. That summer and fall, there were demonstrations protesting these shortages in Warsaw, Łódź and other cities. The economy continued to deteriorate during the last quarter, such that the results for 1981 were grim. National income had fallen by 13% and industrial production by 11%. Foreign trade fell by 20% in 1981, and the debt to capitalist countries increased by $3.5 billion. Wages had increased by 25%, but so had the cost of living, neutralizing that gain. Between the end of 1980 and the end of 1981, employment (in the socialized economy) fell by 54,000, adding to the unfamiliar problem of unemployment. Overall agricultural output actually rose in 1981, as a result of increased yields of grains and root crops, but in the critically sensitive area of meat production and consumption, the figures were down. Animal production was lower due to the cuts in grain and feed imports. Both meat and fish production were down 20–25% from the levels of 1980.

The Polish diet was probably not marginally worse in 1981 than in 1980; but the declines in key areas, particularly of meat, in combination with the perennial problem of distribution, led to continued spot shortages, lines, and rationing. The more open nature of society, and of the press, led to more widespread perception of the problem and its scope.

Popular perceptions of the problem

The number of those describing the economic situation and food supplies as 'bad' had escalated sharply at the end of 1980 and had remained at high levels all during 1981. Before the Gdańsk Agreements, 57% described food supplies as poor and 65% assessed the economic situation as bad. By November of 1980, both of these indicators had risen to over 90% (Kurczewski 1981) and they stayed at the 90% level throughout the next year.

To cope with food shortages and alleviate the problem of hoarding, the regime instituted a system of rationing in April 1981. Rationing was broadly supported by the population, partially because it was expected to improve the availability of food, but more importantly because it was perceived as assuring a more equitable

Table 7.1. *Time required for shopping, May and September 1981*
(%)

Shopping now takes:	May Than before rationing	September Than 2 months ago
Less time	39	11
The same	19	24
More time	39	61
No opinion	3	4

Source: OBOP, 'Zaopatrzenie w żywności w systemie reglamentacji' (November 1981).

distribution of the food that was available. In fact, in the spring of 1981, a large majority of the population (66%) favored expanding the system of rationing (Fuszara, Jakubowska, and Kurczewski 1982). By the fall of 1981, 77% still supported rationing of food, even though the system had not eliminated the lines or the shortages. OBOP polls on the food situation in May and September reveal the popular perception of the worsening situation (see Table 7.1).

That most people supported rationing even though it was not perceived as helping the supply situation suggests again that equity was the major reason for that support. As noted above, egalitarianism is a major element of the Polish political culture; and rationing was a means of sharing the burdens of the economic crisis.

The difficulty of acquiring particular items was also a subject of the September OBOP poll. People were asked whether they could get a list of products, mostly rationed, on the appropriate days of the month. Of 23 listed food items, a majority answered yes for only five of them: sugar, flour, butter, chocolate, and kasza. Fewer than a quarter said they could regularly find sausage, poultry, wine and candy and 12% or less could regularly get most kinds of meat. In this poll, as earlier, most people favored extending the rationing system to other hard-to-find items such as wine, vodka, laundry detergents, and cigarettes (OBOP, 'Zaopatrzenie w żywnosci').

Poles were divided on the reasons for the shortages of food supplies (see Table 7.2).

Table 7.2. *Perceived reasons for the food shortages, by farmers and non-farmers (%)*

	Farmers	Non-farmers
Decline in agricultural production	52	31
Poor government agricultural policy	26	22
Warehousing of food by authorities and directing to export	17	10
Too much use of food for animal feed	17	–
Poor pricing system	13	–
Bad will of farmers, hoarding of food	–	27
Bad system of supply, distribution, rationing	–	12

Source: OBOP, 'Sprzedaż wiązana i stosunki miasto-wieś w opinii społecznej' (November 1981).

Table 7.3. *Opinion on how farmers live, by farmers and non-farmers (%)*

Farmers in Poland currently live:	Farmers	Non-farmers
Well	17	59
Average	37	28
Poorly	46	11
No opinion	0	2

Source: OBOP, 'Sprzedaż wiązana'.

While most farmers identified the problem as one of production, and blamed the government for inadequate support for private agriculture, urban residents were less sure of the causes of the problem. And a large percentage believed that the farmers were deliberately withholding food from the cities. This perception contributed to the growing tension between the cities and the countryside. As the food situation worsened, city residents increasingly found the farmers to be part of the problem. Urban and rural residents had quite different perceptions about life on the farms (see Table 7.3).

Most non-farmers thought the farmers were doing very well; few farmers felt that way. All of these factors led two-thirds of this sample to agree that city residents felt dislike for farmers.

The public also felt strongly that the government's agricultural policies were incorrect. In a September 1981 poll (reported in *Życie*

Table 7.4. *Popular acceptance of price increases, March–November 1981*
(%)

Do you accept necessity of price increases, if compensated?	3/81	9/81	11/81
Yes	59	65	70
No	28	29	24
No opinion	13	6	6

Source: OBOP polls reported in *Życie Warszawy*, November 16, 1981.

Warszawy, September 29), while only 17% condemned official policies generally as incorrect, and a quarter faulted the government's
treatment of Solidarity, fully 51% criticized the government for its
food policy. No doubt these feelings were exacerbated by the
government's decision to cut the monthly meat rations for August
and September from 3.7 kilograms per person to 3 kilograms.

The government was in a difficult position in trying to improve
the food situation. In April it had increased procurement prices for
agricultural products (by as much as 40%), further contributing to
the subsidization of agriculture that was consuming a quarter of the
total state budget (RFER, April 24, 1981). Wage increases since the
Gdańsk Agreements had put further pressure on supplies of food
and other consumer goods. And Poland's huge foreign debt required
cutbacks in imports of both feedgrains and food.

The rationing system had helped somewhat in equalizing the
burdens, but had not solved the supply problem. In the summer and
fall, the government proposed two other delicate policies: food price
increases and 'tied purchases' of produce from farmers. The food
price increases, first proposed in July, were substantial, calling for
increases of 130%–280% on key food items. Public horror at the
scales of the increases led the government to attach a program of
'compensation' for these increases in the form of wage increases
based on family size. Over the course of the year, as the food
situation became worse, there was increasing public acceptance of
the necessity of price increases (see Table 7.4).

This reluctant acceptance, however, was tempered by concern and
pessimism. An overwhelming majority (79%) thought the proposed
price increases were too high, and 59% favored a phased increase of

prices, rather than a one-time increase. Furthermore, the public was split (47% each) on whether or not the price increases would lead to increased supplies and availability of food.

While the 'market solution' of price increases met with reluctant acceptance, the 'tied purchases' (sprzedaż wiązana) scheme was much less popular. Under this program, the state would pay farmers for food with coupons rather than money. The coupons could then be used to acquire deficit consumer goods such as refrigerators, televisions, etc. The authorities saw this 'barter' system as necessary since farmers were increasingly unwilling to sell their produce to the state – there was nothing in the stores for them to buy with the cash they received. Only 26% of farmers and 38% of non-farmers thought this decision was an appropriate one. Non-farmers were against the plan even though a majority of them (54%) thought it would increase food supplies. They criticized the plan for its favoritism to farmers, who were already perceived as being very well off. Farmers thought the plan would neither provide them with more deficit goods nor increase the market supply of food. One result of this was to further increase the tensions and mistrust between the cities and the countryside (OBOP, 'Sprzedaż wiązana'). In fact, some Poles argued that the government had introduced this plan precisely for this reason; by sowing resentment between farmers and workers, the authorities hoped to break up the alliance, through Solidarity, of these two powerful groups.

All of this suggests both a considerable amount of confusion in the population about the food crisis, and a reservoir of sympathy for the government's dilemmas. As the supply situation became worse, tensions in society increased, but there was not necessarily an increased tendency to blame the government. There was a grudging recognition that hard times and sacrifices were necessary before the crisis was overcome, but this did not translate into widespread support for inequitable or hard-line measures to cope with the crisis.

Perceptions of needs

During the year after Gdańsk, most Poles perceived the primary need in Polish society to be an improvement in the standard of living. The *Polacy '80* survey at the end of 1980 revealed that by far the largest number of people believed that the standard of living was 'the most important matter in the country'. An unauthorized survey

Table 7.5. *Most important matters in the workplace, by party and union membership, December 1981 (%)*

Matter	Non-Party members	Party members	Solidarity members
Tools	30.0	27.1	21.9
Economic reform	8.9	15.9	10.4
Wages	9.3	6.9	10.4
Work conditions	7.7	2.1	7.2
Participation in governance	5.7	9.0	7.5
Social conditions	5.8	4.8	6.0
Modernization	5.6	5.8	5.1
Bad relationships	4.7	3.2	4.9
Discipline	3.3	6.4	3.1
Others	19.0	18.8	23.5

Source: Polacy '81, p. 34.

in Poland by *Paris Match* (December 12, 1981) in late 1981 found that improvement in the daily standard of living was the 'wish' most frequently expressed by those polled (33%), ranking ahead of 'hope for greater justice' (24%), 'free and democratic government' (23%), and 'independence for Poland' (19%). OBOP polls in mid-1981 also found 'an improvement of the supply situation' in first place among the most pressing matters in the country (Kania 1981).

By the end of 1981, market supplies were still considered the most important issues at the personal and local level, but not at the national level. In personal and family affairs, the most important need at the end of 1981 was housing (32.6%), just as it had been at the end of 1980. Food supplies had moved into second place, rising from 6.3% in 1980 to 19.2% in 1981. The most important matter for the locality was food supplies (25.1%), followed by roads and communications (18.1%). The only 'political item' on this list, 'territorial self-government, and influence on local authorities', was near last place with 2.1% of the votes (*Polacy '81*).

In the workplace, the most important matters were also ones of supply (see Table 7.5).

By far the major perceived need in the factories was for tools and equipment. After this, demands were spread all over. The next most frequently expressed need by most workers was for better wages.

There was no great support for political changes, either at the national level (economic reform) or at the enterprise level (participation in governance). Interestingly, Party members were much more likely to mention these political needs than were non-Party people or Solidarity members. As noted in Chapter 6, Party members were generally supportive of the demands of Solidarity. Table 7.5 suggests that Party members were even ahead of Solidarity in their interest in political reforms. Although food and material supplies continued to be the most pressing and immediate concern for most people on a day-to-day basis, by the end of 1981, more and more people thought that at the national level, what was needed was a greater measure of political and economic stability. The supply situation came to be viewed more as a *result* of political difficulties rather than the cause of Poland's problems.

THE LAW AND ORDER ISSUE

The economic problem had not been solved during 1981, and popular attention was increasingly focused on the difficulties of making ends meet and finding basic commodities. Over the course of that year, it became apparent that there were no easy solutions to the economic crisis; the problems were long-term ones. Given these perceptions, and the continuing strains caused by economic shortages, it is not surprising that Poles began to yearn for a renewed measure of stability in the society and in the economy.

The interest in 'stabilization' was not new in 1981, but grew steadily from the end of 1980. In the *Polacy '80* survey at the end of 1980, 19% thought that 'stabilization of the situation' was the most important matter for the country; by the end of 1981, over 35% felt that way (see Table 7.6).

The interest in stabilization of the situation had been secondary until the very end of 1981. In the middle of 1981, an OBOP poll found similar kinds of rankings for the most necessary matters in the country. Improvement of the supply situation was first, followed by 'extraordinary steps to resolve the economic crisis', more effective aid for agriculture, more democratization, and further punishment for those responsible for the crisis (Kania 1981). A September 1981 OBOP poll found over 90% expressing feelings of unrest and societal tension. The majority felt that the main source of that tension was 'bad supplies'. Only half as many (25%) attributed the

Table 7.6. *Most important matter in the country,*
December 1980 and 1981 (%)

Most important matter	12/80	12/81
Standard of living	30	21.2
Stabilization of situation	19	35.6
Economic reform	13	12.4
Agriculture	8	
Social-political changes	–	12.6
End to the strikes	–	4.2
Better work	–	4.0
Others	–	10.0

Source: Polacy '80, p. 70; and Polacy '81, p. 41.

tension to the conflicts between the authorities and Solidarity (*Życie Warszawy*, September 29, 1981). By the end of 1981, as revealed in the *Polacy '81* survey, stabilization had replaced the standard of living as the most pressing matter at the national level. This reflects both the popular fatigue with the growing economic difficulties and, perhaps, declining confidence that either Solidarity or the regime could quickly cope with the problems.

The concern for law and order did not, however, translate into support for more rigorous controls. As the authors of *Polacy '81* took pains to point out, 'law and order as understood by the Poles of 1981 was above all *economic* order'. Of those who listed 'stabilization of the situation' in first place, more favored a decentralized political system (41.5%) than a more centralized one (36%); and there was more interest in democratization of the system than in the strengthening of the authorities.[24]

---

[24] When the preliminary results of the *Polacy '81* survey were first reported in seminars at the Academy of Sciences in the spring of 1982, there was extensive and heated discussion of the meaning of the popular support for law and order. As a result of this, the researchers conducted additional analysis of the data by cross-tabulating responses to various questions to get a more accurate reading of the perceptions of those who favored law and order. The phrase 'law and order' itself was changed to 'stabilization of the situation in the country' in the final report. All of this took place in the first months of martial law, when the authorities were asserting that the crackdown was in response to popular needs and wishes. The scientists in the Academy did not want their poll results to become a tool of the regime in this regard.

Opinion on the strikes

Concern about the continuing strikes was one of the main factors behind the support for stabilization. In the first months of Solidarity's existence, the strike tool won widespread support from the population. It was viewed as being the most effective (or the only effective) tool for getting the government to negotiate and compromise with Solidarity. As noted in Chapter 5, however, support for the strike began to wane during 1981. This became particularly the case after both Jaruzelski and Wałęsa appealed for suspension of strikes in the face of the economic crisis. As the strikes continued, often in the face of opposition from Solidarity's national leadership, the public became increasingly weary of the disruptions and tensions engendered by the strikes. They were viewed both as a source of tension and as a contributing factor to the economic decline. As interest in political reform diminished and concern over the standard of living grew, support for the strikes declined. Whereas over 90% of the population had supported the strikes of August 1980, by the end of 1981 slightly more people opposed than supported strikes as a form of protest. Table 7.7. shows the results of a *Polacy '81* question about general support for various kinds of protest.[25]

Table 7.7. *Support for various forms of protest, December 1981 (%)*

Form of protest	Decisive support	Support	Not support	Decisively not
Petitions	27.5	35.7	19.5	4.8
Distributing posters	12.2	30.2	36.5	13.4
Strikes	11.8	34.5	33.2	14.5
Boycott govt. decisions	8.1	19.8	44.5	9.9
Street demonstrations	4.6	17.7	52.3	19.7
Occupying public buildings	4.6	14.4	50.5	22.8
Demonstrating opposition to police, militia, etc.	3.8	13.2	44.7	22.4
Blocking street traffic	1.7	4.4	57.6	30.5
Destroying public objects	0.3	0.2	33.6	63.6

Source: Polacy '81, p. 161.

[25] The question was phrased in such a way as to allow comparison with other countries, based on the cross-national study *Political Action: An Eight Nation Study* (1979).

Table 7.8. *Support for various emergency measures, December 1981 (%)*

The Sejm should:	Agree	Disagree
Guarantee Solidarity access to television and mass media	87.9	7.7
Name new govt. of natl. unity	74.8	15.5
Call new elections to Sejm and Peoples' Councils	71.3	20.3
Obligatory delivery of agricultural products	48.3	38.1
Temporarily suspend free Saturdays	46.4	47.1
Prohibit strikes	46.2	49.0
Temporarily strengthen militia	34.6	59.3
Temporarily limit free speech	12.4	83.0

Source: Polacy '81, pp. 132–45.

As might be expected, the more moderate forms of protest were the most widely supported. The strikes, as an intermediate form, were supported by 46.3% of the sample and opposed by 47.7%. Support for strikes was somewhat higher among young people, skilled workers (54.5%), and members of Solidarity, but even in these groups, opinion was sharply divided.

The declining support for strikes was also manifested in increased receptiveness to the idea of restrictions on strike action. There was little support for an *official* suspension of the right to strike, especially when it was proposed by the Party's Central Committee in the fall. As a Solidarity OBS poll in October demonstrated, Solidarity members were especially dubious of such action: 63% were opposed to such a resolution and only 24% supported it. But after Solidarity's national Presidium appealed for an end to the strikes at the end of October, and as the economic situation worsened, support for a formal ban increased. The *Polacy '81* survey showed 46.2% of the sample favoring a governmental prohibition of strikes, with 49% opposing the idea (see Table 7.8).

The responses to these questions seem to fall into three groups. There is widespread support for the 'democratizing' measures favoring Solidarity: access to the media, a new government of national unity including 'representatives of the most influential political groups and social movements', and for new elections (the last ones had been before Gdańsk). At the same time, there was strong opposition to more rigorous and repressive measures such as limiting freedom of speech and strengthening the powers of the militia and the security services. There is a third middle group of issues on which opinion is divided. These issues, to ban strikes, suspend free Saturdays, and impose compulsory delivery of agricultural goods from the countryside, are all economically related issues. While many people no doubt opposed these measures as a retreat from the gains of the previous year, others supported them as a means of assuring more stability and improvement in the economy. As might be expected, Solidarity members were more strongly opposed to a ban on strikes than non-members, but even 37% of members supported a ban on strikes at the end of 1981. Among occupational groups, the strongest support for a ban on strikes came from unskilled workers (59.3%) and the unemployed (53.6%) who, with relatively low levels of pay were probably most directly affected by the economic problems of late 1981. The strongest opposition to a ban on strikes came from office workers (65.9% opposed) and specialists with a higher education (58.9). These groups, perhaps, saw the strike as a weapon to be used to gain political concessions from the regime, and were probably less concerned with the economic effects of the strikes.

Corruption and crime

Many other factors contributed to the support for greater stability in Polish society. These included the popular perceptions of corruption, crime, societal tension, and external threats. Poles had always been aware of and annoyed at the high levels of corruption in society. These sensitivities were aggravated during 1981 as the economic situation deteriorated. At the end of 1981, when people were asked if there were people or groups who were reaping benefit from the current crisis situation, 69.1% answered yes, and only 6.3% said no. When asked who was benefiting, by far the largest numbers (64.6%) responded that it was 'people in the underground economy' (*Polacy '81*, pp. 84–9). Fewer people identified 'people of influence' (10.6%) and 'people of authority' (9.8%) as benefiting from the crisis, but there was still a strong sense that the authorities lived too well. The high living and fringe benefits of the Party, militia and other official groups had been one of the main targets of criticism at Gdańsk in August 1980. And while the regime had made some moves to deflect this criticism, it remained a source of irritation to many Poles. At the end of 1981, over 77% felt that the differences between the smallest and highest wages in Poland were too large. Almost everyone (91%) agreed that there were wealthy people in Poland, with by far the largest number (31%) identifying 'the authorities' as the wealthy ones. About 19% each identified the wealthy as those earning money dishonestly, or through 'private initiative'[26] (*Polacy '81*, pp. 55–7).

The growth in corruption was accompanied by increased crime and a general decline in compliance with and respect for the law. OBOP polls showed a marked change in the acceptance of law compliance norms between 1978 and early 1981. In 1978, nearly 50% of the respondents agreed that 'one ought always to observe the law even if in our opinion it is unjust'. By 1981, only 36% agreed with that proposition. The number of those believing one is free to break laws considered unjust rose from 16% to 28% during this time (OBOP, 'Prawo i praworządność w opiniach społecznych', June 1981; cited in Jasińska-Kania 1982). In some respects this was a healthy phenomenon, bred of the participatory atmosphere of 1981. It showed that, as with the creation of their own union, Poles were willing to address issues from a moral and principled standpoint rather than simply a legal one. It also reflected the decline in the legitimacy of the official institutions in Polish society.

On the other hand, there were those who took advantage of the greater openness and freedom of Solidarity's Poland to improve their own positions, legally or illegally. What the regime later referred to as the 'anarchization of life' in Poland included increased incidence of crime, in 1981 up by a third over 1980 (*Trybuna Ludu*, February 16, 1982). Perhaps this would have been tolerable in normal circumstances. But the deepening economic crisis created enough difficulties and psychological tensions that many people were willing to return to a more law-abiding society, even at the expense of further democratization.

Threats to Poland's sovereignty

By the end of 1981, a majority of Poles believed that the current

---

[26] The late 1981 *Paris Match* poll found most people (56%) identifying party members as the privileged group in Poland, with 21% mentioning the government and 11% the police and security forces.

Table 7.9. *Is Poland's independence threatened? December 1980 and December 1981 (%)*

	1980	1981
Decisively yes	30.6	36.6
Rather yes	17.0	16.0
Rather no	17.1	17.2
Decisively no	24.0	12.6
Hard to say	11.3	17.4

Source: Polacy '81, p. 129.

Table 7.10. *Whence the threat to Poland?* (%)*

	1980	1981
USSR	49.6	36.0
Socialist countries (CMEA, neighbors, friends, etc.)	13.0	20.2
The government, other internal forces	4.9	10.8
Capitalist countries (NATO, the West, etc.)	9.7	11.4
West Germany	10.7	5.9
Solidarity	–	4.0
The Germans	4.0	2.7
Our creditor countries	1.8	2.3
East Germany	5.1	2.2
Czechoslovakia	3.2	0.9
Don't know	1.5	1.3
Other responses	5.0	8.9

* Multiple responses allowed.
Source: Polacy '81, p. 131.

situation in the country 'constituted a threat to the independence of our state' (see Table 7.9).

For those who answered yes, when asked about the source of the threat, they provided the following responses (see Table 7.10). At the end of 1981, Poles were even more concerned about the survival of the country than they had been at the end of 1980, when there was a wave of rumors both inside and outside Poland that the Soviets were about to invade. In 1981, concern was more widespread, but not as sharply focused on the Soviet Union. In part this reflects the changed nature of the treatment of the threat in the official Polish media. In the fall and winter of 1980, the media and the Party leadership expounded on the threat from outside Poland. (It is amusing, however, that the Poles immediately took this to mean the Soviet Union!) By the end of 1981, media attention was focused on the internal threats to Polish independence. As Table 7.10 shows, most people still perceived the threat to be from Poland's 'friends'; those who did see the threat as an internal one were more likely to blame the government than Solidarity. Regardless of the source of the threat, there was a widespread sense that Poland's very survival was at stake. In these circumstances, it is not surprising that many people favored a calmer atmosphere in the country, to avoid provoking Poland's neighbors.

Personal and social tensions

All of these problems associated with the economy, politics, and Poland's international predicament led to dramatic increases in the population's sense of both societal and personal tensions. This was manifested even in increased incidence of sickness and nervous problems according to the *Polacy '81* survey. Over 87% of the sample thought that peoples' sense of well being and state of health was worse than previously. When asked what factors contributed to that, the respondents most frequently mentioned 'tiredness with the difficulties of daily life', 'tensions over the social-political life of the country', and 'lack of nourishment'. Once again, the economic factors are predominant here. Socio-political tensions were much more frequently mentioned by those occupying leadership positions, and members of the Party (54.8% mentioned this, compared to 40.9% of the overall sample). Most other groups first mentioned the difficulties with daily life (*Polacy '81*, pp. 285–8).

The economic difficulties were also perceived as contributing to societal tensions as well. Almost 87% of the *Polacy '81* sample agreed that the difficulties with food and other supplies contributed to 'discord and disruption' in the society. As seen above, this was particularly true of relations between the cities and the countryside; there was considerable suspicion among urban residents that farmers were withholding food and benefiting from the economic crisis. The frustration with life in Poland was so great that, according to the *Paris Match* (December 25, 1981) poll, 23% of Poles had considered leaving Poland for good, and another 40% temporarily.

Hardline measures?

Despite the trauma and tensions at the end of 1981, most Poles rejected any hardline measures to cope with the crisis. As shown in Table 7.8 above, Poles strongly favored democratizing measures, were divided on the 'administrative' measures affecting the economy, and decisively rejected the repressive measures affecting freedom of speech and the powers of the security forces. As Krzysztof Jasiewicz, the author of this part of the *Polacy '81* (p. 145) report, wrote:

One may interpret this as support for the ideas of consensus and pluralism ... where there does not come into play an immediate threat to group interests, Polish society is (specifically, was in December 1981) inclined to support democratic, pluralistic, anti-autocratic means to overcome the crisis and resolve social conflicts.

These sentiments, and opposition to hardline measures, were characteristic even of most Party members. PZPR members had actually been more involved in acts of protest during 1981 than had the population as a whole (21.6% compared to 18.4%) and remained strongly opposed to repressive measures at the end of the year. Party members were just as strongly opposed to limiting freedom of speech as non-members, and almost as strongly opposed (53.5%) to strengthening the powers of the militia and the security services (*Polacy '81*, pp. 132–45).

As Table 7.7 (above) demonstrated, most Poles opposed the more radical forms of protest. Nevertheless, they overwhelmingly opposed repressive actions by the authorities against such protests (see Table 7.11). The opposition to repressive measures shown here is overwhelming. All of the measures mentioned here were soon thereafter employed by the martial law authorities. These results belie the regime's claims that there was support for such measures.[27]

[27] Similar results were found in the late 1981 *Paris Match* survey. When asked if they would 'accept a return to a hardline, "neo-Stalinist" regime in order to eliminate the shortage of consumer goods and return the country to order, even if it meant limiting liberties', 63% responded 'no, never'; 22% said 'yes, perhaps', and 15% 'yes, certainly'.

Table 7.11. *Support for repression of protestors, December 1981 (%)*

	Decisively support	Support	Not support	Decisively not
A government decree banning public protests and demonstrations	5.8	20.1	36.1	25.2
Severe judicial measures vs. demonstrators not obeying the police or militia	3.0	12.7	40.6	32.5
Use of police, militia units vs. street demonstrations	2.1	11.2	40.5	37.2
Use of the army to break up strikes	1.7	5.4	28.4	55.8

Source: Polacy '81, p. 177.

Table 7.12. *Support for various reform measures, December 1981 (%)*

	Decisively support	Rather support	Rather not support	Decisively not
Increasing role of Church in public affairs	46.3	31.0	12.1	3.7
Limiting the role of the Party	31.2	28.2	13.7	5.7
Expanded private enterprise in industry, trade, etc.	50.0	31.9	6.2	4.3
Allowing foreign capital in Polish enterprises	43.6		26.3	
Full self-government in enterprises	49.8	28.9	5.5	1.3
Strengthening central planning in economy	7.8	11.8	29.5	29.2

Source: Polacy '81, pp. 198ff.

Not only did the Poles of 1981 come out squarely against the repressive measures, but they were generally in favor of most suggestions aimed at decentralization, pluralization, and democratization of Polish society (see Table 7.12).

Though Poles wanted a return to a more stable situation, they viewed reforms as a better way to accomplish this than a crackdown or renewed centralization. One of the most popular methods in this regard, factory self-management, was already being implemented throughout the country. The idea of a 'self-governing society', and especially of enterprise self-management, had been one of Solidarity's strongest themes at the end of 1981. In carrying these reforms out spontaneously, the workers were moving toward a self-governing society in spite of the government. The recognition of this may have been one of the reasons the regime decided to intervene with martial law.

SUPPORT FOR THE REGIME AND SOLIDARITY AT THE END OF 1981

Tensions between Solidarity and the regime increased in the fall of 1981. The first round of the Solidarity Congress in September produced resolutions that were bound to be provocative to the regime. This was particularly so of the open letter adopted by the Congress to workers in the rest of Eastern Europe. This action elicited sharp responses both from the Polish and the Soviet Party leadership. While the Polish authorities were becoming increasingly disenchanted with Solidarity and its leadership, the feelings were mutual by Solidarity members. Solidarity's October poll among its members found over 63% asserting that society's confidence in the government had diminished in the last few weeks. Only 9.5% of this sample thought such confidence had increased (OBS, 'Komunikat', October 1981).

However, as noted in Chapter 5, popular feelings on the dispute were increasingly ambivalent. Support for Solidarity was still strong, but had diminished from late 1980. More and more people were blaming both the government and Solidarity, rather than just the government, for the problems Poland was facing. Solidarity's policies and leadership were not as uncritically accepted as they once had been. After the first session of the Solidarity Congress, for example, OBOP found almost universal acceptance of the union's 7-point program declaration and its resolution of self-management. But opinion was sharply divided on the letter to the working people of Eastern Europe. And while the vast majority (77%) thought the Congress resolutions would be important for Poland, more people (43%) thought the first round of the Congress would increase tensions in society than decrease them (20%) (*Życie Warszawy*, September 29, 1981).

Perhaps in recognition of this phenomenon, both the regime and the Solidarity leadership adopted somewhat more conciliatory stances in the first months after the closing of the Congress's first session. Solidarity's Presidium helped defuse the crisis over self-management by accepting the compromise legislation put forward by the Sejm, even though many Solidarity activists were bitterly opposed to this move. At the second session of the Congress, which opened September 26, despite widespread criticism of Wałęsa's conciliatory positions, he and his mostly moderate colleagues were re-elected to the union's leadership.

There were also conciliatory moves from the authorities. On October 18, Kania was replaced as Party First Secretary by Premier Jaruzelski. In part, this may have been an indication of the regime's intent to consolidate power and deal firmly with the continuing crisis, but it may also have been a tacit recognition of the Party's failure to cope with the crisis and win the backing of the population. Jaruzelski himself was at that time a fairly popular figure in Poland. He had been the top vote-getter in the Central Committee elections the previous summer. And as the leader of the Army, he represented the most popular *official* institution in Poland.

The government made a number of other opening moves in October and early November. On October 10, the government proposed a joint commission of representatives of the government and the labor unions to discuss food supplies, rationing and prices. This looked very much like a response to Solidarity's appeal for a 'social council for the economy' and for consultations on future price increases. Within a week, the government proposal was accepted by the 'autonomous unions' and by the rural and Craftsmen's Solidarity, but was rejected by Solidarity itself (Ruane 1982, p. 248). Shortly thereafter, Jaruzelski proposed a new seven-member 'front of national accord', which Solidarity rejected because the union would have had only one seat on the council. And in an effort to broaden its base of support, the government brought three non-communists into the cabinet, including Edward Kowalczyk, leader of the Democratic Party, as Deputy Prime Minister (Ruane 1982, p. 256). On November 4, there was a meeting of the 'Big Three' of Wałęsa, Glemp and Jaruzelski to seek institutional solutions to the continuing crisis. This meeting was widely reported in the media, and closely followed by the population. Fully 69% of an OBOP sample thought the meeting would reduce social tensions in the country ('Napięcia społeczne').

After early November, however, government–Solidarity talks stalemated and tensions once again increased. A new wave of strikes swept across Poland, spreading even into the universities. On November 27, the Politburo called for emergency legislation to ban strikes. And on December 2, in a show of force that was a prelude to martial law eleven days later, Warsaw riot police raided the firefighters' academy to end an occupation strike by the cadets there.

Responsibility for the crisis

As tensions grew in late 1981, the population became increasingly less willing to assign exclusive blame for the crisis and the conflict to the regime. One sees this phenomenon as early as September, in one of OBOP's polls (*Życie Warszawy*, September 29, 1981). Over 90% of this sample expressed feelings of unrest and societal tension. When asked about the sources of this tension, a majority mentioned 'poor supplies'. The second most frequent response, mentioned by 25%, was 'conflicts between the authorities and Solidarity', which implies equal blame. More people (17%) identified the government's inappropriate policies than Solidarity's (9%) as a source of tension, and in all other polls, Solidarity was rarely assigned the exclusive blame for the problems; but by September, as this poll shows, neither was the government. Even Solidarity members were increasingly less willing to assign exclusive blame to the authorities, as indicated in an October OBS poll of 1000 Solidarity members (see Table 7.13).

Table 7.13. *Who's responsible for conflict between Solidarity and the authorities?* (%)

The authorities exclusively	30.0
Mostly authorities, but also Solidarity	38.5
More or less equally authorities and Solidarity	20.0
Mostly Solidarity, but also authorities	1.5
Exclusively Solidarity	1.0
Someone else	3.0
Hard to say	4.0

Source: OBS, 'Komunikat' (October 1981).

Table 7.14. *Responsibility for the crisis (December 1981)
and the stalemate (December 1980) (%)*

Who's responsible?	December 1981	December 1980
The government	39.7	61.5
Solidarity	3.1	1.1
Both sides	40.0	27.3
Someone else	5.8	5.0
Hard to say	11.4	5.1

Source: Polacy '81, p. 110.

Similar results were obtained in the *Polacy '81* survey just before the imposition of martial law (Table 7.14). While few people blamed Solidarity alone for the 'deepening economic and political crisis', just as many people blamed both sides as the government alone. At the end of 1980, the *Polacy '80* study had asked a similar question about who was responsible for the delays in implementing the Gdańsk Agreements. At that time, far more people blamed the government. By the end of 1981, Solidarity was also believed to be at least partly responsible.[28]

As might be expected, Solidarity members were more likely to blame the government exclusively (47.4%) at the end of 1981, but even so, 36.5% of them blamed 'both sides' for the crisis situation. It is clear that there were strong reservations even among union members about Solidarity's role at the end of the year. But this should not cover over the fact that many more people found the government at fault than Solidarity alone. Even a quarter of all Party members thought that the government was to blame for the crisis (see Table 7.15).

This table provides some indication of the sources of support and opposition to the regime. Solidarity members, farmers, and skilled workers were the most critical of the government and its policies.

[28] The responses for 1980 and 1981 in Table 7.14 are not strictly comparable in that the questions were posed somewhat differently. In the *Polacy '80* survey, respondents were first asked if they thought there had been delays in implementing the Gdańsk Agreements. Those who answered yes were asked who was responsible for the delays. The *Polacy '81* survey simply asked who was responsible for the deepening economic and political crisis.

Table 7.15. *Responsibility for the crisis in public opinion, by various categories, December 1981 (%)*

Social category	Who's responsible?		
	Govt.	Solid.	Both
Overall	39.7	3.1	40.0
PZPR members	25.5	8.7	47.1
Solidarity members	47.4	1.1	36.5
Branch unions	16.4	8.2	54.1
Skilled workers	41.7	1.7	44.8
Unskilled workers	34.3	8.1	44.4
Farmers	47.8	2.3	31.8
Non-believers	25.4	12.7	38.0

Source: Polacy '81, pp. 112–15.

The most supportive of the regime, and most critical of Solidarity, were the members of the old branch unions, to which some 9% of the population still belonged. In fact, on virtually all of the issues raised in the *Polacy '81* survey, the members of the branch unions were the most conservative and the most opposed to Solidarity of any other category. As is apparent from this table, they were considerably more supportive of the regime even than Party members were. Those members of the old unions who had stuck with them through 1981 probably felt even more threatened by Solidarity than the Party did. Continued success for Solidarity would probably have led to the total collapse of the old union structure. As it was, Solidarity had deprived the old unions of most of their influence, resources, and organizational structure (with the dissolution of the Trade Unions Central Council).

Expectations of peaceful resolution

The Ninth Party Congress in July, the Solidarity Congress in September and October, and the conciliatory gestures of the regime and Solidarity in the fall of 1981 boosted popular optimism that a peaceful solution to the crisis could be found. All during this period, some 90% of the population expressed feelings of unrest and tension in society, but successive OBOP polls revealed an increase in those who thought the problems could be settled peacefully (see Table 7.16).

Table 7.16. *How Poland's problems will be resolved*
(%)

Causes of unrest will be resolved by:	September 20	October 5	November 23
Negotiation and compromise	53	65	69
Test of strength and use of force	40	22	19

Source: OBOP, 'Napięcia społeczne'.

Table 7.17. *Responsibility for bad relationship between authorities and Solidarity, September–November 1981 (%)*

Those blaming:	September 19	October 5	November 9
The authorities	35	21	24
Solidarity	5	3	7
Both	53	69	64

Source: OBOP, 'Napięcia społeczne'.

The results here are all the more remarkable in that the last of these polls, conducted just three weeks before the martial law crackdown, showed few people expecting a 'use of force'. The poll was taken, however, after some relaxation of the recent tension, following within a month after Kania's resignation, the meeting of the 'Big Three', and the government's offer of a front of national accord. The popular expectations of a peaceful settlement makes even more tragic and ironic the Government's decision to resort to force.

There was little illusion in the public mind, however, that relations were good between Solidarity and the authorities. In the OBOP polls between September and late November, only 8–15% identified such relations as good. In the November 23–4 poll, 76% thought those relations were 'not too good' or 'bad'. Of those people, many more thought the fault lay with both sides rather than either the authorities or Solidarity (see Table 7–17).

The results here are similar to those of the *Polacy '81* and Solidarity polls mentioned above. Few people identified Solidarity as the culprit. A declining number thought the government was the main cause of the tension. And an increasingly large majority found both sides to be at fault. At the end of November, the overwhelming majority (76%) thought concessions were necessary equally from the government and from Solidarity. Eleven percent thought concessions were necessary primarily from the government and only 7% thought primarily from Solidarity.

These trends are reflected most directly in the OBOP questions on trust in the government and in the leadership of Solidarity (Table 7.18).

Table 7.18. *Trust in the government and leadership of Solidarity, September–November 1981 (%)*

		September 19	October 5	November 23
Trust in government	Have	30	40	51
	Not have	60	51	36
	No opinion	10	9	13
Trust in Solidarity	Have	74	71	58
	Not have	19	15	22
	No opinion	7	14	20

Source: OBOP, 'Napięcia społeczne'.

The data in this table have to be treated with some caution. These polls were taken by the official polling organization during a time of increased tension and difficulties. It is possible people may have been increasingly unwilling to give honest responses in these months. It is even possible, as many Solidarity supporters claim, that the regime altered or manipulated these data, though most Polish sociologists disagree with this.

One needs to be cautious as well with the phrasing of the question in this survey. While there does appear to be increasing support for 'the government', this is a rather ambiguous term in this context. Many people that were disturbed by official policies placed the blame on the Party or the Soviet Union, rather than the government *per se*.[29] The increased support for 'the government', then, does not necessarily reflect increased support for the regime or its policies.

[29] The December *Paris Match* survey, for example, asked who was responsible for the economic crisis. The bulk of the blame was fairly evenly divided between the government (38%) and the Party (35%), with another 16% identifying 'Russia'.

Despite these caveats, the results portrayed here are consistent, in direction at least, with the polls of other organizations too, as noted above. Trust in the government had dipped very low by September of 1981, as the economic crisis was punctuated with hunger marches and the political arena was dominated by the Solidarity Congress. The 30% trust in the government can be compared to the May 1981 poll on trust in institutions, showing 69% expressing trust in the government. Trust in Solidarity's leadership was still very high in September, but had declined somewhat over the course of the year, as discussed in Chapter 5. But during the last months of 1981, there was a sharp increase in trust in the government, and a significant decline in confidence in Solidarity's leadership. The former was no doubt due to the *appearance*, at least, of a conciliatory stance by the government in these months. The decline in confidence in the Solidarity leadership probably reflects two different tendencies: criticism by moderates of the union's unwillingness to compromise and join the government's offer of a national front; and criticism by radicals of Wałęsa's reluctance to employ the strike and other confrontational tactics. Solidarity was still more widely trusted than the government, but was by no means the great hope for salvation that it had been one year earlier.

The only institutions whose support remained both strong and unchanged in latter 1981 were the Church and the Army. The Church was not prepared to play a major political role in Poland, and the communist authorities would not have tolerated such a role. The Army, however, was a popular institution for a number of reasons: it was connected with Poland's nationalist and historical traditions; it was a channel through which all young men passed as part of mandatory military service; and it had a reputation for being apolitical. Jaruzelski, as Defense Minister, had himself benefited from this last myth, when he had supposedly ordered the Army not to fire on Polish workers in 1970.

The popularity of the Army is evident from the 1981 polls on trust in various institutions (see Table 5.3). Both the OBOP and the Solidarity surveys found the Army in a strong third place (of fifteen institutions), behind only the Church and Solidarity. When Army units organized in 'Territorial Operational Groups' (TGO) were distributed around the country in the middle of November, ostensibly to help remedy local economic problems, they were greeted with widespread approval. An OBOP poll found 91% saying the activities of the TGOs would be beneficial for society (OBOP, 'Opinie o TGO'). Most people thought the groups would help uncover and remedy inefficiency, negligence, incompetence, speculation and corruption.

The development of these TGOs may have been both a trial run for martial law a month later, and a 'trial balloon' for public reaction to an interventionist role for the Army. The regime was mistaken, though, if it thought acceptance of the TGOs would lend legitimacy to the much more political role that the Army assumed on December 13. While support for the Army was high, this was in large part because the Army was *non-political*. The use of the Army in a partisan political manner, and against Solidarity, was not likely to win the kind of support as did the use of the TGOs in a non-political, supportive role.

RADICALISM AND COMPROMISE AT THE END OF 1981

Solidarity had always been plagued by a certain ambivalence about its role and mission in Polish society. This ambivalence probably existed within most individual members, and was exacerbated by factions and divisions within the organization. The ambivalence, and even confusion, about Solidarity's role and activities is especially apparent among Solidarity activists, and emerges from their 'self-portrait' presented by French sociologist Alain Touraine and his associates. The Touraine group interviewed Solidarity activists in depth during 1981, and in a series of group discussions, attempted to guide the activists to a self-definition and self-understanding of themselves and the movement. Touraine concludes from this research that the Solidarity militants had a clear awareness of the limits of change in Poland. These included maintaining the leading role of the Party, recognizing Poland's place in the Eastern bloc, and exercising restraint to prevent further damage to the country's economy. Touraine later admits, however, that the first of these limits was 'exploded' at Solidarity's Congress (Touraine 1983, pp. 65, 179). And a strong and sustained theme in the discussions with the union's activists was 'the desire to eradicate the Party from the enterprise' and 'to drive the Party from their lives' (pp. 50–6). As Touraine puts it:

The constantly reaffirmed aim of Solidarity was to free society from the totalitarian domination of the Party. In the factory, rank-and-file militants were just as clear about this as their national leaders. They did not speak of a workers' state, rarely of 'true socialism', and even less of the total independence of Poland. They wanted to drive the Party from their lives, and to limit it to its proper functions within the state, so that a free society might once more exist (p. 56).

This seems at most a contradiction, and at least a failure to recognize the *regime*'s perception of the role of the Party in Polish society. Whether or not it was consistent for Solidarity to speak both of being self-limiting, and wishing to eradicate the Party from their factories and their lives, this was certainly not viewed by the authorities as being consistent with the principle of maintaining the leading role of the Party. Leszek Szymański (1982, p. 73) finds this sort of attitude by Solidarity leaders to reflect an 'unbelievable ignorance of Party semantics and psychology', especially 'for people brought up under Communism'. This is probably too harsh a criticism, given the fluid environment of 1981 and the changes that *had* occurred in the Party already. But it does point to one of the problems that Solidarity faced at the end of 1981.

The ambivalence about Solidarity's role and its relationship with the Party was matched by ambivalence about the extent to which Solidarity should become 'political'. This was a sensitive and divisive issue, as discussed in Chapter 5. It is clear, though, that Solidarity did become more political as time passed. Touraine (1983, pp. 97–8) identifies three stages of Solidarity's growth: the creation and identification of the trade union; the movement for self-management; and the development of political goals. This political phase began in the fall of 1981, and became especially visible at Solidarity's Congress where there were motions and resolutions promoting self-management, denouncing nomenklatura, calling for free elections to the regional councils and the Sejm, and appealing to workers elsewhere in Eastern Europe. All of these were highly political actions, especially in a communist environment, where the boundaries of politics are so much larger than in the West. Wałęsa and other Solidarity leaders continued to claim that Solidarity was not a political movement. They claimed that the organization was more than a trade union, and less than a political party. Rather, they called it a 'social movement'; but the policies and actions of Solidarity in the fall of 1981 make these assertions doubtful.

The ambivalence about its role is one of the reasons, perhaps, why Solidarity became more reactive and defensive in late 1981.

Touraine (1983, p. 134) identifies Solidarity in its third phase as defining itself 'less and less by its hopes and its values, and see[ing] itself increasingly as a force of resistance to threats and provocations'. As Solidarity moved from its positive, goal-setting orientation, to a more negative and defensive one, it was bound to lose some of its luster and dynamism. The new independent union had been dragged into the muck of Polish politics. In doing so, it lost some of the charisma and idealism that had attracted so many people to it in the first place.

The ambivalence within Solidarity was compounded by the problems of factionalism. From its inception, the movement had been torn by competing interests and orientations. The most basic split was between the 'moderates', typified by Wałęsa, and the 'radicals', typified by Jan Rulewski, Andrzej Gwiazda and others. The radicals argued that Solidarity's continued existence, and genuine economic reform, could only be guaranteed by radical political changes; and that these could only be accomplished through constant pressure, threats, and strike action by Solidarity. The moderates argued for a go-slow approach, consolidating the gains of the summer of 1980, and seeking areas of compromise and agreement with the authorities. They feared provoking a hard-line response from the Party or from Moscow. Wałęsa and his colleagues won control of the national leadership at Solidarity's Congress, but were in a difficult position after that point. They were caught between the conservatives in the regime and the radicals within the union. If Solidarity pushed too hard, the regime might harden its position or, worse, resort to repression. If it did not push hard enough, the movement risked an internal rebellion by the 'radicalized horizontal structure' of the union (Misztal 1983). The task of maintaining the balance was all the more difficult because of the lack of political experience by the Solidarity leadership. They were not used to dealing either with the authorities, or with dissenters within the movement. There were frequent debates within Solidarity about whether the union was, or should be 'democratic or dictatorial'.

The radical–moderate split does not do justice, however, to the multitude of tendencies within Solidarity. Touraine (1983, p. 57) calls attention to four main tendencies: defensive, community-based trade unionism (centered in Silesia); broad-based institutional reformism (Gdańsk); nationalist, often aggressive, populism; and independence-minded political democracy (especially among intellectuals). As such a large organization, it was inevitable that Solidarity would encompass a diversity of interests. In its formative year, the spirit of solidarity was enough to mute the competitive and often contradictory trends within the movement. As Solidarity grew and became more institutionalized, these different strands began to unravel and threaten Solidarity's unity.

Radom and Gdańsk, December 1981

At the end of November, the political-atmosphere began to heat up. Government–Solidarity talks were stalemated. The Party's Politburo had called for legislation to ban strikes. And on December 2, Warsaw riot police raided the Firefighters' Academy to arrest the striking cadets occupying the building. In this atmosphere, Solidarity's National Presidium met with the union's regional chairmen in Radom. This was likely to be a stormy meeting anyway, since the Presidium was dominated by Wałęsa and the moderates, and the regional organizations and its leaders tended to be much more radical. In the aftermath of the Firemen's Academy, there was a good deal of discussion about how Solidarity might protect itself against such moves in the future, and about the overall direction of the union. Somebody tape-recorded most of the proceedings, and the government later broadcast and printed what it said were excerpts from various speeches. Jan Rulewski, the Solidarity chairman in Bydgoszcz, talked of setting up a 'provisional government' that should be 'non-party' and which should follow KOR tactics rather than those of the more radical KPN. Zbigniew Bujak and others talked of establishing a 'workers' militia' and was quoted as saying 'the government must at last be overthrown, laid bare, stripped of all credibility' (cited in Szymański 1982, pp. 55–6). Solidarity leaders later said that these were simply ideas for contingency plans, if the regime should ever move to crush the union. But the inflammatory language did reflect the threatening position the union felt itself in. In the statement adopted at the conclusion of the meeting, Solidarity listed its demands, for an acceptable trade union bill, genuine economic reform, democratic elections to the people's councils, and access to the media. At the same time, the union rejected the government's offer of a Front of National Accord. According to the Radom Declaration (printed in *Tygodnik Solidarność*, December 11, 1981).

Talks about a national accord were utilized by the government to conceal the preparation of an attack on the union. In this situation, further negotiations on the subject of national accord are irrelevant. ... A national accord cannot depend on putting the Union into a repainted Front of National Unity ... [this] would only eliminate the union's credibility and independence.

In retrospect, this assertion appears correct, in that ten days later martial law was imposed. Almost certainly the plans for martial law were already in process. However, the radical language and the uncompromising position adopted at Radom simply added ammunition to the arsenal of the hardliners in the regime, and may have accelerated the timing of the crackdown.

The Radom scenario was replayed a week later at a meeting of Solidarity's national leadership in Gdańsk. On Saturday, December 12, the leadership proposed a national referendum on the Jaruzelski government, on establishing a new government with free elections, and on defining Poland's military relationship with the Soviet Union (*Washington Post*, December 20, 1981). All of these issues were close to the hearts of most Poles and would have had to be addressed eventually, but in the tense atmosphere of the winter of 1981, these were provocative and dangerous moves. The regime took advantage of the situation, using the Radom and Gdańsk meetings as an excuse for the establishment of the Military Council of National Salvation (WRON), the arrest of the Solidarity leadership, and the ending of Poland's brief experiment with freedom.

The population's conciliatory mood

The sudden emergence of the radicals in both Solidarity and the regime in late 1981 was particularly ironic in that the Polish population had moved in the other direction. At the end of 1981, Poles were generally optimistic and conciliatory. As seen in Table 7.16 above, there was a growing sense that Poland's problems could be worked out in a peacable manner. The November meeting of the 'Big Three' and the negotiations between Solidarity and the government had engendered hope that social tensions could be reduced. The somewhat restored confidence in the government suggested a reduction in the polarization that had gripped Polish society earlier in the year. And most Poles were cognizant of the risks inherent in Poland's developments, and the limits of change. When *Paris Match* (December 25, 1981) asked Poles what could lead the Russians to intervene in Poland, 44% mentioned 'the risk of contagion of Polish "liberalism" through the Soviet bloc', and 42% said 'because the Polish crisis will endanger the regime'. As shown in Table 7.9, a majority of Poles at the end of 1981 thought Poland's independence was threatened, more than had thought so in the tense days at the end of 1980. Many therefore, were prepared for compromise and conciliation, to avoid endangering the regime or provoking the Soviets. This is evident from popular attitudes on free Saturdays, on political reforms, and on the idea of a government of national unity.

Free Saturdays

Work-free Saturdays had been one of the original 21 Demands at Gdańsk, a source of conflict between Solidarity and the government at the end of 1980, and one of the few concrete gains for the workers in 1981. Despite all of this, when Solidarity's National Commission proposed that workers in key industries (particularly mining) work during the last eight free Saturdays in 1981, the appeal met with a surprising degree of support. When Solidarity's OBS asked workers if they would be willing to work on Saturdays, the vast majority responded positively (see Table 7.19).

Table 7.19. *Will you work on free Saturdays? (%)*

	Workers in:		
Response	Coal mines	Other Silesian industries	Warsaw region industries
Of course	39.9	38.3	52.7
Probably	10.1	11.1	8.5
Depends on decision of factory committee, but personally for	21.0	28.4	22.1
Total yes	71.0	77.8	83.3
No	2.2	1.9	0.3
Probably not	4.3	1.2	1.7
Total no	6.5	3.1	2.0

Source: OBS, 'Wyniki badań' (September 1981).

This shows a remarkable degree of willingness to temporarily give up some of the gains of 1981 to help revitalize the economy and pull the country out of its crisis. Most workers expected a *quid pro quo* from the government. At the personal level, most workers wanted either extra wages for their Saturday work, or the ability to purchase their meat rations without waiting in lines (a typical Saturday ordeal). At the factory level, many workers wanted the factory workers to decide what was produced on the Saturdays. There was also support (by about one-third of the workers in the various regions) for the introduction of real self-management in the factories. And at the national level, the overwhelming majority (64–72%) wanted Solidarity assured of regular access to the mass media, the most burning issue in the fall of 1981. This too indicates a sense of moderation, in that there was much less support for more 'political' changes such as the passage of the new trade union law (15–27% support), allowing Solidarity a role in governing the country (28–37%), and the holding of free elections to the Sejm (17–25%). Solidarity workers were willing to work on Saturdays, and their demands were not radical or escalatory, reflecting their basic needs and the long-standing policies of the union.

As shown in Table 7.8 above, there was considerable support for the suspension of free Saturdays (in mining and other important sectors of the economy) in the *Polacy '81* survey at the end of the year as well. The population was more evenly divided on the issue in this poll than in the Solidarity one, though probably due to the phrasing of the question. Solidarity members had been asked about a *Solidarity* resolution on working free Saturdays. The *Polacy '81* survey asked about a *government* decree to this effect. Most people opposed the idea of any hardline measures to end the crisis, and some of the opposition to this proposition no doubt stemmed from this context of the question. Even so, 40.4% of Solidarity members favored the idea, as did a clear majority of farmers, unskilled workers, and those not employed.

New elections and new parties

At the end of 1981, Solidarity had been calling for new and free elections to the Sejm and People's Councils. This was one of the appeals of the Radom Declaration in early December. The population overwhelmingly supported the idea of new elections, by 71% to 20%, but was much more cautious on the nature of 'free' elections.

Table 7.20. *Do you favor the creation of new political parties?*
(%)

	Yes	No
Overall*	24.5	70.9
PZPR members	23.5	76.5
Solidarity members	31.5	68.5
Educational level:		
Primary	19.8	80.2
General secondary	29.5	70.5
Higher	51.7	48.3

* Excludes 4.5% 'missing data'.
Source: *Polacy '81*, pp. 146–50.

Only 20% supported the creation of a new political party by Solidarity, with 57% opposed to this idea. Solidarity members, in fact, were even more opposed to this proposition (by 63%) than was the rest of the population.

Indeed, most Poles were opposed to the creation of *any* new political parties besides the existing PZPR and its satellite parties, the Social Democratic Party (SD), and the Peasants' Party (ZSL) (see Table 7.20).

This survey shows widespread opposition to the idea of creating any new political parties, even though most Western polls (as unreliable as these may be) show Poles preferring a new Christian democratic, socialist, or 'liberal' party to the communist party (e.g., the unofficial *Paris Match* surveys). This suggests a recognition on the part of Poles in 1981 of the difference between what was desirable and what was possible in those circumstances. It reflected a certain realism about the impact of a multiparty system on Poland's neighbors.

There are some other interesting features to Table 7.20. Even though most people opposed the establishment of new parties, there was still a solid minority of about 25% which favored this idea. As mentioned earlier, there was always a core of a quarter to a third of the population, and of Solidarity, that was anxious to move more directly into the political realm. This is the 'political democracy' tendency in the movement that Touraine refers to. As he noted, this was primarily made up of intellectuals. This is vividly demonstrated in Table 7.20, where those with a higher education are two times more likely to favor additional parties than is the rest of the population. In fact, this is the only subcategory of Poles that favored such a course. Given the role of the intellectuals in Solidarity's formation and development, it is not surprising that this point of view held some currency in the Solidarity leadership as well; but it was not supported by the workers, who wanted to keep the union on a more narrowly trade union course (see above, p. 147, n. 23).

A government of national unity
Instead of creating new political parties, which might well undermine the leading role of the PZPR and be considered provocative by Moscow, most Poles favored the naming of some kind of government of national unity 'which would include representatives of the most influential political groupings and social movements'. A proposition of this sort elicited the support of three-quarters of the population; Solidarity members were even more supportive (88%) of such a government. Most Party members also favored this idea[30] (*Polacy '81*, pp. 132–45). The authors of the *Polacy '81* report, writing after the imposition of martial law, note plaintively that the support for this proposition was so widespread at the end of 1981 that the formulation of such a government would have met with broad support of the population. But in the tense atmosphere of that month, and the emergence of a more radical line on both sides, it is unlikely that such a government would have been supported by either the government or the Solidarity leadership. The latter had rejected the government's offer of a front of national accord, on the basis that the union would have no real power, and would simply be assigned blame for the continuing economic crisis. Perhaps a seat in the government would have been more in accord with Solidarity's demands, though it seems that the same objections would hold. Solidarity was probably not ready to assume such a role. It was still struggling with its identity, and still not sure if it should be directly involved in policy-making.

The Jaruzelski government, on the other hand, had neither the inclination nor the motivation to join in a unity government with Solidarity. Communist governments are not used to dealing with

[30] *Paris Match* asked a similar question in their unofficial poll, and found two-thirds of their respondents supporting a national unity government including the Party and Solidarity.

labor unions on an equal basis, and the Polish regime had found Solidarity to be particularly difficult. A unity government would have further diminished the authority and leading role of the Party, which had already declined to almost nothing. Furthermore, given the divisions within Solidarity and the increased popular frustration with its accomplishments and activities, the regime may have felt it had nothing to gain from an alliance with the union. In declaring martial law, the regime overestimated these divisions and frustrations, and lost an opportunity for reconciliation and popular support.

CONCLUSIONS

Both Solidarity and Polish politics went through a number of phases between August 1980 and December 1981.[31] In the first phase, lasting up to the Bydgoszcz crisis in March, Solidarity was 'an excited crowd', and the union was basically one with society (Misztal 1983). The new union was the first genuinely representative institution in Poland's postwar history, and people enthusiastically turned to it and endowed it with great expectations. In the second stage, through the summer of 1981, the coalition began to weaken somewhat as the economic crisis deepened and, Solidarity struggled with its very identity. The third stage, from the summer on, is characterized by 'destabilization'. Popular feelings of excitement and idealism were replaced by fatigue and apathy. People wanted to see improvements in Polish society, but even more so wanted a reduction of societal tension and a greater degree of calm and stability. Solidarity itself becomes less ideological, defining itself, in Touraine's (1983, p. 134) words, 'less and less by its hopes and its values, and ... increasingly as a force of resistance to threats and provocations'.

Solidarity had been a uniquely democratic institution in Poland, and the PZPR had itself been forced to democratize as well. However, neither institution had much experience with democracy, and there was a tug of authoritarianism within each. Solidarity's association with the Catholic Church, also an authoritarian structure, contributed to such a tendency in the union. As both the union

[31] Misztal (1983) and Touraine (1983) both have identified various stages of Solidarity's developments. They generally agree on the timing of these phases, but differ in their interpretation of each stage.

and the Party came to feel threatened and defensive at the end of 1981, the tendencies toward rigidity and hierarchy began to reemerge in the leadership of each. At the end of 1981, both the Solidarity leadership and the Party leadership were less flexible and conciliatory than the mass membership of those organizations.

The population was still strongly supportive of Solidarity and its policies. The government, and especially the Party, were broadly distrusted. But people showed a growing tendency to fault both sides for Poland's continuing difficulties, and growing sentiment for a conciliatory and compromising position by both Solidarity and the authorities. Popular support for the strikes had diminished sharply over the year, and the population evinced little support for radical changes of either the democratic or authoritarian type. Poles wanted more pluralism in the media and the political system, but recognized the limits to these changes. They opposed regime policies that involved compulsion or recentralization, though they were willing to sacrifice some of the gains of 1981 to achieve a greater measure of stability. The population was in an accommodating mood. It seemed that neither the regime nor the Solidarity leadership was in the same frame of mind.

Both Solidarity and the regime had carried a number of myths into the last months of 1981 (see Misztal 1983). Solidarity, especially in the middle of 1981, believed in 'the endless capacity of the government to negotiate'. The government had indeed negotiated with the workers in Gdańsk, and had agreed to all of their demands. The Gdańsk events had been extraordinary ones, though, and Solidarity would never again muster the unanimity and emotion that surrounded those events and which forced the government to compromise. After that point, both sides had to negotiate and both sides had to compromise.

Solidarity's leaders and activists were also mistaken in thinking that the movement could stay out of politics while formulating demands which, if granted, 'would amount to the abdication of those in power' (Misztal 1983, p. 15). This also emerges from Touraine's (1983, p. 99) interviews with Solidarity activists. Even in Solidarity's 'political' phase, the militants professed not to want to enter the political arena. They felt that 'the movement should continue to represent society in its opposition to the regime, and should not enter political conflict'. But to play the role of opposition *was* a political act. Solidarity probably did need to play a political role, but it also needed to recognize that its role was political. Certainly the regime felt this way, so the myth of apoliticism contributed to the lack of understanding between the two sides. The Solidarity movement was 'self-limited' only in that it did not attempt to seize power. After Radom, even this limitation was in doubt.

Finally, there was the myth that the lack of external intervention in Poland meant that there would be no force available to crack down on the movement (Misztal 1983). This was the most tragic mistake of all. Most Poles thought the Russians would not intervene in Poland and that, if they did, the Polish army would fight against the Russians (*Paris Match*, December 25, 1981). The Army was viewed as being a patriotic and nationalistic force that would defend Poland and the accomplishments of the past year. Few people expected that the Army could be used to crush Solidarity and end the process of renewal. It was a numbing blow to the Polish psyche when it was.

Solidarity did not want or intend to seize power in Poland. It did not, at first, even want to play a political role. The nature of its demands, and the recalcitrance of the regime, drove it into a political role, but the movement was not yet ready to assume the responsibilities as well as the privileges of a political opposition. It was an opposition unwilling to pose alternatives or accept a role in the management of society. Given time, it may well have come to this point, but at the end of 1981, the regime was not willing to accept such a role for Solidarity either.

8

Martial law as a response and the response to martial law

'Bez prowokowania nie ma aresztowania' (Without provocations, there are no arrests)

Slawomir Mrożek, *Policja*

'You know what our people are like. One minute they come together, the other they go back home. Now they'll come back again. Maybe not four hundred straight off, maybe three hundred, maybe two hundred at the worst ...'

Tadeusz Konwicki, *The Polish Complex*

When Premier and Party Secretary Jaruzelski declared a 'state of war'[32] on December 13, he did so without mentioning the Polish United Workers' Party. He himself was introduced only as the head of the Military Council of National Salvation (WRON) and Premier; his title of First Secretary of the Party was not mentioned. The new military government removed the red Party flag from the Party headquarters building in Warsaw and replaced it with the red and white Polish flag. The Politburo and Central Committee did not get around to approving the martial law decree until February 24, almost a month after the Sejm had done so (Kruszewski 1984).

Jaruzelski claimed that martial law was necessary to restore stability to the marketplace and the political arena, and to preclude the possibility of civil war. The General was never very specific about how such a conflict might emerge. It might well have broken out within the Party itself. As noted in Chapter 6, there was some speculation that the apparatchiks were planning their own coup in

---

[32] The Polish constitution had no provision for martial law, as such, only for emergency measures in the case of a 'stan wojenny', which literally means state of war.

late December (Spielman 1982, p. 32). As we have seen above, the Party apparatus was the single biggest obstacle to the renewal process within the Party and without. They were most threatened by the ongoing changes in Poland and by the gains of Solidarity. A seizure of power by the hardliners in the Party might well have led to conflict between the Party and Solidarity. In such an eventuality, if the Army had remained neutral, Solidarity probably would have prevailed, marking the end of Party rule in Poland.

In the aftermath of martial law, Jaruzelski undertook a major purge of the central apparatus, which harbored the opponents of change, and he also restaffed many key positions in the provincial party structure, where many liberals had come to the fore in the previous year. This 'trimming of the wings of the Party' further weakened that organization, leaving the Army with a clear field. For the first time in the Soviet bloc, the military had replaced the Party as the 'leading force in society'.

The regime justified the imposition of martial law on two broad counts. First of all, regime spokesmen argued that Poland might not have survived the forthcoming winter in the face of the continuing economic crisis and strike actions. All of this was contributing, in the words of Mieczysław Rakowski, to the destruction of the Polish economy and to 'a national biological disaster' (*Trybuna Ludu*, February 13–14, 1982). Also, though the government did not publicly make this argument, martial law was felt to insure the necessary control before the government imposed major new food price increases. Most economists, and even Solidarity, agreed that such increases were necessary. In the past, though (e.g. 1970, 1976, 1980) such increases had led to major protest actions. The regime argued that the society could not afford such protests in the critical economic situation. Within two months of the imposition of martial law, major food price increases were announced.

Secondly, the regime contended that Solidarity's increasing political activism was threatening the stability of the state, undermining the Party and the government, and contributing to societal fear and tension. Regime propaganda also implied that the Solidarity leadership had been plotting a seizure of power. As noted above, the media had devoted considerable attention to the alleged transcripts from Solidarity's Radom meeting, quoting Wałęsa, for example, as saying 'confrontation is unavoidable and will take place ... let us realize that we are bringing the system down' (*Washington Post*,

December 20, 1981). This media campaign, which began before martial law, continued after December 13.

Over the course of 1982, the criticism of Solidarity became more harsh. At first, most of the official criticism focused on Solidarity's leaders, implying that they were more radical, political, and anti-socialist than the union's general membership. Later, the criticism was levelled at 'Solidarity' itself rather than simply the union's leadership. In March (6–7th), *Trybuna Ludu* carried a major attack on Solidarity's Program, asserting that 'from beginning to end', the program had only one goal: 'discrediting socialism, attempting to define other, non-socialist paths of development enigmatically named "a self-governing Republic"'.

The regime's initial position was that Solidarity had at first been on the right track, supporting reform, maintaining a commitment to a Polish form of socialism, and maintaining the 'self-limited' nature of the revolution (*Rzeczpospolita*, February 9, 1982). It was only later, this argument went, that the union 'changed itself into a political movement, with an anti-socialist character' (*Rzeczpospolita*, April 8, 1982). Later, however, there were less generous views of Solidarity's genesis. *Trybuna Ludu* (May 12, 1982) implied that Solidarity's goals had been political all along, and that from the beginning, the free trade union movement was in 'strict subjection to oppositional groups and in the first place to KOR'.

In the initial months of martial law the regime also left open some room for compromise with Solidarity. On December 13, government spokesman Jerzy Urban announced that Wałęsa had had high level talks with government officials hours after the declaration of the 'state of war'. 'Wałęsa', he said, 'has not been arrested and is not interned ... He is being treated with all due respect. He is considered the head of Solidarity and Solidarity's activities have only been suspended' (Stefanowski 1982, p. 92). This situation soon changed, of course, but it suggests that the authorities were not certain of their treatment of the independent union, even with the military crackdown. Even Jaruzelski seemed ambivalent on the future of the unions. In a Christmas Eve speech he declared that there was room in Poland's socio-economic system for 'self-governing and genuinely independent trade unions'.

While arrests, internments, and repression continued, there were still conciliatory messages from the regime up through the spring of 1982. The new government newspaper *Rzeczpospolita* (April 8, 1982) argued for 'restoring the principle of partnership which would mean not only rights for both parties in carrying out negotiations but also in respecting each partner and understanding his reasons'. An official statement from the Sejm on May 4 called for 'cooperation of all the nation's forces', including 'all people of good will, *no matter their ideas and organizational alliance*' (*Życie Warszawy*, May 4, 1982; stress added). And an article in *Życie Warszawy* (April 6, 1982) on the creation of a 'Front of National Agreement' went so far as to say that such a front was 'in a certain sense *mainly for those who "don't like socialism"*, for those who have other notions of the social order, or have none' (stress added). This was a remarkable statement, and may not have reflected an official position. But it did indicate some realization of the depth of alienation and apathy in Poland that led to the creation of Solidarity in the first place.

This accommodating mood gradually disappeared as it became clear that the regime would not win the confidence of Solidarity or its leaders. In the first five months of martial law, the population had remained remarkably quiescent, partly out of shock and partly from the economic hardship of the price increases, the winter, and the restrictions of martial law. The regime may have been lulled into thinking the quiet indicated support, or at least acquiescence. This illusion was shattered with the outpouring of protest in the spring.

In spite of some signs of conciliation, the actions of the martial law regime became more and more harsh and repressive as time went on. The early reference to Wałęsa's freedom was soon belied by Wałęsa's isolation and internment. A large number of industries, including most of those in transportation and communication, as well as the ports, refineries and mines, were militarized, so it became a capital offense for workers to strike in these workplaces. As it became clear that the universities were a major center of opposition to martial law, the authorities clamped down there as well. In January, the Ministry of Higher Education dissolved the pro-Solidarity Independent Students' Union (N.Z.S.) and in April the popular rector of the University of Warsaw (Samsonowicz) was dismissed. After the demonstrations of early May, in which many students participated, the regime bluntly challenged the cherished freedom of academia. Central Committee Secretary Hieronim Kubiak, himself an academic, asserted that:

pedagogical ethics [do] not provide for teachers sharing their concerns and doubts with their students, but on the contrary, they should protect the young against dilemmas and ideological/moral frustration, particularly when these lead to legal violations (*Trybuna Ludu*, May 14, 1982).

In March, the independent minded Polish Journalists' Association was dissolved and replaced by a more malleable organization. The regime also began to move against some of its other nemeses, including Leszek Moczulski's Confederation for an Independent Poland (KPN). Trial proceedings against Moczulski and his colleagues began in February.

THE ROLE AND PERCEPTION OF THE POLISH ARMY

The regime's increasing reliance on repression became necessary as it became clear that the martial law regime could not win the popular support and image of legitimacy necessary to restore growth and stability in the country. General Jaruzelski had been banking on a certain amount of support for WRON, simply because of the popular support for the Army in the population. This support was evident from both regime and Solidarity polls conducted in 1981. Surveys on trust in institutions conducted in May 1981 by OBOP and in October by Solidarity's OBS showed the Army ranked high, along with the Church and Solidarity (see Table 8.1).

Table 8.1. *Trust in institutions, May and October 1981 (%)*

	Do you trust these institutions?				
OBOP Poll (May)	Yes	Rather yes	Rather no	No	Hard to say
Catholic Church	81	13	1	2	3
Army	64	25	2	1	8
Solidarity	62	29	3	2	4
OBS Poll (Oct.)	Decisively yes	Rather yes	Rather no	Decisively no	Hard to say
Catholic Church	68	26	2	1	3
Army	22	47	13	4	14
Solidarity	68	27	2	1	2

Source: See Table 5.3.

Both of these polls show the Army in third place overall, though in the OBOP poll, those expressing unqualified confidence in the Army is even higher than that for Solidarity. The Solidarity poll, asking for stronger levels of commitment by phrasing the top response as *decisively* yes, found a lower level of unqualified confidence in the military. But still, that institution was placed a strong third of the fifteen institutions asked about.

Confidence in the Polish military had grown substantially in the years since 1956, largely as a result of the refusal of the military to side against the workers in times of trouble. The Army had always been a popular institution in Poland before World War II, but had lost much of its sheen in the aftermath of that catastrophe.[33] The 'organic unity' between the Polish people and their army began to return somewhat after the 1956 disturbances, when regular army troops refused to disperse Polish workers, and in some cases joined them.

In 1970, the Polish army ignored commands from Politburo member Kliszko to use repressive force, and the high command refused to support Gomułka against Gierek. Defense Minister (since 1968) Jaruzelski's retention of his ministry and his Politburo seat was a 'reward for the military's refusal to prevent the change-over' (Korbonski 1982, p. 117). Similarly, during the disturbances of the summer of 1976, General Jaruzelski was reported to have said that 'Polish soldiers will not fire at Polish workers.' Whether or not this story is apocryphal, it was a well-known one in Poland, and further enhanced the reputation of the military, and of Jaruzelski himself.

Finally, in the summer of 1980, Gierek's accession to the demands of the striking workers was in large measure due to the military's refusal to use force against the workers. Apparently both Defense Minister Jaruzelski and Central Committee Secretary Kania, in charge of military and security affairs, favored a peaceful and political solution to the crisis (Korbonski 1982, p. 119).

This history of the Army's benevolent role in times of crisis contributed to the positive image of the military. While there are no pre-1981 polls to compare to those above, there is indirect evidence of this improved image of the military. Surveys of occupational prestige, for example, show considerable gains for the military profession. In 1958, army officers were ranked 20th out of 27

[33] For a discussion of the role of the military in Polish society, see Herspring (1981) and Korbonski (1982).

occupations by urban residents. A similar poll in 1975 ranked the Army 13th of 21 (Korbonski 1982, p. 126). The confidence polls in Table 8.1 suggest that confidence in the Army had increased even further as a result of its role in the 1976 and 1980 events.

Andrzej Korbonski (1982, p. 210) suggests that the military had become the 'supreme arbiter' in Polish politics, passing judgment at times of political deadlock, and that this role had come to be accepted by the various factions within the party and the government. The Jaruzelski regime used the Army in this role in December 1981, but it miscalculated in its assessment of the 'deadlock'. There was not really an equal balance of public opinion for and against Solidarity. It was still a popular institution that represented the wishes of the majority of the population. In this situation, the Army was no longer a neutral arbiter, but a partisan, buttressing a regime and a Party that had little support from the population. The reputation of the Army was based on its support for the workers. Now that it was turned against them, its past popularity could not be used to lend legitimacy to martial law.

PUBLIC OPINION ON MARTIAL LAW

Survey research polls suddenly became much less frequent and much less reliable upon the imposition of martial law. Solidarity's OBS, of course, was prohibited from further activity, so any future Solidarity polls were conducted illegally underground. Virtually all academic survey research, like most other academic activities, was terminated or suspended as a result of martial law. Only the official OBOP continued public opinion polling, but in the tense atmosphere of early 1982, the validity of the results is doubtful. Even so, few of the official surveys were reported publicly and those that were received only selective and fragmentary treatment. One cannot, therefore, treat the polls of 1982 with the same confidence as those of the Solidarity era.

A month into martial law, OBOP conducted its first survey under the new circumstances, among the residents of Warsaw. This was probably not a representative sample; Warsaw residents are somewhat more conservative than those of other cities; and the atmosphere in the middle of January was still tense and depressing. So one should treat these results with a great deal of caution. The results, presented three weeks later in the Warsaw press, showed that 51%

Table 8.2. *Opinion on most painful restrictions of martial law, January 1982 (%)*

Restrictions on:	% mentioning
Freedom of movement and travel	49
Telephone communications	35
Curfew	24
Personal freedom and civil rights	14
Cultural activities, press, media	12
Gasoline sales	10
Activities of trade unions	8
Censoring of phone and mail	3
Freedom of speech and criticism	3

Source: Życie Warszawy, February 6–7, 1982.

of the respondents considered the decision to introduce martial law 'justified' and only 19% thought it was unjustified (*Życie Warszawy*, February 6, 1982). Few people in Warsaw believed the results of this poll and most professionals involved in survey research (in conversations with the author) doubted that *any* polls in the rigid atmosphere of January 1982 could be considered reliable. The regime had no such qualms, however, and the official press indirectly referred to these results in contending that 'the absolute majority' of the Polish nation 'fully supported the decision of the Military Council of National Salvation' (*Żołnierz Wolności*, February 23, 1982).

OBOP asked which of the martial law regulations were the most painful for society. The results, presented in Table 8.2, indicate that for most people, the worst part of martial law was the restrictions on daily activities rather than those on political freedom and on Solidarity. The actual figures in this table are probably not reliable at all, since many of the respondents, fearful of reprisal, probably told the pollsters what they wanted to hear. There may be some truth, however, in the general pattern of responses. Most people, in the difficult days of January, were mainly concerned about *managing*, rather than an immediate renewal of political activities. The most immediate concern was with transportation and communication, reflecting the frustration Poles felt with the inability to see and talk with friends and relatives elsewhere in the country and abroad. The OBOP poll also asked if there had been any positive changes in the

Table 8.3. *Opinion on changes accompanying martial law*

Changes	% mentioning
No positive changes	22
Greater sense of security, less crime and hooliganism	54
Peace, order	22
Ending of strikes and partial normalization of economy	11
Intensified struggle with speculation	8
Some improvement in food supplies	6
Greater order in stores	6
Introduction of obligation to work	5
Greater productivity of labor	5

Source: Same as Table 8.2.

country as a result of martial law. A bold 22% asserted that there had been none. The positive responses (see Table 8.3), however, tended to bolster the regime's propaganda and policies.

The Jaruzelski regime had claimed that the major purpose of martial law was to restore peace, stability and order to Polish society. It was able to refer to polls such as this, however unreliable, to bolster that position.

The results of other official polls in 1982 must not have been so favorable for the authorities, since no others were reported in the press until the end of 1982. An official survey of attitudes towards trade unions including Solidarity, conducted by OBOP and the Academy of Sciences at the end of March 1982, produced results surprising enough to the regime to preclude their publication. Apparently the poll showed that over 70% of the population favored immediate reinstatement of Solidarity.[34]

The Party's IPPML conducted its first survey in May and June of 1982, among 4000 workers in major enterprises. These results were also not officially released in 1982, but some did leak out in Western publications the next year (e.g. Powiorski 1983, p. 116). This survey asked about the conflict and tensions that led to martial law. A third of the sample thought that primarily the authorities were to blame; only 9% assigned primary blame to Solidarity. The largest number,

[34] I saw the questionnaire before it was administered, but not the results. This figure was mentioned to me by several people who did see them.

though, 44%, thought both the government and Solidarity were at fault. Again, the official nature of this survey makes the results somewhat unreliable. On the other hand, this pattern of responses closely matches the opinions on responsibility for societal problems in surveys conducted before martial law, as discussed in Chapter 7. Few people blamed Solidarity exclusively, but most felt Solidarity shared some of the blame with the government. Nevertheless, the May 1982 survey showed that Solidarity still enjoyed a good reputation. About 80% said Solidarity had looked after the interests of the workers 'well' or 'very well'.

The negative assessment of martial law was especially strong among young people, who had also been the most vigorous supporters of Solidarity. A Warsaw University survey of youth attitudes on martial law, conducted in February 1982, showed 70% believing the crackdown was 'totally inappropriate' and 80% contending that this action by the government was contrary to the interests of society. These results were not made public until the middle of 1983 (*Rzeczpospolita*, July 20, 1983) when another comparable survey was able to show that 'nearly 40%' of young people gave a positive assessment to martial law, citing the strengthening of social discipline and the beginning of economic reform as their main reasons. Even if these results are accurate, they still indicate that a large majority of young people continued to be critical of martial law, even sixteen months after the crackdown.

OBOP apparently conducted periodic polls all through 1982, but did not report on any of them until a year-end interview of its Director, Albin Kania, in *Życie Warszawy* (December 30, 1982). Kania referred to several dozen OBOP polls during 1982, but cited no figures at all until he discussed some polls done in November and December. He characterized 1982 as being divided into three periods: the first to the spring of 1982; the second to November 10; and the third from that date until the end of the year. In discussing the first period, his description of the public mood was obviously based on the January OBOP poll of Warsaw residents, discussed above, even though he did not directly refer to that poll and even though, as noted above, the results of that survey are highly suspect. Thus, Kania described the public's concerns over restrictions on daily life more than on union activities and political freedoms; and described 'the public's' recognition of the necessity of martial law based on the growth in the sense of security, etc. To refer to these poll results as representing the national mood, and as characterizing the whole period up to the spring of 1982, is a blatant misuse and misrepresentation of these data. It should also make us suspicious of the other official surveys of martial law.

Kania claimed that the second period, from the spring of 1982 until November 10, was characterized by increasing unrest and uncertainty as a result of strikes and street demonstrations. He asserted, without citing specific figures or surveys, that the underground Solidarity movement gradually lost support during this period, but he also admitted that 'the authorities' had not won the confidence of the population either. People were increasingly disinclined to support the idea of a general strike. Without citing figures, he asserted that the regime's decision to abolish all former trade unions and create a new set of labor unions 'may be accepted with understanding by a large part of society'. The wording of this sentence suggests that most people actually opposed that decision.

Kania dated the third period of 1982 from November 10, which was the day of the last major effort of Solidarity to mount a general strike and protests against martial law. The outcome was somewhat less than a success for the resistance movement. Kania claimed that this third period was characterized by the isolation of the underground from society, as well as an improved popular mood, a decline in tension, and growing confidence in the authorities.

Kania finally did cite figures from several polls done at the end of November and the end of December 1982, without however indicating the nature of the questions or of the sample. The November poll apparently included questions on trust in institutions, similar to those of OBOP's May 1981 survey. He said the poll showed the military 'maintaining very high authority' and the government winning the confidence of 'a majority' of the population. The latter is a surprising statement, though it could be that confidence in the *government* as such, rather than 'the authorities' or the Party, had recovered somewhat by the end of 1982. Even so, 50% support would have been much lower than the 69% expressing trust in the government in the 1981 OBOP poll.

OBOP's December 21 survey asked about the forthcoming suspension of martial law. Fifty-four percent approved the idea; 27% thought martial law should be completely terminated; and 11% thought the suspension was still too early. This December poll asked people how they assessed the year 1982. Fully 44% said that 1982 had been 'bad' for the country, while only 17% rated it as good. But Kania contended that these results were actually relatively good compared to ratings of past years. Although 44% had rated 1982 as bad, 86% felt that way about 1981, and 78% rated 1980 as bad. These are puzzling figures, and Kania does not give the dates that the polls on 1980 and 1981 were conducted. It seems unlikely that 1980 could have been rated as bad in the months after August, and equally unlikely that 86% would have called 1981 bad before the imposition of martial law. If these figures are drawn from samples before and after Solidarity, then, they do not provide an adequate comparison of feelings before and after martial law.

When asked why 1982 would have been rated better than the previous two years, Kania referred to the decline in fear, unrest, concern for personal security and for the fate of the country. There was a sense, he said, of some improvement in food supplies, and that Poland was emerging from its economic and political crisis. On the other hand, the larger number of those who rated the year badly pointed to the continued problems with food supplies and manufactured products, price increases, declines in real incomes and a sense that the crisis had not yet been resolved. As Kania understated the situation, 1982 'was not a year free from controversial decisions and social unrest'. Nevertheless, there was some improvement in public optimism between the end of 1981 and the end of 1982; those expecting the following year to be better increased from 20% to 41% (Kania 1982).

In this interview OBOP Director Kania called attention to the strong differentiation in opinion between the intelligentsia and the rest of society. As he pointed out, there had always been some such differentiation in public opinion polls, but never as significant as in 1982. 'In regard to basic social and political problems', Kania said, 'in their attitudes toward the authorities, towards martial law, and in regard to the labor movement, a significantly greater segment of the intelligentsia than other classes and social strata had a critical position'. Such differences were bigger than differences in opinion on the basis of age, party membership, or union membership. This is not perhaps very surprising, given the strong support for Solidarity from intellectuals, and the strong support for democratization of society from this quarter during 1981. As shown in Table 7.20 above, intellectuals were far more likely than any other groups to favor radical political changes in Poland. It is not surprising, therefore, that they were the most critical of martial law.

Kania's mention of this fact marks a renewed tendency on the part of the authorities to use public opinion polls for political purposes. With the imposition of martial law, the authorities tried to drive a wedge between Solidarity and the intellectual community. This took numerous forms. One tactic was to put the blame on Solidarity's intellectual advisors for leading the workers astray, and in particular for trying to radicalize and politicize the Solidarity movement. Another was to try to woo some of Solidarity's more moderate advisors away from the union in the aftermath of martial law, sowing seeds of bitterness against the advisors. The official press, for example, used some of the 1981 writings of Solidarity's advisors to criticize the union and its political tendencies in late 1981. And it encouraged other intellectual advisors to break the press boycott by appearing in the pages of *Polityka* and other newspapers. Finally, the regime moved very hard against the members of KOR, the Workers' Defense Committee. Jacek Kuroń, Adam Michnik and other KOR members were arrested and charged with the capital offense of treason. KOR was also singled out as being a false prophet of the workers, using them for its own insidious and political motives. The use of these public opinion polls, then, was part of this general campaign to discredit intellectual supporters of Solidarity, and to widen the gap between the workers and the intellectuals. It was the union of these two groups that had brought about Solidarity in the first place. The regime wanted to avoid a repetition of this phenomenon.

Solidarity's martial law surveys

Solidarity, underground and illegal, could no longer produce the kinds of representative sample surveys that the OBS had done before martial law. The polls that Solidarity did conduct were necessarily circumspect, and relied on Solidarity members interviewing only those they absolutely trusted. The results, therefore, are hardly representative, though they do give some indication of the thinking and mood of those active in the underground movement.

One of the first such surveys to be reported in the underground press was an informal poll conducted by Solidarity members in three factories in Warsaw between January 20 and March 3 of 1982. This survey showed almost unanimous opinion on every issue, including support for the continued existence of Solidarity under its old statutes and for the leadership of the organization ('Wyniki Badań', *KOS*, April 2, 1982). A separate but similar survey among Solidarity members shortly after the declaration of martial law showed 54% identifying the Soviet Union as the main stimulus for martial law, compared to only 14% who thought extremists in the Party were the main factor ('Społeczeństwo wobec przemocy', 1982).

Another poll among Solidarity members in Wrocław found a peculiar channel for publication: the army newspaper *Żołnierz Wolności* (June 9, 1982). The paper was attempting to ridicule the results, harping on the fact that the percentages added up to more than 100%. This was an inane remark since many surveys, including those done by OBOP, invite multiple responses, resulting in totals that exceed 100%. But in ridiculing the results, *Żołnierz* reported them as well. When asked about the strategy Solidarity should pursue, a majority of blue-collar workers (54%) favored a general strike, 32% favored 'passive resistance', and 22% favored an 'armed uprising'. White collar workers were more in favor of a general strike (62%) and passive resistance (38%), but much less supportive of the idea of armed uprising (7%). Presumably, this story was reported to show the continued existence of a radical and violent element in the underground, though the paper did not specifically comment on that aspect of the results. What the results in both Warsaw and Wrocław show, though, is the continuing support among Solidarity activists for the leadership, policies, and tactics of the underground leadership, well into the spring of 1982. At this point, there was little inclination to withdraw from the struggle with the regime.

By the fall of 1982, there was a somewhat different orientation among Solidarity members. By that time, perhaps out of frustration with the results of the strikes and demonstrations of the spring and summer, support had grown for the idea of building an underground community rather than directly confronting the authorities. This is evident from the results of one of the most thorough Solidarity polls of martial law. The questionnaire was designed by the underground organization KOS, the Committee for Societal Resistance (Komitet Oporu Społecznego), which consisted mostly of Solidarity members, and which aimed at creating a network of self-supporting 'cells' in Polish society. The questionnaire appeared in the Committee's

Table 8.4. *Participation in various forms of protest*
(% positive response)

Forms of protest	Took part
Boycotting press on Wednesdays	67
Extinguishing lights on 13th of month	43
Strikes at workplace	35
August 31 demonstrations	30
Wearing buttons, resistors, etc.	28
Going for walks during TV news	22
May 3 demonstrations	22
May 1 demonstrations	15
Letters of protest to authors	13
Others	9
Didn't take part in any	4

Source: 'Wstępne wyniki ankiety Komitetu Oporu Społecznego "KOS"', reported in *Biuletyn Informacyjny* (New York), nr. 74 (June 1983), pp. 19–21.

underground newsletter *KOS*, and 1400 persons responded. The authors cautioned that the results were not representative, in that the survey was restricted to the Warsaw region, it reached only those 'certain persons' who read *KOS*, and it overrepresented those with a middle or higher education (81% of the total) and 'mental workers' (72%) rather than blue collar ones (17%).

The survey asked a number of questions about past involvement in protest and suggestions for future directions. The respondents were asked in which forms of protest they had taken part.

These results illustrate the power of intimidation by the martial law authorities. Even among these 'certain people' who read *KOS*, presumably the more active Solidarity supporters, there was little willingness to engage in risk-taking protest behavior. While most people exhibited some form of symbolic protest, through boycotting the press or extinguishing lights at night on the 13th of every month, less than a third of these respondents had participated in more direct forms of protest. This may be due in part to the makeup of the sample: there were few of the more radical and activist blue-collar workers in this survey. Certainly it also reflects the fear of retribution and the psychological exhaustion caused by the sudden military crackdown. Curiously, though, participation in street demonstrations among this group *increased* over time. More people partici-

Table 8.5. *Support for various forms of protest (%)*

Form of protest	% support
Activity to build an underground society	77
Symbolic acts of protest	43
Active resistance on a societal scale (e.g. general strike)	41
Reprisals with the use of force (e.g. individual terrorism)	19
Other	4

Source: Same as Table 8.4.

pated in the May 3 protests than in the May 1 ones, and even more turned out for the August 31 demonstrations on the anniversary of the Gdańsk Agreements. This is surprising in that most reports of these events suggest that the number of participants in these demonstrations decreased as the year went on and the forceful reactions of the militia intensified.

The survey went on to ask the respondents what kinds of protests they 'decisively' supported (see Table 8.5).

Two thirds of the respondents thought that their workplace colleagues would participate in symbolic acts of protest and in building an underground society. Only a fifth believed they would support societal-wide acts of resistance. This perception may help explain why there was such growing interest in the creation of an underground society. This was not always illegal, and was less of a direct challenge to the regime. It was therefore less dangerous for the participants. This was also a long-term strategy that might well bear fruit in the future at a time when active resistance seemed not to be having much success.

The idea of an underground society, which *KOS* promoted, included some of the following activities: organizing aid for those 'repressed' and their families; producing 'independent' publications; organizing independent education; organizing work for underground Solidarity; and collecting information and news for the underground press. Many Solidarity supporters were already engaged in such activities during 1982. The support for an underground society apparently grew over the course of the year. When the respondents to this survey were asked what course of action toward the authorities they would actively support in the near term,

Table 8.6. *Short-term strategies toward the authorities*

Strategy	% supporting
Full cooperation with authorities, including participation in official structures (e.g. PRON)	0.4
Cooperation only in those areas conducive to development of labor unions and other forms of societal activity	18
Ignore authorities and work only for self	17
Ignore authorities and undertake activities outside official structures	63
Oppose authorities through boycott of work	21
Struggle with authorities through acts of terror	15
Other possibilities	6

Source: Same as Table 8.4.

the vast majority (63%) favored 'ignoring the authorities and undertaking social activities outside official structures – participating in the construction of an underground society' (see Table 8.6).

These survey results, almost a year into martial law, show remarkable similarities to those of the last weeks of 1981. At the end of 1982, as at the end of 1981, there was a minority of 30% or so whose position was hardline and uncompromising: total non-cooperation or active resistance to the authorities. A slightly smaller faction favored some limited cooperation with the regime, apparently in hopes of returning some measure of stability and growth to the economy and the society. Most people, while still highly supportive of Solidarity, favored a 'go-slow' approach in building autonomous institutions in society. In favoring this 'realistic' strategy over the 'idealistic' one of revolution and resistance, the population was buckling down for the long haul against a regime that had all the instruments of power.

THE RESPONSE OF THE POPULATION AND OF SOLIDARITY

The initial popular response to martial law was one of shock and depression. With the arrest and internment of most of Solidarity's national and regional leadership, a coordinated response to the military crackdown was impossible. Spontaneous demonstrations and strikes occurred throughout the country, but the authorities cracked down hard on such activities, and they largely ceased by the end of December 1981. According to the official press, protests took place in 180 workplaces in 19 voivodships on December 15, but these numbers steadily declined to six factories in two regions by December 20 (*Polityka*, February 20, 1982).

The strongest resistance came from the traditionally radical and activist miners and dockworkers. During an occupation strike in the Wujek mine near Katowice on December 16, the militia fired on the workers, killing seven and wounding 39. There were occupation strikes in other mines as well, though these ended more peacefully. Major demonstrations near the dockyards in Gdańsk in mid-December resulted in one death and, according to official figures, the injury of 163 'civilians' and 160 militiamen (*Polityka*, February 20, 1982). The last major strike ended on December 28, when miners at the Piast mine came out after a two-week holdout. By the end of the year, active resistance had ended.

The suddenness and efficiency of the crackdown had surprised most Poles and the use of the *Polish* army caused uncertainty, confusion and resignation. An unofficial survey conducted by *Paris Match* (December 25, 1981) before martial law found 74% of the respondents saying they would 'resist' if the Soviets intervened in Poland. Although many people would have resorted to violence and other forms of active resistance against a foreign occupier, there was no consensus on how to react to the Polish Army and a Polish military regime. The authorities had apparently counted on the 'psychological exhaustion of the masses' in imposing martial law. They expected that the turmoil, dislocations and shortages of 1981 had wearied people enough that they would not actively resist the crackdown on Solidarity. Certainly many people did feel this way; and these people were therefore not inclined to further struggle anyway. For others, martial law led to a sense of resignation, withdrawal or despair that effectively prohibited mass action. For those that did resist, the brutal reaction of the militia, the summary sentences under martial law, and the long internments were sufficient to end most of their activities (see Misztal 1983).

Repression and debate: January–May

Protests, demonstrations and strikes continued through the first half of 1982, though these were scattered, decentralized, and ineffectual.

A demonstration in Poznań on February 13 resulted in the arrest of 194 persons. Strikes or strike preparations were met with arrests of the organizers and dismissal of factory directors. There were some cases of 'terror' as well, though these also were scattered and found little support in the population. The only reported case of a violent act of terror was the murder of a militia man on a Warsaw tram in February.

After the initial shock of marital law had passed, the Solidarity underground began to work out a strategy. About 90 of the 107 members of Solidarity's National Coordinating Commission had been rounded up on December 13, and some others were subsequently apprehended. On January 13, some of the at-large members, including the ranking leader not interned, Zbigniew Bujak, met to establish a Temporary Coordinating Commission (TKK) to direct Solidarity activities until the union could reemerge in its old form. The group called for an end to martial law, the release of all internees, and a commitment by the regime to dialogue with Solidarity's official leadership. The Warsaw Solidarity leadership later declared that negotiations with the regime about possible new unions could only take place with the elected leaders of Solidarity, and that Solidarity insisted on three conditions in any new union structure: democratic elections of its leaders; a regional structure (as Solidarity had been); and reactivization of the statutes passed by Solidarity's First Congress (*Wiadomości*, March 17, 1982). These conditions meant, effectively, that the underground would only accept the return of Solidarity.

Bujak himself was a moderate among the underground oppositionists. He feared the organization of terrorism, and called for the struggle to be peaceful. It was necessary, he said, for Solidarity to organize itself underground, and to be prepared for a long-term struggle. In an interview with John Darnton of the *New York Times* (reported in *The Times* (London), January 18, 1982) he asserted that 'truly independent unions can exist only in conditions of democracy. Thus, to continue and to remain independent, the union must fight for democracy and become its guardian.' He and others signed an 'Occupation Code' which called for Solidarity members to organize underground to provide help to those interned and dismissed from work, to collect and disseminate information about repression and opposition, to engage in passive resistance at work, and to refuse cooperation with the regime and its collaborators (*Wiadomości*, January 15, 1982).

Many Solidarity members followed these suggestions in the first half of 1982, after the initial strikes and demonstrations had proved fruitless. Underground Solidarity units were reconstituted in workplaces all around the country. Dues were secretly collected, and funds disbursed to help the families of the interned and fugitive leaders. The churches also participated in this enterprise, collecting funds and ration cards for those in need.

Almost immediately after martial law, illegal Solidarity brochures began to appear, and by the middle of 1982, there were hundreds of different titles 'published' by various factory organizations and other groups. This was in spite of strict martial law restrictions on the use of photocopying machines (all of which were locked and sealed in the first months of the new regime), and severe penalties for production and distribution of such materials. By April 1982, the underground had even begun broadcasting 'Radio Solidarity' over the airwaves. This program was more a taunting of the authorities than an effective means of communication, as the broadcasts lasted only a few minutes before they were interrupted by jamming. Nevertheless, every Sunday night, thousands of Warsaw residents tuned their radios for this pirate broadcast, as motorized army and militia units with monitoring equipment fanned across the city trying to locate the source of the transmitter.

Many workers also engaged in Bujak's suggested passive resistance, by deliberately slowing down production or simply boycotting official activities. This strategy was potentially most effective among blue-collar workers, and many did initially engage in such activities. A letter from Solidarity workers at the Ursus tractor factory near Warsaw to the workers at Massey-Ferguson in England, for example, asserted that 'the workers of Ursus are adopting passive resistance', and that in the first two weeks after martial law, they had produced only two tractors (*Solidarność Information Bulletin*, January 22, 1982). There were also boycotts of the press by journalists, of the stage by actors, and of filmmaking by actors, actresses and technicians.

During the winter of 1982, though, the military regime appeared to consolidate its power. Solidarity did not manifest its existence, and there was much talk about Solidarity being 'dead'. In this environment, there emerged in the underground challenges to Bujak's conception of building an underground society and preparing for the future. Jacek Kuroń, the interned leader of KOR was the major spokesman for a more activist and confrontational strategy for Solidarity. He argued for building a strong, centralized underground Solidarity for the eventual seizure of power. Kuroń thought that the military authorities would never sit down at the conference table except under pressure of force so Solidarity must demonstrate its ability to bring pressure to bear on the regime. There needed to be *public* demonstrations of society's opposition to the regime.[35] Increasing support for the Kuroń line led to more active forms of demonstration in the spring and summer of 1982.

All during the winter, Solidarity activists had promoted the slogan 'zima wasza, wiosna nasza' (the winter is yours, the spring will be ours). After the initial strikes and demonstrations in December and January, there was little overt political activity. The only 'demonstrations' allowed under martial law were religious processions, so during the winter months, these became a tacit form of solidarity and protest. In Warsaw, tens of thousands of people joined in processions celebrating religious holidays and other events. These often took on political overtones in the homilies of the priests or the hymns and songs of the participants, but they were generally orderly and solemn and did not challenge the regime or confront the police, who kept a low profile at such gatherings.

This suddenly changed at the beginning of May. The first of May is the 'official' workers' holiday celebrated in communist countries. In the past, it had been an occasion for well-organized parades past daises where Party and government leaders looked down on the proceedings. In 1981, in the spirit of democratic renewal, the leaders (First Secretary Stanisław Kania included) had come down off the platforms to march with the workers in a happy and ragtag celebration. A year later, under martial law, Solidarity called for a boycott of the official parade and for Solidarity supporters to attend church services that day instead. In Warsaw, the churches were filled to overflowing at noon that day, and afterwards, tens of thousands of people proceeded to a Solidarity counter-demonstration. This was the first large-scale and overt manifestation of support for Solidarity since early in the year. That day, the militia did not move against the demonstrators.

The Solidarity underground then called for Solidarity's own day of celebration on May 3, the day commemorating Poland's demo-

---

[35] A discussion of the Bujak–Kuroń debate appears in the underground weekly *Tygodnik Wojenny*, May 6, 1982.

cratic constitution of 1791. The official press, on May 2 and 3, warned the population not to participate in these events, and that there would be penalties for those who did. Nevertheless, in Warsaw, thousands of people assembled in the Cathedral of St John in the Old Town, and proceeded from there to a demonstration of support for Solidarity, marching through the center of the city waving banners and flags and chanting slogans of support for the union and its leaders. This time, the ZOMO (motorized riot police) reacted with force, dispersing the crowd with water cannon, tear gas, and truncheons. Hundreds of protestors were arrested. Similar demonstrations and similar results occurred in other cities.

The forceful, often brutal reaction of the police to the May 3 demonstrations dampened the enthusiasm of many people for this strategy of protest. There were more such demonstrations through the summer and fall of 1982, but it seemed that fewer and fewer people were willing to assume the risks of arrest, internment, and job loss that faced those who participated. Increasingly, only the 'die-hard' activists joined the open demonstrations.

The next major planned demonstrations were on August 31, the anniversary of the signing of the Gdańsk Agreements, and November 10, the anniversary of the legal registration of Solidarity. In neither case, though, was the turnout and participation as large as Solidarity activists hoped for. The November 10 events, planned long before by the TKK, were to include an 8-hour nationwide strike and subsequent demonstrations. The results were a disappointment for the Solidarity underground. Strikes were scattered and short in duration, nowhere lasting the whole day. Major demonstrations occurred only in a few cities and were quickly dispersed by the ZOMO.

Both the fact of the illegal demonstrations and the less-than-expected size of the demonstrations, encouraged the Jaruzelski regime to further restrict the union. The Solidarity underground remained committed to a negotiated settlement. A statement from the TKK after the August 31 events asserted that 'agreement remains our goal and the only chance of emerging from the crisis ... Such a nation cannot be ruled by force. If the rulers won't understand this, and if they do not begin talks with the national commission for Solidarity headed by Lech Wałęsa, we may lose the chance for the peaceful resolution of the conflict' (*New York Times*, September 11, 1982). Government spokesman Jerzy Urban responded that, as a result of the continuing protests, 'our opinion of Solidarity leaders is that they are not a good partner for talks', foreclosing any remaining possibility of negotiation. Soon thereafter, the regime formally banned Solidarity and instituted new trade unions more directly under government and Party control.

In the aftermath of the demonstrations of May and August, many Solidarity supporters returned to the passive resistance strategy advocated by Bujak. Many people continued to extinguish their lights briefly in the evenings on the thirteenth of every month, to boycott the press on Wednesdays, and to take walks during the evening news. There were other non-confrontational forms of protest as well. In Warsaw's Victory Square one night, for example, someone replaced one of the pavement stones with a plaque commemorating the miners who had been killed at the Wujek mine on December 16, 1981. The plaque was removed the next day by the authorities, of course, but for weeks after that, people would decorate the spot where the plaque had been with flowers, candles, chunks of coal, and an occasional Solidarity sign. Each night, the authorities would clear all this away, but the next day, new flowers, candles and signs would gradually accumulate. Finally, the authorities closed off the square completely, 'for repairs'.

By the end of 1982, it had become clear that the regime was not going to accommodate the demands of the Solidarity underground, and that the public was becoming weary of strikes and demonstrations that appeared to yield few results. After the disappointing November 10 protests, and the regime's subsequent release from internment of Lech Wałęsa, the TKK called off any further protest action for the rest of the year. The TKK statement, signed by Zbigniew Bujak of Warsaw, Władysław Hardek of Kraków, Bogdan Lis of Gdańsk and others, said the policy statement was a result of 'a new political situation in Poland'. With the apparent failure of the November 10 strikes, the release of Wałęsa, the prospect of the lifting of martial law, and the population's weariness with protests, the underground needed to reassess its strategy.

At the same time, the population increasingly supported a less confrontational strategy of developing an 'underground society' and working within the system to achieve smaller scale goals. Wałęsa himself suggested that the movement 'loosen up a bit' and concentrate on four main areas: factory work; the development of factory self-management councils; a struggle against censorship by keeping alive independent organizations of artists, writers and intellectuals; and the development of various programs for young people (*New York Times*, December 23, 1982, p. 6). All of these were legal activities, within the framework of the 'renewal' promised by the martial law regime. Instead of the all or nothing approach advocated by the more radical Solidarity supporters, which so far had achieved mostly nothing, Wałęsa was arguing for trying to make the best of a bad situation.

The position of the intellectuals and the church

The intellectual community was largely unanimous in censoring martial law, but divided on how to react to it. As noted above, many writers, journalists and artists refused to participate in regime-sponsored activities after December 13, adopting an implicit strategy of nonviolent resistance and non-cooperation. The unspoken assumption behind this strategy was that the regime could not survive without the support, or at least the neutrality, of the intelligentsia. Others felt that if moderates in the intellectual community refused to cooperate with the regime, policies would be dominated by bureaucrats and hard-liners, who would eliminate all of the gains of 1981. The division between these two groups was a bitter one: the regime referred to the dissidents as 'the internal emigration' while the latter branded those who cooperated as 'collaborators'.

The Jaruzelski regime moved quickly to bring intellectuals, and particularly the universities, into line. The academic community had been a major source of protest at the end of 1981, and many universities had been on strike during the last months of the year. In the first months of martial law, the regime dismissed a number of university rectors (chancellors) who had been most closely associated with Solidarity and the reform movement. Many of these had been elected by the faculty under new democratic procedures adopted in 1981. The dismissal of the University of Warsaw's rector, Henryk Samsonowicz, was met by almost unanimous opposition from the deans and faculty of that university. First the deans, then the faculty senate, then the faculties of most major departments, addressed letters to the Minister of Education, protesting Samsonowicz's dismissal. There were some short and symbolic strikes of students and faculty as well. The faculty, by adopting a common front, was also able to block any significant purge of the university community during 1982.[36] In this case, the issue was one of academic freedom and autonomy more than support for Solidarity as such. Consequently, the university community was virtually unanimous on these issues.

On political matters, however there were deep divisions. Many intellectuals refused to write for official publications, and others were prohibited from having their material appear. Others who adopted a more moderate stance were allowed to make statements that were mildly critical of the authorities. Jan Szczepański, Polands most eminent sociologist, who became chairman of one of the government's new advisory councils, spoke against the tendency to identify Solidarity with 'opposition groups' outside the union. 'Solidarity brought together millions of people who were concerned that the slogans of social justice, respect for dignity, and co-participation in decision-making on public affairs, the same slogans which were marked on the flags of socialism, were really accomplished' *Życie Warszawy*, May 6, 1982). Janusz Reykowski, a prominent psychologist, made a similar argument for understanding the appeal of Solidarity in a paper presented first to a closed meeting of Party members, and later published in the official *Tu i Teraz*. One of the most interesting cases of the accommodationist position was Andrzej Tymowski, a Warsaw sociologist and advisor to Solidarity from the very beginning (during the Szczecin strikes). In June 1982, while he still considered himself a Solidarity advisor, he participated in a lengthy interview with the weekly *Polityka* (June 12, 1982). At that time, many Solidarity supporters were refusing to *buy* that publication, much less write for it. Tymowski, on the other hand, argued that, as an 'expert', he was obliged to provide honest advice to whomever asked for it; that the scientist was not responsible for the use to which his advice is put. 'Not to participate', said Tymowski, 'is to have no influence.' At the same time, he was forthright in his recommendations: the regime must create democratic institutions, representative of 'real social forces'.

The debate over resistance versus accommodation was also evident in the Roman Catholic Church. Many parish priests were quite vocal in their opposition to martial law, and often criticized the regime in blunt terms in their Sunday homilies. Churches often acted as starting points for Solidarity demonstrations and havens for

[36] For a description of these events in the university, see Mason (1983c).

those on the run from the ZOMO. They also exhibited their own forms of protest. On Easter weekend, for example, when every church has a display depicting the tomb of Christ, there were numerous blatantly political statements. One such display depicted outlines of bodies lying dead or bleeding on a black pavement underneath Christ's tomb. Each body was marked with a different date: 1956, 1968, 1970, 1976, 1980, 1981. The last figure had blood oozing from the head. Other churches had Solidarity banners draped around the altar, or included in the tomb display.

The Polish episcopate was not quite so overtly supportive of Solidarity, but frequently called for the release of internees, respect for human rights, and a 'dialogue between the authorities and society'. In such discussions, said a May communique from the bishops, there must be a place for the labor unions, without whose voice it would be impossible to plan an effective and realistic renewal. ('Komunikat ze 184 Konferencji Episkopatu Polski'). This communique was reported in the Polish press, though the reference to the labor unions was omitted.

Archbishop Glemp was also critical of the restrictions and violence of the martial law regime. Nevertheless, he himself was often criticized by Solidarity supporters for not being more vocal in his criticisms of the regime and his support for the union. After the May demonstrations, for example, Glemp was quoted in the official press as criticizing the 'manipulation of patriotic feelings' of young people, and cautioning them to 'keep out of the disputes of older people'. 'One needs no wisdom to throw stones at another man', said the Archbishop (*Trybuna Ludu*, May 10, 1982). Solidarity supporters found this homily offensive in that it did not level equal criticism at the use of violent force by the ZOMO on the other side; but as Glemp later told a Western journalist, his primary motive was to help avoid violence and bloodshed in the tense atmosphere of martial law.

My first task after martial law was to avoid bloodshed, to prevent violent revolution . . . And I think we were helpful in attaining that end. We do not want there to be the creation of an underground of terrorists. We want to work toward a national reconciliation to help to breach the terrible and increasing gap between the government and the people (quoted in N. Darnton 1982, p. 23).

In this respect, Glemp's position sounds similar to that of Tymowski, and even of Wałęsa at the end of 1982.

In early November, several days before Solidarity's scheduled strike, Glemp met with Jaruzelski and issued a communique setting the June 1983 date for the Pope's visit to Poland and calling for 'peace, social order and also honest work' (deWeydenthal, Porter and Devlin 1983, p. 273). At the end of that month, in one of his sermons, Glemp called on radio and television performers to end their year-long boycott of the official media. Early in December, Glemp held several meetings with parish priests to explain the new position of the Church, which apparently included a disassociation from the cause of the free trade union movement. In answering criticism from some priests, Glemp contended that the Church was in no position to help restore Solidarity as such; rather, the Church would work to uphold the democratic ideals that Solidarity had promoted (Stefanowski 1983, p. 179). The accommodationist position seemed to be winning out over the resistance one.

THE REGIME'S RESPONSE

The declining support for Solidarity's protests at the end of 1982 led the regime to adopt a more confident and forceful approach to the union. The authorities pursued a two-track strategy: increasing its criticism of the TKK leadership, attempting to isolate the underground from the population; and relaxing some of the restrictions of martial law. On October 8, the Sejm formally disbanded all former trade unions, including Solidarity, and established the framework for new factory level trade unions. At the 10th Plenum of the Party's Central Committee on October 28, General Jaruzelski criticized 'subversive foreign centers and the anti socialist underground' for their planned protest actions which he said were aimed at undermining the economy and the process of normalization. He said that 'the duration of martial law will be determined by the situation, and the situation will be determined by the people' (Stefanowski 1983, p. 157).

The day after the November 10 protests, it was announced that Lech Wałęsa would be released. The regime, apparently feeling confident that the Solidarity underground had played its last card, moved toward easing martial law. On December 19, the Council of State approved the formal suspension of martial law, to take effect on December 31.

On December 30, in one final effort to discredit the Solidarity underground on the eve of the suspension of martial law, Warsaw radio broadcast tape recordings of secret meetings of the underground leaders. The tapes revealed serious divisions among the underground leaders on the direction Solidarity should pursue. Bogdan Lis, the Gdańsk leader, admitted that people were tired of strikes and demonstrations and argued for a 'ceasefire' with the authorities. Besides the demoralizing content of the tapes, the very fact of their existence was also a blow to the underground, suggesting that its security had been breached. The Solidarity underground seemed to be both divided and defeated.

SOCIETY'S MOOD IN THE AFTERMATH OF MARTIAL LAW

Only in 1983 did there begin to appear reports indicating the depths of public malaise in the aftermath of Solidarity and martial law. A survey of youth attitudes conducted in May of 1982 showed far fewer young people than before willing to support the ideals of socialism (Gołębiowski 1983). When asked if 'the world ought to develop in the direction of socialism', only half answered positively, compared to 78% in 1977 (see Table 3.3), while 28% responded negatively, compared to only 8% in the earlier survey. Another youth survey at the end of 1982 yielded similar results and led one analyst (Nowacki 1983) to suggest that this was a 'new generation' with different behavior patterns and political attitudes from previous generations of young people; 'They are suspicious of all public institutions and important persons.' It was clear that the shock of martial law had led to widespread disillusionment with the official ideology and institutions among a large and crucial sector of Polish society.

With Solidarity banned and the official institutions discredited, there was little sense of hope for improvements in Poland after 1981. A late 1983 survey asked respondents if they had learned anything recently which had caused them to be anxious about the fate of the country. Three quarters of the sample answered yes. On a similar question about hopeful signs, the same percentage saw none. Most people expected no basic changes in Poland before the year 2000. Of those who did, only half expected positive changes (Goban-Klas 1984). Two years after the declaration of martial law, there were few optimists in Poland.

Other surveys in 1982 and 1983, even official ones, reported widespread alienation, apathy and hopelessness. A survey on 'social behavior' by the Party's IPPML found a popular sense that 'interpersonal relations have grown extremely brutal' and a perception of recent growth in bribery, callousness, greed, drug abuse, drunkenness, red tape, profits drawn from informal relations, logrolling, and crime (Engel 1984). Poland's traditional values of community and generosity were also threatened. A large majority of those polled believed that 'openness in stating one's opinion, willingness to make sacrifices for the public good, and generosity' had become rare in Polish society. In the face of all of these problems, people felt passive or helpless:

people who claim they are passive with regard to social ills justify their passivity either by helplessness ('What can I do by myself?', 'This is more than I can deal with') or by fear of the consequences in view of past experiences ('When I was young, I took many risks, but now I don't want to get knocked down, my health and family are more important').

A 1983 survey of workers in industrial enterprises found a similar downbeat mood (Sarapata 1984). Many workers, in fact, refused to talk at all with the interviewers. Most who did complained that they had no influence in their workplaces, despite the erstwhile economic reforms. Employee willingness to work hard was declining. In short, wrote the sociologist in charge of this survey, 'apathy and disenchantment are spreading'. 'The official view', he wrote, 'is that the current situation (inside the factories) is better than it was a year or a year and a half ago. This is a mistaken belief.'

The government had hopes that the new institutions of its economic reform program, the new trade unions and employee self-management, would eventually lead to greater support and participation by the workers. Such support, however, was low and grudging. The new unions did attract some four million members by the end of 1983, but this was less than half the membership Solidarity had enjoyed, and many of those who did join were not enthusiastic. A 1983 survey by the new Centrum Badania Opinii Publicznej (CBOP) found just 60% of the *members* of the new trade unions believing the new trade union legislation to be 'democratic and assuring broad rights for the trade unions'. Only a fifth of non-members assessed the law positively (*Nowe Drogi*, October 1983). Both members and non-members saw widespread distrust and skepticism that the new unions would genuinely represent the interests of the workers. Even many of the members of the new unions (25%) were in favor of reactivating all of the old trade unions, including Solidarity.

Workers were even less interested in 'employee self-management' and factory work councils which had been promoted by Solidarity, temporarily suspended under martial law, and then reactivated. An early 1983 survey on self-management by the Party's IPPML found that only a quarter of the workforce was supportive of enterprise self-management (Malak 1983). In every case, a small minority felt they had any influence in management decisions, *wanted* to participate in such decisions, or even knew who their representatives were on the work councils.

Much of this negative mood was due to the popular antipathy toward the martial law regime and its 'reform' institutions. However, it also reflects a return of some degree of authoritarianism in Polish society that had been in evidence even in the days of Solidarity. The IPPML poll mentioned above detected a strong sense of the need for a 'trustee method of governing' in spite of the regime's attempt to foster participation in the trade unions and self-government. In that survey nearly three-quarters of the sample agreed 'that people are mostly interested in being well governed'. One sees this in particular cases as well. When a May 1983 OBOP poll on the economic reform asked who should determine the prices of manufactured goods, 54% selected 'the government only' compared to 19% who said 'partly the government and partly the enterprises, as at present' and only 11% for the enterprises alone (*Polityka*, September 30, 1983).

The popular mood of resignation, apathy, and disengagement is understandable after the exhilaration and disruptions of 1981 and the devastation and depression of 1982. After one year of martial law, it was clear to most people that Solidarity would not return, at least in the short term. Surveys of young people, for example, showed the vast majority expecting 'the opposition' to pursue extended activity in Poland. By 1983 only about 10% thought there were favorable conditions for such activity (*Rzeczpospolita*, July 20, 1983). At the same time, few people expected any genuine political or economic reforms to emanate from the top of the political structure. Without the opportunity for meaningful participation, most people retreated from public life, and turned their attention to protecting their own personal or family interests.

Indeed, after the flood of participation and hope in 1981, Poland now was overcome by anomie. Anomie has been defined (MacIver 1950, p. 84) as: 'the state of mind of one who has been pulled up by his moral roots ... The anomic man has become spiritually sterile, responsive only to himself, responsible to no one. He lives on the thin line of sensation between no future and no past.' All of this aptly applied to Poland in 1983. Poles had been pulled up by their roots with the crushing of Solidarity. The regime had destroyed Solidarity, but had also discredited itself, and the socialist ideology from which it claimed legitimacy. Poland, once again, had been cut off from its past, and faced a future without promise.

CONCLUSIONS

The year 1982 was one of depression punctuated by the temporary exhilaration of mass protests and strikes. At the beginning of the year, Poles were hostile toward the martial law authorities, and angry about the loss of their union and its leaders, but there was also a widespread sense of resignation. The economy had deteriorated to such a point at the end of 1981 that many Poles no longer had time for politics. The initial thrill of popular power and participation at the beginning of the year had given way under the grind of daily life, so when martial law was declared, most people were too tired and weary to respond.

The spring of 1982 saw some revival of the spirit of protest, caused partly by the slightly improved economic situation and also, no doubt, by the weather. The May 1 protest was largely spontaneous, happy, and optimistic. The police let them demonstrate. On May 3, though, the protests were confrontational and violent. Over 1300 protestors were detained by the police, and most of them were tried and sentenced. The protests were no longer a lark, and henceforth, fewer and fewer people were willing to join in them. When it became clear that the authorities meant business, and that they would not tolerate the kinds of strikes and demonstrations that Solidarity had led in 1981, even more people resigned from the political field.

By the end of the year, the declining support for the TKK and the increasing confidence of the regime led the government to formally ban Solidarity and formally suspend martial law. It seemed that the regime had calculated correctly that a forceful policy on the part of the regime would contribute to the psychological exhaustion of the population and allow the termination of the troublesome union. Instead of confronting the regime, many Poles adopted psychological defense mechanisms such as resignation, withdrawal, or despair (Misztal 1983).

While the regime could stop the participation of the masses, it could not end their belief in the ideals of Solidarity. As T. G. Ash (1983b, p. 279) has said, 'beyond the single monumental organisational fact of Solidarity's existence, the most fundamental changes were all in the realm of consciousness rather than being'. He characterizes the events of 1980–1 as 'a revolution of the soul'. Most Poles still supported the ideals of Solidarity, if not the organization itself. A considerable proportion of the population continued passive forms of protest and supported the idea of building an underground society. In the face of power, force, and terror, Poles had retreated from idealism to realism, and were biding their time. But the idea of Solidarity remained alive. The independent self-governing trade union had been the first genuinely representative institution in Poland in 35 years. It upheld principles and values that were cherished by the vast majority of the population. For sixteen months, Solidarity tried to build a society in accord with those values. The martial law regime was able to crush the organization, but it could not eliminate the idea of Solidarity.

9

Conclusions

Public opinion and public opinion surveys played an important political role in the events of 1980–1982. Before 1980, public opinion as such had never played a major role in the Polish political process except through the medium of public protests, as in 1956, 1970 and 1976. With the creation of Solidarity and the opening up of Polish society after August 1980, public opinion was more directly heard both through Solidarity and through public opinion research. In fact, Solidarity was a necessary vehicle for public opinion to have influence. As James Oliver (1969) has pointed out, in order for public opinion to have an impact, there need to be autonomous groups to aggregate and process societal demands into a program that can serve as an alternative to that of those in power. Without such groups, the demands are processed within the political system, reducing the pressures of public opinion on the authorities. Solidarity provided such a channel.

At first Solidarity was able to point to public opinion polls as evidence of the overwhelming support that the movement enjoyed. Indeed, in the early exciting months of the strikes and the formation of the union, Solidarity was exceedingly popular. During 1981, however, a number of factors contributed to the erosion of the early unanimity in Polish society, putting the public opinion data up for grabs in the political arena. As it became clear that Solidarity could not accomplish everything that it promised, some of the luster and charisma of the movement began to wear off. During 1981, political tensions increased and the economy continued to deteriorate, leading many people to wish for a more peaceful and stable environment. The rapid growth in Solidarity, and the multiplication of its activities, inevitably led to factions and divisions within the organization, putting stress on the solidarity that brought it to life in the first place.

All of these tendencies became apparent through survey data, particularly as the surveys became more sophisticated and more penetrating. Some of the early public opinion surveys simply asked about the level of support for Solidarity, without examining the sources of such support. The lopsided responses in the surveys in late 1980 made it difficult to discover differences based on occupation, political affiliation and other social and economic characteristics. By the middle of 1981, partially because of the changes in public opinion, and partially due to the improved size, representativeness and sophistication of the surveys, the divisions and complexity in public opinion became more evident.

By the end of 1981, both the regime and Solidarity were able to use public opinion surveys to bolster their positions. Solidarity could point to the continued strong support for the union and for its most important demands. The regime could use survey data to show the population's declining support for Solidarity, its willingness to assign Solidarity part of the blame for Poland's continuing crisis, and the significant amount of support for more 'law and order' in society. It seems likely that the Jaruzelski regime relied on these data not only for propaganda purposes, but also in making the decision on martial law. Jaruzelski justified martial law as a response to the civil strife and economic disorder in the country and to the politicization and radicalization of Solidarity. All of these were factors of concern to the population, as reflected in the public opinion surveys. As both Solidarity and many sociologists later pointed out, however, the forceful response of martial law was not what society expected or wanted. After the imposition of martial law, public opinion research was much more circumscribed and the results were much less frequently made public. As before 1980, the regime could once again control all aspects of public opinion research.

This was the kind of situation to which the regime was accustomed. Before 1980, the authorities had not had to deal with, and counter, the claims of public opinion. Since all of the media, including public opinion research institutes, were controlled by the authorities, public opinion itself could be defined and shaped by the authorities. After August, this was no longer the case, and the authorities were forced to deal with public opinion as an autonomous political variable. The demands of Solidarity, in conjunction with the claims of public opinion, created a certain 'demand overload' on the Polish political system. As David Easton (1965, p. 120) has pointed out, this can threaten a political system that is 'compelled to try to process a greater volume of business than its organization permitted'. The Polish Party and government were simply not equipped to cope with the outpouring of uncontrolled demands from society.

Typically, a political system can regulate and manage such stress by relying on 'diffuse support', a reserve of good will toward the system, or by obtaining 'specific support' through demand satisfaction, structural change, or coercion (Easton 1965, pp. 124–6; Devine 1972, p. 28). By the end of 1981, the Jaruzelski regime was unable or unwilling to use any but the last of these options. Any good will toward the system had washed away with the emergence of Solidarity and the regime's intransigence toward the union's demands. The economy was so depressed by the end of 1981 that the regime could hardly afford to meet any more economic demands. This reduced the alternatives to structural change or coercion. A change in the structure of the system would have meant granting Solidarity a role in governmental decision-making, or perhaps allowing the emergence of genuine political parties to contest the role of the PZPR. Either of these options would have provided channels for the burgeoning expression of public opinion, and therefore reduced the overload on the government and the Party. But they would also have jeopardized the (already weakened) leading role of the Party, something the regime, and the Soviets, were unwilling to sanction. By resorting to coercion, the regime temporarily eliminated the demand overload and the pressures of public opinion, but the basic problems remained. Coercion is not a technique that can be used forever. As Samuel Huntington (1970, p. 44) has argued, 'in an established single-party system, as in a democratic, competitive party system, political stability is measured by the degree to which the system possesses the institutional channels for transforming dissenters into participants'. In Poland, the regime seems intent on excluding the dissenters from the political process altogether. Given the number of such people, this solution cannot be a long term one.

The public opinion data from Poland support many of the generalizations about public opinion and political culture drawn from Western countries. Political attitudes in Poland were unstable, and subject to change under the impact of events. Support for strikes, for example, diminished sharply during 1981 as the economy continued to deteriorate. The overwhelmingly positive image of Solidarity weakened somewhat during 1981 for the same reason as people came to feel that the union was partly to blame for the continuing crisis. Certainly some of these changes were a result of the deliberate effort to manipulate public opinion by the regime through the official media, which harped on the damaging effects of the strikes and the intransigence and radicalization of the Solidarity leadership. However, since most Poles had access to Solidarity publications and other unofficial media, and were highly skeptical of the official media, the changes in public opinion cannot be explained entirely as a result of official propaganda. In fact, the strikes were disruptive, and economic and social tensions did increase during 1981, and this had a direct impact on popular perceptions and attitudes.

Studies of public opinion in the West have generally found that while specific attitudes change quite easily, more basic beliefs will remain more stable (Almond and Verba 1980). In Poland, however, even some basic beliefs and orientations seem to have changed, especially under the impact of martial law. All through Poland's postwar experience, for example, support for the ideals (if not the practice) of socialism remained strong. After the imposition of martial law, however, there appears to have been a fundamental decline in support of this value. In the long term, this may turn out to be a temporary deviation from the norm, and an expression of popular distaste for all things connected with the regime that crushed Solidarity. There is considerable evidence, however, that this is a fundamental change in the political culture of Poland. The rejection of socialism is particularly strong among young people, who previously had been the strongest supporters of this ideal. The regime has recognized this problem: at a 1983 Party conference on ideological problems, one eminent ideologist talked of an 'ideological crisis' manifested in 'the undermining of the faith of a large part of the Polish society in the value of socialist ideals and socialism itself' (*Nowe Drogi*, October 1983). One reason for this was the interruption of the process of political socialization during the sixteen months of Solidarity. As another speaker at the same party conference contended, during 1981 'the teachers were not teaching history to youth; instead they taught it how to strike'. He also complained about the continuing strength of 'the Catholics' in schools 'on a scale that simply cannot be compared with the pre-war scale'. 'This is a bitter pill', he admitted.

Political socialization is the process by which political attitudes and values are transmitted from one generation to the next. This has always been a weak point in the Polish political system, but seems to have virtually collapsed in the years since 1980. During the Solidarity era, young people were flooded with a whole new set of values regarding openness, participation, political debate, and democracy. Since December 1981, discussion of these ideas in the schools has continued, though on a lesser scale and partly 'underground'. Perhaps more importantly, the role of the Church and Roman Catholic values have become more important, both because of the Church's support of Solidarity during 1980–1 and since then because the Church is now the only widely popular institution in Poland. So, as the regime has continued difficulties in propagating and inculcating official values in the young people, the chain of cultural transmission is broken. Even some of Poland's basic political values are subject to change.

At the same time, as noted in Chapter 8, there is a widespread sense of anomie in Polish society in the aftermath of martial law. Robert Merton(1957, pp. 162–3) sees anomie as the result of:

a breakdown in the cultural structure, occurring particularly when there is an acute disjunction between the cultural norms and goals and the socially structured capacities of members of the group to act in accord with them ... When the cultural and the social structure are malintegrated, the first calling for behavior and attitudes which the second precludes, there is a strain toward the breakdown of the norms, toward normlessness.

Solidarity had helped align the cultural and social structures in Poland, by creating an institution that genuinely reflected the values of most Poles. Martial law abruptly broke that link, once again setting societal norms at odds with the official ones. Many Poles now lost the inclination to be involved in or attentive toward politics. Public opinion polls after martial law show high degrees of pessimism, bewilderment, alienation, anxiety, hostility, and a sense of political futility, which are all associated with anomie (McClosky 1969). This is not an environment conducive to reconciliation and renewal, as the authorities seem to hope. From the regime's point of view, though, apathy and anomie is better than opposition. At the moment, this may be the most the regime can expect.

THE ENDURING CONSEQUENCES OF SOLIDARITY

Solidarity, in promoting the principles of egalitarianism, participation, and non-violence, incorporated the most important values of Polish society. The organization represented the goals and interests of Poles as no other organization had; it became, therefore, a symbol as well as an institution. The institution itself was vital in the effort to make permanent the gains of August 1980. In the past, the gains from worker protests had been ephemeral. The regime had promised change, and then gradually moved away from those promises. This time, the workers in Gdańsk and Szczecin insisted on an independent trade union to guarantee the implementation of the Gdańsk Agreements. The banning of the union meant an end to the compact, and the end of any institutionalized pressure on the regime to keep its part of the bargain.

As a symbol, though, Solidarity remains alive. The union brought out into the open the concerns, goals, and values of the Polish population, and held the official institutions to account. It showed once and for all the hollowness of the regime's propaganda about the unity, health and optimism of Polish society. It forced the leadership and the Party to admit that the reality of Polish life did not live up to the ideals of socialism and democracy. It exposed cynicism, corruption, greed, and the manipulation of power in the political system. Solidarity raised and aired the most sensitive and critical questions relating to Poland's destiny: the nature of socialism; the role of the Party; the role of religion and the Church; and Poland's relationship with the Soviet Union. On all of these issues, the public was allowed to express its views, both through Solidarity and other institutions (even the Party), but also through public opinion surveys. Poles were able to voice their opinions, and see them reflected in the media and in political debates. The regime could no longer claim that it represented the interests of the workers or society, or that Poles were united on all important issues. The polls, and the political process, showed otherwise. So while the institution of Solidarity may have been crushed with martial law, the idea of Solidarity and the experiences of those sixteen months remain with Poles. Henceforth, they will be a factor in the Polish political process, whether the regime likes it or not.

The events of 1980–2 and the public opinion polls reveal other things about Polish society as well. Poles wanted a more open society which would include room for a freer press, greater pluralism in the political arena, and more participation by workers and citizens in decision-making in the factory and the community. Each of these changes was a challenge to the regime and to the status quo. On the other hand, Poles supported, or at least accepted, many of the institutional· and ideological features of the postwar political system. They generally supported the principles of socialism, particularly the elements of egalitarianism and social welfare. Many Poles accepted the leading role of the communist party in the political system, though they rejected the monopoly of power by that organization. There was even a grudging recognition of the necessity of Poland's alliance with the Soviet Union, and even substantial support for that relationship. In sum, while Poles wanted serious and far-reaching reform in their society, they recognized the limits to those changes.

A major reason for this realistic appraisal of the limits of change was the strong and widespread interest in economic issues. Economic difficulties and price increases had sparked the 1980 protests in the first place, and economic issues maintained their prominence all through the Solidarity era and beyond. As Renata Siemieńska (1982) has pointed out, the relationship between the masses and the leadership in socialist societies is determined primarily by 'the extent of need satisfaction on a national scale', and these needs are mainly material and economic ones. When the Polish regime failed on this count, the workers created Solidarity. Solidarity's leadership was also held to the same standards. While the workers could be more forgiving and patient of their own organization, they also expected an improvement in the economy and the standard of living. For most Poles, Solidarity and popular participation in decision-making were only *instruments* for achieving the larger goal of an economic system that was more successful and more equitable. The principle of participation was never a value ranked as highly as economic well being or a more just (e.g. equitable) social order. When, at the end of 1981, these values seemed as elusive as they had been a year earlier, popular enthusiasm for Solidarity began to diminish somewhat. It was becoming clear that there were no easy

solutions to Poland's economic problems, and that greater democracy was not by itself going to solve these problems.

The ideal of participation *had* become the principal goal of many
of Solidarity's leaders, however. This was to be expected. As the
union matured and began to develop a cadre of leaders, their
primary interests became political ones. For many of them, pluralism and political participation was a necessary prerequisite for
economic change. They were probably correct in this assessment,
but the kinds of reforms that they envisaged went far beyond what
most Poles wanted. Major political reforms were a long-term
process. In putting the political issues ahead of the economic ones,
Solidarity leaders ran two risks. On the one hand, they risked losing
the support of an impatient public that saw the political issues
interfering with the (more important) economic ones. On the other
hand, in pressing the political issues, they risked frightening an
insecure regime into a forceful response. In the end, Solidarity lost
on both counts. Support for the Solidarity leadership waned and the
Party leadership, sensing this, moved to crack down on the movement.

Solidarity wrestled all during its existence with an identity
problem. This is evident both from the public opinion polls and from
the in depth interviews with Solidarity activists conducted by Alain
Touraine's group of sociologists. Solidarity members and activists
were unsure whether Solidarity was a trade union, a social movement, or even a political party. In fact, the organization at times
played all three roles, which were often conflicting. Even as a trade
union, Solidarity sometimes acted as a militant Western style union
'putting forward impossible economic demands', and sometimes as
a genuine socialist-type union and 'potential partner in government'
(Nuti 1982, pp. 39–40). In part, this confusion of self-identity was
due to the lack of experience in the formation of independent
organizations. As some Solidarity leaders pointed out, Solidarity
was inherently political, for the simple reason that its existence
challenged the monopoly of power of the Party. Since the Party
treated Solidarity as a challenger and a threat, and behaved toward
it in that way, Solidarity necessarily acquired some characteristics of
a political opposition just to defend itself. In doing so, it jeopardized
its trade union functions of promoting the interests of the workers in
their factories. Solidarity was more than a trade union, but less than
a political party. It represented a large number of interests, and

lobbied on issues that were not always related to living standards and workplace conditions. In that sense, the organization was like a large Western interest group. The difference between an interest group and a political party is that the latter attempts to put its people into public office. This Solidarity did not attempt. Most Poles and most Solidarity members favored new elections, but were opposed to Solidarity creating a political party, or to the creation of any new political parties. Most members of the union favored a retraction of Solidarity's activities to the narrower boundaries of a trade union. Given these pressures, over time this probably would have happened, and the regime might not have found it necessary to take such drastic action.

One of the most disturbing elements of this whole period, for both Solidarity and the authorities, was the open manifestation of political conflict. In the closed and monocentric political systems of Eastern Europe, political conflict is hidden from view, and restricted to the governing elite. Solidarity, in acting as an alternative center of power and authority, brought political conflict out into the open. This was unsettling all around. The workers, now given an institutional forum for confronting the authorities, were uncertain of the rules of the game. In the past, they had won concessions only by acting outside official and legal channels, through protests, strikes and demonstrations. Their successes had been won through confrontation and obstinacy. They assumed that nothing could be achieved without threats. The men and women who were thrust into positions of leadership in Solidarity were workers with this kind of background. With few exceptions, they had no political experience, and therefore were not used to the political practice of bargaining and compromise. Consequently, Solidarity's demands were often extreme and uncompromising. When the union's leaders found the authorities unwilling to accept their initial demands, they accused them of bad faith, further poisoning the relationship between them. In this respect, at least, Solidarity's leaders were out of touch with their supporters. As 1981 wore on, Poles increasingly came to accept the necessity of compromise and to fault both Solidarity and the regime for lack of progress.

The Party elite had similar problems with bargaining and compromise. With a monopoly of power, the Party had never before bargained with the workers. Even when forced to grant concessions or make political changes in 1956 and 1970, when the stimulus for change came from outside the Party, the direction and pace of the changes were determined from within. With the birth of Solidarity, the Party had lost the initiative; it was now Solidarity that was the leading force in society. So the Party was not only uncomfortable with the new rules, as Solidarity was, but also felt threatened by them. The legitimacy of the organization was based on its claim of representing all forces in society and in being the guiding force in the political system. Feeling threatened, the Party leadership was even less willing to compromise, fearing further erosion of its power, image and legitimacy.

The year 1981 also saw unprecedented divisions and conflict within both the Party and Solidarity. The Party leadership was more willing to tolerate political conflict within the organization than outside it; inside, it was easier to control. The result was unprecedented change and reform of Party leadership, rules and policies. Party members were exposed to an unprecedented degree of political debate and political conflict both inside and outside the organization. Much of the initiative for change in the Party came from the grass roots; this also was a new phenomenon and an experience that remains with the Party.

Solidarity also experienced, perhaps unexpectedly, the divisions of political conflict. Initially, the very name of the organization symbolized the unity and common purpose of the nation. However, almost as soon as the union was formed, there emerged divisions on which policies Solidarity should press, which tactics should be used, whether to focus on local or national concerns, or whether to stress political or economic goals. These differences were not just attitudinal. To a large extent, the differences coincided with social and occupational distinctions. As Frank Parkin has pointed out, efforts to gain power 'of a purely class nature are especially difficult to sustain on the industrial front because of the tendency towards fragmentation along occupational lines' (Parkin 1979, p. 81). Indeed, after the initial flush of excited support for Solidarity's program of economic welfare and political participation, the workers began to divide on these issues. The relatively highly paid skilled workers tended to favor the political elements of Solidarity's program for broader participation from the factory to the national level. Unskilled workers, more poorly paid and still struggling to make ends meet, were more concerned with the purely economic issues. As the economy and standard of living continued to deteriorate, they were more likely to favor a return to stability and order and to focus on solving the immediate economic problems.

All of this conflict, within Solidarity and the Party and between Solidarity and the regime, was a healthy, if short-lived, process for Poland. Political conflict is a necessary concomitant of a pluralist political system. For a while, Poland experienced pluralism, and became acquainted with open political and social conflict. In most cases, this conflict was manifested in legitimate, legal, and peaceful ways. Such conflict raised and opened issues for public discussion as never before in Poland. The discourse was sophisticated and penetrating, touching on the most important issues of Poland's politics, its place in Europe, and even of human nature. Few societies anywhere have undergone such a fundamental assessment of their past and future. For Poland, this was a trial run with democracy.

1980–1: SOCIETY IN CONTROL

The years 1980–2 in Poland were unprecedented for the Soviet bloc and have left a permanent mark on the regimes of that area. The events of these years were unique in several key respects. For the first time in Eastern Europe, workers used the strike to wrest major concessions from the Party leadership. In the past, workers in Poland and elsewhere in Eastern Europe had engaged in short protest strikes and street demonstrations to force political and economic changes. In Poland, in fact, riots and demonstrations had become almost a legitimate form for the expression of demands by the workers and for achieving political change. In the summer of 1980, however, workers for the first time relied exclusively on the strike to achieve their demands. The technique was not only effective, but highly embarrassing to a regime that claimed to be acting on behalf of the workers. A general strike in a socialist state was an ideological and political anomaly.

The summer strikes were also unprecedented in the scope of the demands from the workers. In the demonstrations of 1956, 1970 and 1976, Polish workers had put forward largely economic demands. The political issues were secondary, and fit within the existing parameters of the system; e.g. demands for the strengthening of workers' councils. In 1980, however, the workers went beyond such limits, and intruded into the political arena in demanding the creation of an independent and self-governing trade union. Solidarity was the first independent trade union in the communist world. Even more, it was the first officially sanctioned independent organization of any kind in the Soviet bloc. In societies where the communist party has a constitutional role as the 'leading force in society', the Polish United Workers' Party in fact relinquished this leading role to Solidarity. In doing so, the whole nature of the political system was changed and challenged.

The formation of Solidarity unleashed many other changes in Polish society. The 'renewal' that swept through Poland affected not only the political system, but also economic management, the arts, the media and the Church. Censorship was relaxed, at first spontaneously and unofficially, then legally with a new censorship law in the fall of 1981. The freer atmosphere in the press allowed a remarkably open discussion of political, social, economic, and cultural issues. The movement toward a more open official press was accelerated by the enormous quantity of unofficial publications, many published by local or factory Solidarity organizations, which were completely free of censorship. As more and more people came to read and rely on Solidarity publications for information, the official press was forced to become more honest simply in order to compete with the unofficial press.

The increased availability and diversity of information and ideas stimulated public discussion and popular participation in the political arena. Membership in Solidarity expanded at a phenomenal rate until it included some nine million members. This made the organization one of the largest trade unions in the world; as a proportion of the population, it was probably the largest independent trade union anywhere. Membership in Solidarity was not a passive act. Most of those who joined were involved, at least in the early months, in Solidarity meetings, discussion groups, publishing and other activities. Factory level Solidarity meetings were usually crowded, noisy, and boisterous. This was an exuberant democracy.

Democratization and participation occurred outside the union as well. The long-standing writers' and artists' unions were revitalized by the renewal and new leadership. The old student organizations were challenged by a new one, the Independent Students' Union (NZS), set up by Solidarity supporters. The whole structure of the university system was affected by new procedures for electing department heads, deans and rectors that were far more democratic than those prevailing in most Western countries. Even the Polish United Workers' Party was seized by the spirit of participation and renewal. Many members left the Party during 1981, but most of those who stayed were intent on reforming the organization to make it more representative of the workers and more responsive to the grass roots.

What all this meant was that *society* had taken control in Poland, and this is perhaps the most unique feature of the Polish experience. The direction and pace of reform was directed from below. While the Party elite managed to slow the pace and to block some reforms, these efforts were reactive rather than initiatory. The workers had become the 'leading force in society'; the Party was, for the first time, following the workers.

This was unique for Poland and the rest of Eastern Europe, but was an unusual and important phenomenon in the broader context as well. Even in Western societies, it is rare that a broad social movement directs the course of change in a society. Revolutions result from such social movements, but revolutions replace the old leadership with the revolutionaries. In Poland, such a transforma- tion of leadership did not occur. Yet revolutionary changes con- tinued, initiated from below. The leadership could only stall or accommodate, as they did during 1981, or react with force, as they did at the end of that year. The year 1981 was a revolutionary one, but the revolution was not complete; it was a frustrated, incomplete or, as Jadwiga Staniszkis describes it, 'a self-limiting revolution'.

In some respects, the phenomenon of Solidarity, while unique in the Soviet bloc, may be compared to other grass-roots social movements in other countries. Solidarity, in its actions, philosophy, and programs, had much in common with 'the Greens' in West Germany, with the peace movements in Western Europe and the United States, and, historically, with Mahatma Gandhi's indepen- dence movement in India. Even in the Western democracies, many people are disenfranchised, or feel that way. Solidarity, like the Greens, attempted to change the system through mass activism, and with a 'people-oriented' program of democracy, participation, equality, and non-violence. In that respect, Solidarity may be a precedent for political change in the West as much as it will be in the East.

Yet another unique feature of the events of 1981 was the takeover by the army at the end of the year. Never before in the communist world (with the possible exception of the Cultural Revolution in China in the 1960s) had the military played a major political role. The declaration of martial law was evidence both of the inability of the Party to reestablish control, and of the fear of a possible Soviet military intervention in the absence of a Polish crackdown on Solidarity. The year 1981 had been a revolution by stages, in which Solidarity had subtly and gradually chipped away at the traditional role of the Party. Solidarity had accomplished gradually what the Soviets had refused to permit in Hungary in 1956 and Czechoslovakia in 1968 when the authority of the Party was more directly challenged. By the end of 1981, it was too late for the Party to reassert its leading role. That left the task to the Army, as the only institution with the authority, power, and legitimacy that was acceptable to the Polish and Soviet leadership. The long-standing popularity of the Army and its history of unwillingness to side with the Party against the workers, gave Jaruzelski a certain grace period to restore order and stability. By the time that grace period had ended, the Military Council of National Salvation had managed to crush Solidarity and return power to the Party.

The intervention of the Army into politics will have long-term effects on the rest of Eastern Europe as well. The Polish Army set a precedent: the military can and will play a political role. In this sense, the politics of Eastern Europe may begin to resemble the politics of third world countries, where the armies frequently seize power to 'restore order and stability'. While mass politics in Poland began to resemble similar phenomena in the industrial democracies, elite politics came to resemble politics in the developing countries. The clash between these two tendencies is bound to be disruptive for both Poland and the rest of the Eastern bloc.

The declaration of martial law brought home forcefully the limits to radical change in Poland. Solidarity had tried to conduct a 'self-limiting revolution', but the internal contradiction of that phrase eventually became all too evident. In trying to limit itself, Solidarity made an attempt at 'cramming that radical wave of protest and class war ... into a trade union' (Staniszkis 1982, p. 183). This proved to be impossible in the short time. Solidarity had available. In retrospect, though, 1981 may prove to be a catharsis for Poland, in that the revolutionary strain may have run its course. Most Poles, supporters of both Solidarity and the regime, now recognize the given features and the limits of Polish society. An article in

Życie Warszawy shortly after the imposition of martial law (Bartosze-wicz 1982) identified 'four truths' from the post-August period: first, that Poland was, is and will be a socialist state, based on the social ownership of the means of production; secondly, that the country must maintain the leading political role of the PZPR; third, that Poland is a Catholic country, in which the overwhelming majority of people are believers; and fourth, that the authorities may not govern without the acceptance of society and taking into account its aspirations and convictions. Certainly, virtually all Poles would agree with the third and fourth 'truths' of this statement, most would accept the first, and most recognize the necessity of the second. The necessity of maintaining the leading role, if not the monopoly, of the Polish United Workers' Party is probably the most painful and emphatic lesson of the 1980–2 period. This is largely conditioned, of course, by Poland's 'geopolitical situation', as Polish writers refer to the country's relationship to its eastern neighbor. The Soviets have demonstrated time and again, in 1956, 1968, and 1981, that the Warsaw Pact states must remain in the Pact and must retain the leading role of the Party. In Hungary and Czechoslovakia, Soviet troops insured those conditions. In Poland, the Polish Army did so, probably preempting Soviet action. The relationship with the Soviet Union remains a given, a 'truth' of European geography and international politics. As Tymowski described the situation in 1981, the Poles find themselves in a sort of shotgun marriage with the Soviets: 'even if we divorced, we would still have to live together'. Tymowski cautioned that Poles must recognize not only what is desirable, but what is possible 'in our part of Europe' (Tymowski 1981d, p. 12).

Given the limits, it is remarkable just how much the Polish workers did accomplish. They formed an organization and a movement that was at the same time Christian, democratic, and socialist. They brought together three ideals that pull against each other most other places in the world. The Christian principles included respect for the dignity of the individual, rejection of methods of violence, and concern for the poor and the weak. Socialist ideals included the importance of community, material well being, and egalitarianism. Democracy, interpreted perhaps even more broadly than in the West, incorporated the principle of citizen participation in all phases of life and all levels of government. It developed into the concept of 'a self-governing society' in which workers were to be given a say in how their factories were run as well as the affairs of state.

The Polish workers drew on the best elements of Western democracies and Eastern socialism, and rejected the worst. They rejected the Eastern pomp, the restrictions on freedom, and the concentration of power. They also rejected the selfish individualism, the inequality, and the violence of the West. The new Polish society was based on a new constellation of values, and as such, entailed a rebuilding of the social order. This was a threat to the established order in Poland, as it would have been a threat to the establishment in any society, East or West. Solidarity posed a new alternative that was a challenge to all societies and all ideologies. The institution of Solidarity is moribund, but the idea of Solidarity is alive. What Wałesa has said about the institution is probably more true of the idea: 'for the moment, they have stopped us. But we shall win.'

Appendix: Summary of major public opinion polls used in this book

The following list includes some of the major survey polls cited in this book. They are listed by author or authoring agency, as they are referenced in the text and in the list of references below. Each entry includes as much information as available on authors, sample size, sampling method, and date of survey.

Beskid and Sufin 1981. These studies were conducted by the Institute of Philosophy and Sociology of the Polish Academy of Sciences (IFIS PAN), statisticians at the Main Statistical Office (Główny Urząd Statystyczny – GUS), and the Central Committee's Institute of Basic Problems of Marxism-Leninism (IPPML). The analyses are based on a survey of household budgets conducted by GUS in 1974 and a followup questionnaire sent in 1975 to all adults in the first survey. The 1975 sample consists of some 10,000 households with 22,000 adults (e.g. Chapter 2 and Table 6.1).

Bucholz 1983. December 1980 poll of 548 shipyard workers in the Gdańsk–Gdynia–Sopot region, conducted by the PZPR Voivodship Committee in Gdańsk (e.g. Chapter 4).

Gołębiowski 1982 and 1983. Gołębiowski, the director of the Sociology of Politics Department at the University of Warsaw, in cooperation with the Institute of Research on Youth, conducted a survey in May 1982 of 1200 high school, vocational and technical students nationwide (e.g. Chapters 1, 8).

Jasiewicz and Jasińska 1981. This research was part of a larger project on local government conducted by the Institute of Sociology of the University of Warsaw. This study was based on a survey implemented in July 1977 in six medium-sized cities with over 300 citizens selected randomly from each city. The interviews were conducted by sociology students from the University (e.g. Chapter 2).

Kawecki 1981. This research was based on an April 1977 survey conducted by the Party's IPPML of a representative sample consisting of 12,000 secondary school students responding to an 'anonymous questionnaire'. These surveys were repeated in later years (1977–80) and the subject of other publications by Kawecki and others (e.g. Table 3.5).

Krasko 1981. This poll was conducted in April and May of 1981 by the Public Opinion Research Section of the Center for Social Research of Solidarity's East-Central Region (Ośrodek Badań Społecznych Regionu Środkowo-Wschodniego). The sample consists of 697 Solidarity members from two voivodships in the Lublin area. The questionnaires were sent to the factory Solidarity commissions for implementation (e.g. Tables 5.7 through 5.9).

Łódź '76 and *Łódź '80*. These are the most recent of four surveys conducted periodically by the Institute of Sociology of the University of Warsaw and the Institute of Philosophy and Sociology of the Academy of Sciences. The samples consist of about 1000 working males in the city of Łódź. Interviews were conducted by sociology students at the University of Warsaw (e.g. Table 2.6 and Chapter 6).

Olędzki 1981. This research on 'the extent of political consciousness of the young generation' is based on a questionnaire administered in December 1978 to a national representative quota sample of 2500 persons between the ages of 15 and 29 (e.g. Chapter 3).

OBS. Decyzje w strzymania i odwołania strajku w opiniach zatrudnionych w przemyśle warszawskim. This survey was conducted by Bohdan Ofierski and Andrzej Radźko on behalf of the Center for Social Research (Ośrodek Badań Społecznych) of Solidarity's Mazowsze region. The communique does not mention the size of the sample, which consisted of workers in industrial enterprises in the Warsaw voivodship, interviewed in April 1981 (e.g. Chapter 5).

OBS. Sprawy podstawowe w oczach członków związku. Survey conducted in August 1981 among a 'representative sample' of 1000 members of Solidarity from the whole country. The interviews were conducted mostly at the homes of the respondents, by 'qualified and experienced pollsters' (e.g. Tables 5.2, 5.4, 5.6).

OBS. Socjologiczne badania pogladów delegatów na I-szy Zjazd Delegatów NSZZ Solidarność. Survey administered by Ofierski and Radźko during the second session of Solidarity's Congress in October 1981. The sample consisted of 271 delegates to the Congress (e.g. Tables 5.2, 5.4).

OBOP. Społeczne zaufanie do instytucji politycznych, społecznych i administracyjnych (May 1981). This is one of many surveys conducted by OBOP, the Center for Public Opinion Research and Program Studies of Polish Radio and Television. OBOP's communiques rarely provided data on sample size, etc., but according to Albin Kania, the OBOP Director, during 1981 the organization conducted surveys two or three times monthly, using a national representative sample of several thousand adults. About 200 numbered copies of the communiques were distributed to government and party officials, the media, academics, and to Solidarity (e.g. Table 5.3, Chapter 7).

Paris Match, 1981. This 'clandestine survey' was conducted in Poland by representatives of the French magazine. Eighteen interviewers talked with 600 persons in Poland between November 3 and December 5, 1981. The sample was then 'weighted' by demographic and occupational characteristics to be representative of the population at large (e.g. Chapter 7).

Polacy '80. This study was based on questionnaires from a representative quota sample of 2500 adults. It was conducted in late November and early December 1980 by sociologists at the Institute of Philosophy and Sociology of the Polish Academy of Sciences (e.g. Tables 3.4, 4.1, 7.6).

Polacy '81. A followup survey to *Polacy '80*, this one was conducted in the weeks leading up to martial law, November 20 to December 12. Of a planned 2000 interviews, 1895 had been completed at the time martial law was imposed. This 'representative, national random sample' asked many of the same questions posed in *Polacy '80*, allowing comparisons over the intervening year (e.g. Tables 5.1, 6.3, 7.7).

Sufin 1981b. The reports in this volume edited by Zbigniew Sufin, a sociologist at the Academy of Sciences, are based on ten major surveys conducted by the Party's IPPML between 1975 and 1980. Each of these were national representative samples consisting of 2000 to 5000 persons randomly selected from voting lists after elections to the Sejm and peoples' councils (e.g. Tables 2.2, 3.6).

Wstępne wyniki ankiety Komitetu Oporu Społecznego 'KOS'. The questionnaire for this survey appeared in the underground newsletter *KOS* in the fall of 1982. The results, which also appeared in *KOS*, were based on 1400 responses from the Warsaw region. The authors caution that the results were not representative, in that the survey was restricted to that region, and only reached those persons who read *KOS*. As such, it overrepresented 'mental workers' who constituted 72% of the sample (e.g. Tables 8.4, 8.5).

References

BOOKS AND ARTICLES

Albinowski, Stanisław. 1982. Economy in the Grips of Crisis. *Trybuna Ludu*, February 18, 1982.

Almond, Gabriel and Verba, Sidney. 1963. *The Civic Culture*. Princeton: Princeton University Press.

Almond, Gabriel and Verba, Sidney. eds. 1980. *The Civic Culture Revisited*. Boston: Little Brown.

Ascherson, Neal. 1981. *The Polish August*. London: Penguin.

Ash, Timothy G. 1983a. Poland's Hope. *The New Republic*, July 18 and 25, 1983, pp. 17–21.

Ash, Timothy G. 1983b. *The Polish Revolution: Solidarity*. New York: Scribners.

Bartoszewicz, Tomasz. 1982. Co dalej? *Życie Warszawy*, 15 March, 1982.

Bell, Daniel. 1968. Socialism. In *International Encyclopedia of the Social Sciences*, vol. 14. New York: Macmillan.

Beskid, Lidia. 1976. Stopień rozpiętości płac realnych netto w Polsce w okresie 1956–1972. In Lidia Beskid and Zbigniew Sufin, eds., *Ekonomiczne i Społeczne Problemy Spożycia*, pp. 187–214. Wrocław: Polska Akademia Nauk.

Beskid, Lidia. 1982. Sprawiedliwy czy egalitarny. *Polityka*, 20 March, 1982, p. 5.

Beskid, Lidia and Sufin, Zbigniew, eds. 1981. *Warunki Życia i Potrzeby Społeczeństwa Polskiego w Połowie Lat Siedemdziesiątych*. Warsaw: Instytut Podstawowych Problemów Marksizmu-Leninizmu.

Bielasiak, Jack. 1984. The Evolution of crises in Poland. In Jack Bielasiak and Maurice Simon, eds. *Polish Politics: Edge of the Abyss*, pp. 1–28. New York: Praeger.

Bielasiak, Jack and Simon, Maurice, eds. 1984. *Polish Politics: Edge of the Abyss*. New York: Praeger.

Bielski, Marcin, Caban, Wiesław, and Lutynski, Jan. 1981. NSZZ Solidarność: związek zawodowy i ruch społeczny. In *Krajowa Konferencja nt. Program Solidarność* Łódź.

Brown, Archie and Gray, Jack, eds. 1977. *Political Culture and Political Change in Communist States*. New York: Holmes and Meier.

Brumberg, Abraham, ed. 1983. *Poland: Genesis of a Revolution.* New York: Vintage.

Bucholc, Stanisław. 1983. Shipyard workers on causes of the crisis. *Tu i Teraz,* 28 September 1983. Translated in Joint Publications Research Service, *East Europe Report,* November 1, 1983.

Bunce, Valerie. 1980. The succession connection: policy cycles and political change in the Soviet Union and Eastern Europe. *American Political Science Review* 74: 966–77.

Chmielewski, Krzysztof. 1981. From the vantage point of the director. *Zarządzanie,* 6:8–11. Translated in Joint Publications Research Service, *East Europe Report,* July 23, 1982.

Connor, Walter D. 1977. Opinion, reality and the communist political process. In Connor and Gitelman 1977, pp. 167–87.

Connor, Walter D. 1979. *Socialism, Politics and Equality: Hierarchy and Change in Eastern Europe and the USSR.* New York: Columbia University Press.

Connor, Walter D. and Gitelman, Zvi., eds. 1977. *Public Opinion in European Socialist Systems.* New York: Praeger.

Czuma, Łukasz. 1981. Kto nas karmi? *Biuletyn Informacyjny.* March 23, 1981. Lublin: MKZ, NSZZ Solidarność.

Dahl, Robert A. 1956. *A Preface to Democratic Theory.* Chicago: University of Chicago Press.

Darnton, Nina. 1982. The subtle power of the Polish church. *New York Times Magazine,* June 6, 1982, pp. 23ff.

Davies, James. 1962. Toward a theory of revolution. *American Sociological Review,* 27: 5–19.

Davison, W. P. and Leiserson, Avery. 1968. Public opinion. In *International Encyclopedia of the Social Sciences,* vol 13, pp. 188–204. New York: Macmillan.

Devine, Donald J. 1972. *The Political Culture of the United States.* Boston: Little Brown.

The Directions of the Operations of Solidarity in the Current Situation of the Country. *Tygodnik Solidarność,* April 17, 1981. Translated in Radio Free Europe Research, *Background Report,* no. 210, July 22, 1981.

Dissent in Poland: Reports and Documents in Translation, December 1975–July 1977. London: Association of Polish Students and Graduates in Exile, 1977.

Dorn, Ludwik. 1981. Polling the Poles: a report from Solidarity headquarters. *Public Opinion,* 4:5–7.

Drążkiewicz, Jerzy. 1975. Udział klasy robotniczej w aktywności społecznej. In Jan Malanowski, ed., *Nierówności społeczne w Polsce w świetle badań empirycznych,* pp. 9–21. Warsaw: Polska Akademia Nauk.

Easton, David. 1965. *A Framework for Political Analysis.* Englewood Cliffs, New Jersey: Prentice Hall.

Engel, Janusz (interview). 1984. Ani ja, ani samorząd. *Polityka,* 19 May 1984, p. 4.

Fallenbuchl, Zbigniew. 1982. Polish economic crisis. *Problems of Communism,* 31 (March–April): 1–21.

Flakierski, Henryk. 1981. Economic reform and income distribution in Poland: the negative evidence. *Cambridge Journal of Economics* 5:137–58.

Fleron, Frederic J., ed. 1969. *Communist Studies and the Social Sciences*. Chicago: Rand McNally.

Fuszara, Małgorzata, Jakubowska, Iwona, and Kurczewski, Jacek. 1982. Sprawiedliwość czasów reglamentacji. Warsaw: unpublished manuscript.

Gadomska, Magdalena. 1981. Świadomość nierówności. *Przegląd Techniczny*, 24 May 1981, pp. 19–21.

Gawronski, Jas. 1983. Walesa's Nobel. *New York Times*, October 8, 1983.

Gitelman, Zvi Y. 1977. Public opinion in communist political systems. In Connor and Gitelman (1977), pp. 1–40.

Gitelman, Zvi Y. 1981. The world economy and elite political strategies in Czechoslovakia, Hungary, and Poland. In Morris Bornstein, Zvi Gitelman and William Zimmerman, eds., *East–West Relations and the Future of Eastern Europe*, pp. 127–61. London: Allen and Unwin.

Goban-Klas, Tomasz. 1984. The hopes and fears of the Poles. *Polityka*, January 14, 1984, p. 3. Translated in Joint Publications Research Service, *East Europe Report*, February 29, 1984.

Gołębiowski, Bronisław. 1976. Aspiracje i orientacje zyciowe młodziezy. *Przekazy i Opinie*, no. 1 (January–February).

Gołębiowski, Bronisław. 1982. (Interview) Looking for a perspective. *Życie Warszawy*, November 30, 1982. Translated in JPRS *East Europe Report*, January 24, 1983.

Gołębiowski, Bronisław. 1983. *Trybuna Ludu*, January 22–3, 1983, p. 6.

Gulczyński, Mariusz. 1980. *Literatura*, October 16, 1980.

Hart, Henry O. 1980. *Emergent collective opinion and upheaval in Eastern Europe and the role of radio communication*. Munich: Radio Free Europe.

Herspring, Dale. 1981. The Polish military and the policy process. In Maurice Simon and Roger Kanet, eds., *Background to Crisis: Policy and Politics in Gierek's Poland*, pp. 221–38. Boulder: Westview.

Huntington, Samuel P. 1970. Social and institutional dynamics of one-party systems. In Samuel Huntington and Clement Moore, eds., *Authoritarian Politics in Modern Society*, pp. 3–47. New York: Basic Books.

Huszczo, Adaline. 1977. Public opinion in Poland. In Connor and Gitelman (1977), pp. 41–82.

Informator biuletynu MKZ NSZZ Solidarność (East central region, Lublin), January 30, 1981.

Inglehart, Ronald. 1977. *The Silent Revolution*. Princeton: Princeton University Press.

Inkeles, Alex. 1958. *Public Opinion in Soviet Russia: A Study in Mass Persuasion*. Cambridge, Mass.: Harvard University Press.

Jacob, P. E., ed. 1971. *Values and the Active Community: A Cross-National Study of the Influence of Local Leadership*. New York: Free Press.

Janicka, Krystyna. 1981. Przemiany potocznej percepcji ruchliwości międzypokoleniowej w latach 1964–1976. *Studia Socjologiczne*, January 1981.

Jasiewicz, Krzysztof and Jasińska, Aleksandra. 1981. Problemy zaspokajania potrzeb i funkcjonowanie władz lokalnych w percepcji mieszkańców. In Krzysztof Jasiewicz, et al., *Władza Lokalna a Zaspokajanie Potrzeb: Studium sześciu miast*, pp. 183–240. Warsaw: Polska Akademia Nauk.

Jasińska-Kania, Aleksandra. 1982. National identity and images of world society: the Polish case. *International Social Science Journal*, 34: 93–112.

Jerschina, Jan. 1980. The impact of universities on Polish students' attitudes towards their own nation and the Catholic religion. *International Journal of Political Education* 3; 271–86.

Johnson, A. Ross. 1971. Polish perspectives, past and present. *Problems of Communism* 20 (July–August): 59–72.

Jones, T. Anthony, Bealmear, David and Kennedy, Michael D. 1984. Public opinion and political disruption. In Jack Bielasiak and Maurice Simon, eds., *Polish Politics: Edge of the Abyss*, pp. 138–68. New York: Praeger.

Kania, Albin. 1981. (Interview). *Życie Warszawy*, August 1, 1981.

Kania, Albin. 1982. (Interview). Opinie o roku 1982. *Życie Warszawy*, December 30, 1982.

Kawecki, Zenon. 1981. Postawy światopoglądowe i społeczne-polityczne młodzieży. In Zbigniew Sufin 1981b, pp. 88–131.

Kemme, David. 1984. The Polish crisis: and economic overview. In Bielasiak and Simon 1984, pp. 29–55.

Kemp-Welch, A. 1983. *The Birth of Solidarity*. New York: St. Martins.

Key, V. O. 1961. *Public Opinion and American Democracy*. New York: Knopf.

Kolankiewicz, George. 1981. Renewal, reform or retreat: the Polish communist party after the Extraordinary Ninth Congress. *The World Today*, 37: 369–75.

Kolankiewicz, George. 1982. The politics of 'socialist renewal'. In Jean Woodall, ed., *Policy and Politics in Contemporary Poland*, pp. 56–75. New York: St. Martins.

Kolankiewicz, George and Taras, Ray. 1977. Poland: socialism for everyman? In Brown and Gray 1977, pp. 101–30.

Komunikat ze 184 Konferencji Episkopatu Polski. May 4, 1982. Jasna Góra.

Koralewicz-Zębik, Jadwiga. 1982. Potoczna percepcja nierówności. Unpublished manuscript. Warsaw: Polska Akademia Nauk.

Korbonski, Andrzej. 1982. The Polish army. In Jonathan Adelman, ed., *Communist Armies in Politics*, pp. 103–27. Boulder: Westview.

Krasko, Nina. 1981. Oceny, szanse, niebezpieczeństwa. *Ruch Związkowy* (zeszyt nr. 1 Ośrodek Prac Społeczno-Zawodowych KKP NSZZ Solidarność, Warsaw).

Krejci, Jaroslaw. 1982. *National Income and Outlay in Czechoslovakia, Poland and Yugoslavia*. New York: St. Martins.

Krencik, Wiesław. 1980. *Gospodarka Planowania*, April 1980.

Kruszewski, Z. Anthony. 1984. The communist party posture during the 1980/81 democratization of Poland. In Bielasiak and Simon 1984, pp. 241–67.

Kurczewski, Jacek. 1981. W oczach opinii publicznej. *Kultura*, March 1, 1981.

Kuśmierski, Stanisław. 1980. *Teoretyczne Problemy Propagandy i Opinii Publicznej*. Warsaw: Państwowe Wydawnictwo Naukowe.

Kwiatkowski, Stanisław. 1983. (interview). *Słowo Polskie* (Wrocław), January 4, 1983, p. 4.

Lane, David. 1971. *The End of Inequality? Stratification Under State Socialism.* Harmondsworth and Baltimore Md.: Penguin.

Lane, David. 1976. *The Socialist Industrial State: Towards a Political Sociology of State Socialism.* Boulder: Westview.

Łódź '76 and *Łódź '80.* Surveys of about 1000 working males in the city of Łódź, conducted in the fall of 1976 and the fall of 1980 by the Institute of Sociology of the University of Warsaw and the Institute of Philosophy and Sociology of the Academy of Sciences.

MacIver, Robert M. 1950. *The Ramparts We Guard.* New York: Macmillan.

Malak, Zdzisław. 1983. Self-government: what do they think of it? *Polityka.* July 30, 1983, p. 4. Translated in JPRS, *East Europe Report*, September 6, 1983.

Malanowski, Jan, ed. 1975. *Nierówności społeczne w Polsce w świetle badań empirycznych.* Warsaw: Polska Akademia Nauk.

Marody, Mirosława et al. 1981. *Polacy '80.* Warsaw: University of Warsaw.

Mason, David S. 1982. Membership of the Polish United Workers' Party. *Polish Review* 27: 138–53.

Mason, David S. 1983a. Policy dilemmas and political unrest in Poland. *Journal of Politics* 45: 397–421.

Mason, David S. 1983b. Solidarity, the regime, and the public. *Soviet Studies* 35: 533–45.

Mason, David S. 1983c. The University of Warsaw fights back. *Change: The Magazine of Higher Learning*, January/February 1983, pp. 43–5.

Mason, David S. 1984. Solidarity and Socialism. In Bielasiak and Simon 1984, pp. 118–37.

Maziarski, Jacek. 1981. Do we want strong authority? *Kultura*, January 25, 1981. Translated in JPRS, *East Europe Report*, March 18, 1981.

McClosky, Herbert. 1969. *Political Inquiry: The Nature and Uses of Survey Research.* New York: Macmillan.

Merton, Robert K. 1957. *Social Theory and Social Structure*, revised edition. Glencoe, Ill.: Free Press.

Mickiewicz, Ellen. 1983. Feedback, surveys, and Soviet communication theory. *Journal of Communication* 33: 97–110.

Mieczkowski, Bogdan. 1975. *Personal and Social Consumption in Eastern Europe.* New York: Praeger.

Mieczkowski, Bogdan. 1978. The relationship between changes in consumption and politics in Poland. *Soviet Studies* 30: 262–9.

Milic-Czerniak, Roza. 1981. Płaca i zakładowe świadczenia społeczne jako motywy pracy. In Zbigniew Sufin, ed., *Diagnozy Społeczne w Okresie Narastającego Kryzysu*, pp. 101–26. Warsaw: IPPML.

Miller, Joanne, Slomczynski, Kazimierz and Schoenberg, Ronald. 1981. Assessing comparability of measurement in cross-national research: authoritarianism-conservatism in different sociocultural settings. *Social Psychology Quarterly* 44: 178–91.

Mink, Georges. 1981. Polls, pollsters, public opinion and political power in Poland in the late 1970's. *Telos* 47: 125–32.

Misztal, Barbara and Misztal, Bronisław. 1984. The transformation of political elites. In Bielasiak and Simon 1984, pp. 169–85.

Misztal, Bronisław. 1983. Apathy and participation: the natural history of

Polish Solidarity movement. Paper presented at the annual meeting of Midwest Slavic Association, Chicago, May 1983.

Montias, John. 1980. Economic conditions and political instability in communist countries. *Studies in Comparative Communism* 13: 283–99.

Morawski, Witold. 1980. Society and the strategy of imposed industrialization. *The Polish Sociological Bulletin*, no. 4.

Morawski, Witold. 1981. O źródłach i naturze kryzysu 1980–1981 w Polsce. *Literatura*, September 24, 1981, pp. 5–6.

Morawski, Witold, ed. 1983. *Demokracja i Gospodarka*. Warsaw: University of Warsaw.

Nowacki, Grzegorz. 1983. (Interview) *Życie Warszawy*, April 25, 1983, p. 3.

Nowak, Stefan. 1971. Społeczna przydatność badań postaw i opinii. *Nowe Drogi*, no. 9.

Nowak, Stefan. 1980. Value systems of the Polish society. *The Polish Sociological Bulletin*, no. 2: 5–20.

Nowak, Stefan. 1981. Values and attitudes of the Polish people. *Scientific American* 245: 45ff.

Nuti, Domenico M. 1982. The Polish crisis. In Jan Drewnowski, ed., *Crisis in the East European Economy*, pp. 18–64. New York: St. Martins.

Olędzki, Jerzi. 1981. Opinie młodzieży polskiej o demokracji burzuazyjnej i socjalistycznej. *Kultura i Społeczeństwo*, nos. 1–2, pp. 245–60.

Oliver, James H. 1969. Citizen demands and the Soviet political system. *American Political Science Review*, 63.

Ośrodek Badań Społecznych (OBS, of Solidarity's Mazowsze Region). Członkowie związku o błędach krajowych władz związku. Warsaw, November 23, 1981.

OBS. Decyzje w strzymania i odwołania strajku w opiniach zatrudnionych w przemyśle Warszawskim. Warsaw, no date (April 1981?).

OBS. Komunikat z badań. Warsaw, no date (October 1981?).

OBS. Socjologiczne badania poglądów delegatów na I-szy Zjazd delegatów NSZZ Solidarność. Warsaw, October 25, 1981.

OBS. Sprawy podstawowe w oczach członków związku. Warsaw, no date (September 1981?).

OBS. Wyniki badań opinii na temat zawartego w apelu KKP wezwania do podjęcia pracy w wolne soboty. Prepared by Bohdan Ofierski and Andrzej Radźko. Warsaw, September 1981.

Ośrodek Badania Opinii Publicznej i Studiów Programowych (OBOP). Napięcia społeczne i stosunki władza- Solidarność w opinii publicznej. Warsaw: November 1981.

OBOP. Opinie o Terenowych Grupach Operacyjnych. Warsaw, November (?) 1981.

OBOP. Społeczne zaufanie do instytucji politycznych, społecznych i administracyjnych. Warsaw, May 1981.

OBOP. Sprzedaż wiązana i stosunki miasto-wieś w opinii społecznej. Warsaw, November 1981.

OBOP. Zaopatrzenie w żywność w systemie reglamentacji. Warsaw, November 1981.

Paczkowski, A. 1981. Quoted in *Komunikaty*, NSZZ Uniwersytet Wrocław. 20 May 1981.

Paris Match survey. 1981. Un grand sondage clandestin. *Paris Match*, December 25, 1981, pp. 37–9.

Parkin, Frank. 1971. *Class Inequality and Political Order: Social Stratification in Capitalist and Communist Societies*. New York: Praeger.

Parkin, Frank. 1979. *Marxism and Class Theory: a Bourgeois Critique*. New York: Columbia University Press.

Pelczynski, Zbigniew. 1973. The downfall of Gomulka. *Canadian Slavonic Papers* 15:1–23.

Persky, Stan. 1981. *At the Lenin Shipyard*. Vancouver: New Star Books.

Persky, Stan and Flam, Henry, eds. 1982. *The Solidarity Sourcebook*. Vancouver: New Star Books.

Piekalkiewicz, Jaroslaw. 1972. *Public Opinion Polling in Czechoslovakia, 1968–69*. New York: Praeger.

Pitus, Wiktor, Smrokowski, Tadeusz and Tuora, Tadeusz. 1975. Nierówności społeczne w dziedzinie położenia materialnego. In Jan Malanowski, ed., *Nierówności Społeczne w Polsce w Świetle Badań Empiricznych*, pp. 50–64. Warsaw: Polska Akademia Nauk.

Plano, Jack C. and Greenberg, Milton. 1976. *The American Political Dictionary*, 4th ed. Hinsdale, Ill.: Dryden.

Polacy '80: Wyniki Badań Ankietowych. Author team: Władysław Adamski, Ireneusz Białecki, Krzysztof Jasiewicz, Lena Kolarska, Andrzej Mokrzyszewski, Andrzej Rychard, Joanna Sikorska. Warsaw: Polska Akademia Nauk, Instytut Filozofii i Socjologii.

Polacy '81. Authors: W. Adamski, I. Białecki, J. Sikorska, L. Beskid, E. Skotnicka-Illasiewicz, E. Wnuk-Lipinski, K. Jasiewicz, A. Mokrzyszewski, L. Kolarska, A. Rychard, A. Titkow. Warsaw: Polska Akademia Nauk, Instytut Filozofii i Socjologii.

Poland Today: The State of the Republic. Compiled by the Experience and the Future Discussion Group. Edited by Jack Bielasiak. Armonk, New York: M. E. Sharpe, 1981.

Political Action: An Eight Nation Study, 1973–1976. Cologne: University of Cologne, 1979.

Powiorski, Jan (pseudonym). 1983. The Poles of '81: public opinion on the eve of martial law. *Poland Watch*, no. 3, pp. 109–32.

Poznań 1956–Grudzień 1970, Dokumenty, no. 35. Paris: Instytut Literacki, 1971.

Pravda, Alex. 1981. East–West interdependence and the social compact in Eastern Europe. In Morris Bornstein, Zvi Gitelman and William Zimmerman, eds., *East–West Relations and the Future of Eastern Europe*, pp. 162–90. London: Allen and Unwin.

Pravda, Alex. 1982. Is there a Soviet working class? *Problems of Communism* 31 (November–December): 1–24.

Preibisz, Joanna M. 1982. *Polish Dissident Publications: An Annotated Bibliography*. New York: Praeger.

Pye, Lucian W. 1968. Political culture. *International Encyclopedia of the Social Sciences*, vol 12, pp. 218–24. New York: Macmillan.

Raina, Peter. 1978. *Political Opposition in Poland, 1959–1977*. London: Poet and Painters' Press.

Robinson, William F., ed. 1980. *August 1980: The Strikes in Poland*. Munich: Radio Free Europe.

Rocznik Statystyczny, annual. Warsaw: Główny Urząd Statystyczny.

Ruane, Kevin. 1982. *The Polish Challenge*. London: British Broadcasting Corporation.

Sanford, George. 1982. The response of the Polish communist leadership and the continuing crisis. In Jean Woodall, ed., *Policy and Politics in Contemporary Poland: Reform, Failure, Crisis*, pp. 33–55. New York: St. Martins.

Sanford, George. 1983. *Polish Communism in Crisis*. New York: St Martins.

Sarapata, Adam. 1984. (interview). *Życie Warszawy*, February 3, 1984, pp. 1, 3.

Sicinski, Andrzej. 1963. Public opinion surveys in Poland. *International Social Science Journal*, no. 1.

Sicinski, Andrzej. 1967. Developments in East European public opinion research. *Polls*, 3.

Siemieńska, Renata. 1982. Mass-authority relationships in the Polish crisis: anatomy of social consciousness. Paper presented at annual meeting of the American Political Science Association, Denver, September 2–5, 1982.

Simon, Maurice. 1981. Polish student attitudes and ideological policy. In Maurice Simon and Roger Kanet, eds., *Background to Crisis: Policy and Politics in Gierek's Poland*, pp. 137–76. Boulder: Westview.

Simon, Maurice and Kanet, Roger, eds. 1981. *Background to Crisis: Policy and Politics in Gierek's Poland*. Boulder: Westview.

Singer, Daniel. 1981. *The Road to Gdansk: Poland and the USSR*. New York: Monthly Review Books.

Sisyphus: Sociological Studies. 1982. Vol. III: Crises and Conflicts; The Case of Poland 1980–81. Warsaw: Państwowe Wydawnictwo Naukowe.

Słomczyński, K., Miller, J. and Kohn, M. 1981. Stratification, work and values: a Polish–United States comparison. *American Sociological Review*, 46: 720–44.

Smolar, Alexander. 1983. The rich and the powerful. In Abraham Brumberg, ed. *Poland: Genesis of a Revolution*, pp. 42–53. New York: Vintage.

Spielman, Richard. 1982. Crisis in Poland. *Foreign Policy*, no. 49: 20–36.

Społeczeństwo wobec przemocy. *CDN* (Warsaw), January 1982.

Staniszkis, Jadwiga. 1981. The evolution of forms of working-class protest in Poland: sociological reflections on the Gdansk–Szczecin case, August 1980. *Soviet Studies* 33: 204–31.

Staniszkis, Jadwiga. 1982. Polish peaceful revolution: an anatomy of polarization. *Journal of Peace Research* 19: 181–95.

Staniszkis Jadwiga. 1984. *Poland's Self-Limiting Revolution*. Princeton: Princeton University Press.

Starski, Stanislaw. 1982. *Class Struggle in Classless Poland*. Boston: South End Press.

Stefanowski, Roman, ed. 1982. *Poland: A Chronology of Events, August–December 1981*. Munich: Radio Free Europe.

Stefanowski, Roman, ed. 1983. *Poland Under Martial Law: A Chronology of Events*. Munich: Radio Free Europe.

Sufin, Zbigniew, ed. 1981a. *Diagnozy Społeczne w Okresie Narastającego*

Kryzysu. Warsaw: Instytut Podstawowych Problemów Marksizmu-Leninizmu.

Sufin, Zbigniew. 1981b. *Społeczeństwo Polskie w Drugiej Połowie Lat Siedemdziesiątych; Raporty z Badań.* Warsaw: Instytut Podstawowych Problemów Marksizmu-Leninizmu.

Szafnicki, K. and Mach, B. 1982. Modele determinacji dochodów z pracy. Unpublished manuscript. Warsaw: Institute of Sociology, University of Warsaw.

Szczepański, Jan. 1970. *Polish Society.* New York: Random House.

Szczepański, Jan. 1979. Założenia i środki kształtowania socjalistycznego sposobu życia. In Włodzimierz Wesołowski, ed. *Marksizm i Procesy Rozwoju Społecznego,* pp. 177–89. Warsaw: Książka i Wiedza.

Szczepański, Jan. 1982. Kontynuować politykę ugody. *Zycie Warszawy,* May 6, 1982.

Szczypiorski, Andrzej. 1982. *The Polish Ordeal: The View from Within.* London: Croom Helm.

Szymański, Leszek. 1982. *Candle for Poland: 469 Days of Solidarity.* San Bernardino, California: Borgo Press.

Szymański, Łukasz. 1982. (interview) Władza a opinia publiczna. *Rzeczpospolita,* no. 25, p. 5.

Tarkowski, Jacek. 1981. Patrons and clients in a planned economy. In S. N. Eisenstadt and R. Lemarchand, eds., *Political Clientelism, Patronage and Development.* London: Sage.

Tarkowski, Jacek. 1983. Władze terenowe po reformie. In Jerzy Wiatr, ed., *Władza Lokalna u Progu Kryzysu,* pp. 23–76. Warsaw: University of Warsaw.

Tarniewski, Marek. 1982. *Słownik Polityczny.* Warsaw: Wydawnictwo Głos.

Touraine, Alain. 1983. *Solidarity: The Analysis of a Social Movement: Poland 1980–81.* Cambridge: Cambridge University Press.

Turski, Jerzy. 1983. *Polityka,* August 13, 1983, p. 4.

Tymowski, Andrzej. 1981a. Ku czemu wolny. *Przegląd Techniczny,* May 24, 1981, pp. 10–12.

Tymowski, Andrzej. 1981b. Polityka społeczna po Sierpniu 1980. *Kultura,* November 15, 1981.

Tymowski, Andrzej. 1981c. Problem egalitaryzmu konsumpcji w rzeczywistości społeczno-gospodarczej. *Roczniki Instytutu Handlu Wewnętrznego i Usług,* zeszyt 3, pp. 23–37.

Tymowski, Andrzej. 1981d. Strzały do Pana Boga. *Czas,* November 8, 1981.

Uncensored Polls Take Poland's Pulse. *Wall Street Journal,* July 6, 1981.

Vanous, Jan. 1982. Letter in *Problems of Communism,* 31 (November–December): 86.

Ward, Barclay. 1981. Poland. In William A. Welsh, ed., *Survey Research and Public Attitudes in Eastern Europe and the Soviet Union,* pp. 389–435. New York: Pergamon.

Welsh, William A., ed. 1981. *Survey Research and Public Attitudes in Eastern Europe and the Soviet Union.* New York: Pergamon.

deWeydenthal, Jan. 1979. *Poland: Communism Adrift.* Beverly Hills, California: Sage.

deWeydenthal, Jan B., Porter, Bruce, and Devlin, Kevin. 1983. *The Polish Drama: 1980–82*. Lexington: Lexington Books.
Wheeler, Michael. 1976. *Lies, Damn Lies and Statistics: The Manipulation of Public Opinion in America*. New York: Dell.
Wiatr, Jerzy J. 1980. The civic culture from a Marxist-sociological perspective. In Almond and Verba 1980, pp. 103–23.
Wiatr, Jerzy. 1981. Poland's party politics: the Extraordinary Congress of 1981. *Canadian Journal of Political Science* 14: 813–26.
Widera, Wojciech. 1983. Stare związki zawodowe wobec potrzeb pracowniczych. In Witold Morawski, ed. 1983, pp. 289–330.
Wojtasik, Lesław 1980. Ways to gauge, influence public mood discussed. *Polityka* 4:137–44, April 1980. Translated in Joint Publications Research Service. *East Europe Report*, no. 75781.
Wolski, Wojciech. 1980. Portrait sketch of the young generation. *Kultura* (Paris), 1, 2:123–132; translated in JPRS, *East Europe Report*, 1980.
Woodall, Jean. 1981. New social factors in the unrest in Poland. *Government and Opposition* 16: 37–57.
Woodall, Jean, ed. 1982. *Policy and Politics in Contemporary Poland: Reform, Failure, Crisis*. New York: St Martins.
Wstępne wyniki ankiety Komitetu Oporu Społecznego KOS, *Biuletyn Informacyjny* (New York), no. 74, June 1983.
Wyniki badan. *KOS Solidarność*, April 2, 1982.

PERIODICALS

Biuletyn Informacyjny (New York: Committee in Support of Solidarity).
Christian Science Monitor.
Joint Publications Research Service, *East Europe Report*.
KOS Solidarność (Warsaw: Komitet Oporu Społecznego Solidarność), 1982.
Komunikaty (Wrocław: NSZZ Uniwersytet Wrocław), 1981.
Kultura (Warsaw).
Kultura (Paris).
Kurier Polski (Warsaw).
Literatura (Warsaw).
New York Times.
Nowe Drogi (Warsaw), 1983.
Odra, 1980.
Paris Match, 1981–2.
Polityka (Warsaw), 1980–3.
Przekazy i Opinie (Warsaw).
Radio Free Europe Research, *Background Reports*, 1980–3.
Rzeczpospolita (Warsaw), 1982–3.
Solidarność Information Bulletin (London), 1982.
The Times (London), 1982.
Trybuna Ludu (Warsaw), 1981–3.
Tu i Teraz (Warsaw), 1982–3.
Tygodnik Solidarność, 1981.

Tygodnik Wojenny (NSZZ Solidarność Region Mazowsze), 1982.
Wall Street Journal.
Washington Post.
Wiadomości: Biuletyn Informacyjny NSZZ Solidarność (Warsaw), 1982.
Życie Partii, 1981.
Życie Warscawy, 1981–2.
Żołnierz Wolności, 1982.

Index

This is primarily a subject and name index. Authors are listed only when they were referred to in the text. The events of the years 1956, 1968, 1970, 1976 and 1980 appear at the end of the index, after the alphabetical listings.

macropolitics, 7
Main Statistical Office, 24, 249
Man of Iron, 42
market supplies (*see also* food supplies),
    44, 170–2
martial law, 102, 162
    instruments of, 179, 204, 208
    interrupts *Polacy '81* survey, 29
    justification for, 23, 159, 161, 198,
        201–3, 234
    plans for, 193
    protests during, 204, 215, 218, 220,
        222–3, 231
    and public opinion, 27, 31–3, 207–13
    response to, 217–18
    suspension of, 211–12, 227
    trust in institutions during, 211
Marxism, 7, 13, 75, 103, 104, 154
mass media, 10, 67, 178, 244
    control of, 136
    criticism of Solidarity, 202–3
    martial law boycott of, 227
    and public opinion, 18, 23, 25–6, 236
    public opinion on, 14, 96, 123–5
    Solidarity access to, 89n, 123, 124,
        133, 152, 174, 192, 195
    (*see also* press)
mass transit strike, 130
materialist and post-materialist values,
    14, 60–1, 81
Maziarski, Jacek, 20, 96, 137
Mazowiecki, Tadeusz, 115
McClosky, Herbert, 1
meat (*see also* food), 45
    consumption of, 48, 54
    polls on, 166
    supplies of, 43–4, 164–5
medical care, 47
Merton, Robert, 237
Michnik Adam, 213
micropolitics, 7
Mieczkowski, Bogdan, 38
Military Council of National Salvation
    (WRON), 193, 201, 205, 208, 246
military, *see* army
militia
    during martial law, 218, 221–2
    polls on, 174–5, 179
    privileges of, 67, 87–8
miners, 218
minimum wage, *see* wages
Ministry of Higher Education, 204
Misztal, Bronisław, 81, 108, 136

MKS, *see* Interfactory Strike Committee
mobility, social and occupational, 39–40,
    58, 62, 76, 81, 88
Moczar, Mieczysław, 40
Moczulski, Leszek, 205
Modzelewski, Karol, 111, 134
Morawski, Witold, 58, 86, 103
Movement for the Defense of Human
    and Civil Rights, *see* ROPCiO
Mrożek, Slawomir, 201

national unity government, 174, 197–8
nomenklatura, *see* Polish United
    Workers' Party
non-violence, 247–8
Nowak, Stefan, 15, 17, 18, 20, 34, 65, 69,
    75

OBOP, *see* Ośrodek Badania Opinii
    Publicznej
OBS, *see* Ośrodek Badań Społecznych
Ochab, Edward, 50
Ofierski, Bohdan, 250, 251
Oliver, James, 233
Olszowski, Stefan, 133
On Human Labor, 115
optimism, 22, 193, 212, 228
Organizing Committee for Social
    Justice, 110
Ośrodek Badań Społecznych
    (Solidarity's Center for Social
    Research)
    polls on free Saturdays, 194;
        important issues, 122; mass media,
        125; responsibility for crisis, 183;
        Solidarity, 94, 108, 118, 120, 123,
        126, 128, 132; strikes, 127, 174; trust
        in institutions, 30, 118, 181, 205
    public opinion research by, 11, 29, 30,
        34, 250–51
    under martial law, 207
Ośrodek Badania Opinii Publicznej
    (OBOP), 11, 13, 14, 16, 20–4, 34, 251
    during martial law, 31–33, 207,
        210–11
    polls on crime, 176; economic
        problems, 16, 94, 166–8, 230;
        equality and justice, 63, 87; martial
        law, 207–9, 212; national priorities,
        171–2; politics, 47, 71; privilege,
        66n; public mood, 56; responsibility
        for crisis, 183; Solidarity, 128, 181,
        186–7; solving problems, 186;

For EU product safety concerns, contact us at Calle de José Abascal, 56–1°,
28003 Madrid, Spain or eugpsr@cambridge.org.

www.ingramcontent.com/pod-product-compliance
Ingram Content Group UK Ltd.
Pitfield, Milton Keynes, MK11 3LW, UK
UKHW010346140625
459647UK00010B/864